Brigham Young

MORMONISM:

ITS LEADERS AND DESIGNS.

BY

JOHN HYDE, Jun.,

FORMERLY A MORMON ELDER AND RESIDENT OF SALT LAKE CITY.

SECOND EDITION.

NEW YORK:
W. P. FETRIDGE & COMPANY,
No. 281 BROADWAY,
OPPOSITE STEWART'S.
1857.

STEREOTYPED BY
THOMAS B. SMITH,
82 & 84 Beekman-st., N.Y.

PRINTED BY
J. APPLEBY,
82 & 84 Beekman-st.

DEDICATION.

TO THE

HONEST BELIEVERS IN MORMONISM.

My Friends:

In writing the following work, I was not actuated by the base design of helping to malign an unpopular people, nor by the unworthy one of administering to mere idle curiosity. I wrote it neither to feed public prejudice, nor to supply public scandal. I wrote it for you; to you, therefore, I dedicate it.

I know your sincerity; I know also your delusion. As sincerely deceived as yourselves, I have preceded you to Salt Lake City. Some things of what I there saw, with the reflections they have suggested, are contained herein. Of the much that ought to be said, I have endeavored to say a little. The subject, however, is by no means exhausted.

While it is better to learn by personal experience than ever to remain ignorant, it is far wiser to profit by the experience of others. Although the practices of individuals can not determine the principles of communities, yet, when those practices are criminal and those individuals assume to be prophets and apostles, all men ought to hesitate before committing themselves to their jurisdiction, believing their pretensions, or imitating their examples.

If the following pages, for which I solicit your serious and candid perusal, accomplish no more, may they at least lead you to a thorough and careful re-investigation of your grounds of faith; while they teach you to remember that *new* thoughts are not, *therefore*, *true* thoughts; nor *new* light *true* light. To industriously declaim against the evils existing in the world, does not render proposed remedies necessarily good; and wise men should deliberate before rushing

> "——— from evils that we know,
> To those we know not of."

I am your sincere well-wisher,

THE AUTHOR.

NEW YORK, *July*, 1857

INTRODUCTION.

It is interesting to learn the peculiarities of a remote nation or an ancient age. It is far more important, however, that we should correctly understand the character and practices of any extraordinary people of our own day. Mormonism and the Mormons are subjects that not only deserve attention or excite interest, but demand the most serious consideration. The meanness of its origin, the singularity of its history, its present anomalous position, its still increasing dissemination, the mysterious influence it exercises on its followers, and its ultimate destiny, should commend its investigation to all persons. As a curious example of successful imposture, and a stern proof of human fanaticism, it must interest the philosopher. As a system of absolute autocracy in the center of a republic, it must attract the attention of politicians. As ensuring human misery, and consummating human degradation, in the cases of thousands of credulous men and women, and thousands more of helpless children, it should be noticed by the philanthropist. As a religious delusion increasing very rapidly, and entailing not only present suffering, but eternal loss on its infatuated adherents, it ought to arouse the divine to thought and action.

Mormonism is no longer a myth; and however wise the policy of contemptuous disregard for its mental delusion or its moral contaminations may have previously been, it is wise no longer. It has become a fact, and is every day growing more substantial and consolidated. As such a fact it deserves to be examined, and demands to be met. In so far as it is erroneous, it needs refutation; or wicked, it needs exposure; or criminal, it needs punishment.

To be met it must be understood; and to be understood it must be investigated. There is much falsehood circulated about the Mormons. This every one must perceive. Knowing this, many truthful accusations are successfully denied by their apologists, disbelieved by their followers, and rejected by impartial persons, accustomed to newspaper exaggerations. In such case the testimony of an eye and ear witness, if credible, must be important. As such, the following work is submitted. The author has endeavored to exhibit the people of Utah as they are; and while he has *much*

> "Extenuated,
> Has set down naught in malice."

Prophetic assumptions must be sustained by prophetic conduct, or they fail The validity of bombastic pretensions to superior purity can only be determined by the extent of that purity. While this is inevitably true, still the correctness of principles does not depend on consistency of practice. A theory may be admirable and practicable however much neglected or despised. Many sincere believers in Mormonism, *as a system*, deplore its exhibitions *as a practice*. To prove to such that the practices of Mormons are the natural consequents of their theory, is another object of this work.

Circumstances throw many persons into controversy with believers of this system, but the press of whose occupations prevents any elaborate and personal investigation of their tenets and history, or of the opposing arguments. In order to supply, to a small extent, such information, and briefly to indicate whence such arguments may be drawn, has been another design of the author.

And if the great Source and Ultimatum of all truth will accept and bless this work, to the inducing any mind to shake off the bondage of a miserable delusion the author will feel abundantly repaid.

CONTENTS.

PAGE

INTRODUCTION, ...

CHAPTER I.

THE AUTHOR.

MORMONISM IN ENGLAND AND AMERICA—EMBRACES MORMONISM—IS ORDAINED AND PREACHES—GOES AS A MISSIONARY TO FRANCE—LEAVES ENGLAND FOR AMERICA—VISITS NAUVOO AND CARTHAGE—THE SMITHS—ICARIANS—THE PLAINS—THE INDIANS—ARRIVES AT SALT LAKE—IS INITIATED INTO MORMON MYSTERIES—EFFORTS TO LEAVE SALT LAKE CITY—APPOINTED A MISSIONARY TO THE SANDWICH ISLANDS—LEAVES FOR CALIFORNIA—DOUBTS AND DIFFICULTIES—PACIFIC OCEAN—ARRIVES AT SANDWICH ISLANDS—RENOUNCES MORMONISM—BRIGHAM'S CERTIFICATE—MOTIVES FOR ACTING—CONDUCT OF THE AUTHORITIES TOWARD HIM, ... 13

CHAPTER II.

SALT LAKE CITY.

"THE BIG MOUNTAIN"—EMIGRATION KANYON—THE BENCHES—GREAT SALT LAKE—THE CITY WALL—THE CITY—THE INHABITANTS—THE HOUSES OF THE LEADING MEN NEAR TEMPLE BLOCK—KIMBALL'S CITY PROPERTY—BRIGHAM'S LION HOUSE—THE MANSION AND WHITE HOUSE—MORMON THEATER AND DANCING-HALL—PUBLIC BUILDINGS—TITHING OFFICE AND SYSTEM OF TITHING—COMMUNISM AND CONSECRATION—PUBLIC LANDS—TEMPLE BLOCK—TABERNACLE AND SABBATH SERVICES—ENDOWMENT HOUSE AND TEMPLE—THE SOIL—CAPACITY TO SUPPORT INCREASED POPULATION—STARVATION—MANUFACTORIES—LIQUOR MAKING AND CONSUMING—IRON AND COAL FOR THE PACIFIC RAILROAD—MINERALS—WEAPON MANUFACTORIES—THE MORMON CENSUS AND LYING—MORMON PROSPERITY AND PURITY, ... 27

CHAPTER III.

PRACTICAL POLYGAMY.

FAMILY ARRANGEMENTS—FAVORITES—DOMESTIC HAPPINESS—SLEEPING ALONE—MAKING TABERNACLES—MORMON SALVATION—WIFE HUNTING—MOTHERS

PAGE

AND DAUGHTERS SEALED TO ONE MAN—HALF-SISTER WIFE—EFFECTS OF POLYGAMY ON FIRST WIVES—WHISKY—TERMAGANTS—ADULTERY—JEALOUSY—BRIGHAM ON CONNUBIALITIES—PROPORTION OF THE SEXES IN UTAH—ARGUMENTS USED TO INDUCE YOUNG GIRLS TO MARRY POLYGAMISTS IN PREFERENCE TO YOUNG MEN—WHY THEY DO NOT LEAVE—EFFECTS OF POLYGAMY ON THE CHILDREN—MORTALITY—STERILITY OF WOMEN—EARLY MARRIAGE—DIVORCE—MRS. MCLEAN AND PARLEY P. PRATT—MRS. COBB AND BRIGHAM—UTAH MARRIAGES, ... 51

CHAPTER IV.

MORMON MYSTERIES.

SEALING FOR ETERNITY—WOMEN SEALED TO ONE AND MARRIED TO ANOTHER HUSBAND—SPIRITUAL WIVES—CAUSE OF SMITH'S DEATH—SMITH'S WIDOWS—"PROXY DOCTRINE"—MARRIAGE AND SEALING FOR THE DEAD—THE ENDOWMENT—WASHING AND ANOINTING—FIRST DEGREE OF AARONIC PRIESTHOOD—SECOND DEGREE OF AARONIC PRIESTHOOD—FIRST DEGREE OF MELCHISEDEC PRIESTHOOD—SECOND DEGREE OF MELCHISEDEC PRIESTHOOD—"BEHIND THE VAIL"—OBEDIENCE WITH EXAMPLES—SEALINGS AT THE ALTAR—MURDERS—INITIATION LECTURES—SEALINGS TO INDIAN SQUAWS—ADOPTION—SELLING DAUGHTERS, ... 83

CHAPTER V.

EDUCATION.

PRACTICAL EDUCATION—SCHOOL SYSTEM—BRAGGADOCIO—SCHOOL TEACHERS—THREE MONTHS' TERMS AND NINE MONTHS' VACATIONS—EVENING SCHOOLS—DANCING SCHOOLS—ORSON PRATT *v.* BRIGHAM YOUNG—KIMBALL ON EDUCATED MEN—PRATT'S MATHEMATICAL CLASS—GRAMMAR SCHOOLS—CULTIVATED FEMALE SOCIETY—HOME EDUCATION—FEMALE "BAS BLEUS"—LITERARY INSTITUTIONS—NOVEL-READING—DESERET ALPHABET—NEWSPAPERS—BOOK OF MORMON—SMITH'S REVELATIONS—NEW TRANSLATION OF THE BIBLE—BOOK OF ABRAHAM—KEY TO APOCALYPSE OF ST. JOHN—PROPHECIES OF ENOCH—GOSPEL OF ADAM—WRITTEN LAW *v.* ORAL LAW—CONTROVERSIAL WORKS, 115

CHAPTER VI.

BRIGHAM YOUNG AT HOME.

HIS BIOGRAPHY—BIRTH AND EDUCATION—EMBRACES MORMONISM—MEETS SMITH THE PROPHET—JOURNEY TO MISSOURI—IS ORDAINED AN APOSTLE—PREACHES—APPOINTED PRESIDENT OF THE APOSTLES—FLIES FOR HIS LIFE—RELAYS FOUNDATION OF TEMPLE IN JACKSON COUNTY, MISSOURI—MISSION TO ENGLAND—RETURNS TO NAUVOO—BRIGHAM AND SMITH—BRIGHAM AND SIDNEY RIGDON—BUILDS UP NAUVOO—CONDUCTS EMIGRATION—MORMON BATTALION—SALT LAKE CITY—BRIGHAM'S LEADERSHIP—APPOINTED PRESIDENT

PAGE

OF CHURCH—QUARRELS WITH JUDGES AND EXPELS THEM—COLONEL STEPTOE —"MODUS OPERANDI"—SHOULD HE DIE, FATE OF THE CHURCH—PERSONAL APPEARANCE—IN COUNCIL AND IN PULPIT—SATELLITES TO THIS PLANET—HIS MANNERS—STYLE OF ORATORY—AS A WRITER—AS A HUSBAND AND FATHER—DOMESTICITIES—HIS WIVES—HIS FAVORITE—WOMEN COURTING THE MEN—OCCUPATIONS AND PROPERTY—UNIVERSAL CONFIDANT AND ADVISER—ADMINISTRATIVE BLUNDERS—SECRET OF SUCCESS, ... 136

CHAPTER VII.

BRIGHAM THE PROPHET.

INTENTION OF MORMONISM—SMITH'S PREDICTION AND DESIGN—MORMON PRAYERS—CHRIST COMING IN 1890—WHERE HE SHALL DESCEND—BRIGHAM'S POSITION—BRIGHAM ON HIMSELF—DRAWING THE SWORD OF THE ALMIGHTY—SHEDDING BLOOD—BRIGHAM ON PROSPECTS OF UTAH—FANATICISM—HIS ARMY—HIS INTENTION IF ARRESTED—HIS METHOD OF GOVERNMENT—STEALING—BRIBERY—DEBT-PAYING—FRIGHTENING APOSTATES—MORMON MISSIONS AND MISSIONARIES—BRIGHAM'S POLICY—HIS SUCCESSOR—JOSEPH SMITH, JUN.—HEBER C. KIMBALL—O. HYDE—P. PRATT—JOSEPH A YOUNG—BRIGHAM'S GOD—ADAM THE FATHER OF CHRIST, ... 172

CHAPTER VIII.

CHRONOLOGICAL HISTORY OF MORMONISM, 199

CHAPTER IX.

ANALYSIS OF INTERNAL EVIDENCES OF BOOK OF MORMON.

INTRODUCTION—NATURE AND PURPORT OF THE BOOK—CONTRADICTION AS TO PLATES—AS TO URIM AND THUMMIM—AS TO HEBREW LANGUAGE—JEWISH MATERIALS FOR WRITING—LABAN'S PLATES AND THEIR CONTENTS—GENEALOGIES—COPIES OF THE LAW—HISTORY OF JEWS—VARIOUS PROPHETS OF BIBLE AND BOOK OF MORMON—CONTRADICTION IN PREDICTION—LEHI'S COMPASS OR LIAHONA—NATURAL HISTORY OF BOOK OF MORMON—OF AMERICAN NATURAL HISTORY—IMPORTATIONS OF STOCK—ELEPHANTS IN AMERICA—ASTRONOMICAL ANTICIPATIONS—CONTRADICTIONS BETWEEN THE PRETENDED AUTHORS OF THE BOOK OF MORMON—SOLOMON'S TEMPLE IN AMERICA—GIFTS OF THE SPIRIT BEFORE CHRIST—JARED'S BARGES, WHAT THEY WERE AND WHAT THEY BROUGHT—PLAGIARISMS FROM THE BIBLE—INCONSISTENCIES—PROPHETIC APOLOGIES, ... 210

CHAPTER X.

EXTERNAL EVIDENCES OF BOOK OF MORMON.

MORMON STYLE OF ARGUMENT—ATTACKS ON THE BIBLE EXAMINED—LAWS OF EVIDENCE—CONTRADICTIONS BETWEEN STATEMENTS—URIM AND THUMMIM—

PAGE

AFFIDAVITS OF SMITH'S ACQUAINTANCES—CONTRADICTIONS OF PROBABILITIES—SMITH'S PREVIOUS CHARACTER—AFFIDAVITS OF ELEVEN CITIZENS—OF FIFTY-ONE—OF DIFFERENT INDIVIDUALS—SMITH'S THREE WITNESSES—CONTRADICTIONS—OLIVER COWDERY—MARTIN HARRIS—DAVID WHITMER—OF THE EIGHT WITNESSES—ANALYSIS OF TESTIMONY—FALSE GROUNDS OF THE MORMONS—THEIR PROPHETIC EVIDENCE—SUMMARY, ... 237

CHAPTER XI.

REAL ORIGIN OF THE BOOK OF MORMON.

CREDIBILITY OF TESTIMONY—MONEY-DIGGING IN NEW YORK—CHASE'S "PEEP-STONE"—SMITH'S MODE OF TRANSLATING—PAGE'S STONE—SMITH'S PLATES—WILEY'S PLATES—CUPIDITY OF SMITH'S FAMILY—SMITH'S OBJECT—MARTIN HARRIS'S INDUCEMENT—OLIVER COWDERY'S INDUCEMENT—ORIGIN OF NAME—ORIGIN OF MATTER—SPALDING'S RELATIONS' TESTIMONY—SMITH'S MEANS OF OBTAINING SPALDING'S MSS.—INCIDENTS OF BOOK OF MORMON—RELIGIOUS DECISIONS—RELIGIOUS STYLE—GRAMMATICAL CONSTRUCTION—THE BIBLE, . 262

CHAPTER XII.

THEORETICAL POLYGAMY.

POSITION — ANTI-SCRIPTURAL — ADAM — NOAH—LAMECH—ABRAHAM—JACOB—DAVID—CHRIST—PAUL—CHRISTIAN DISPENSATION—ANTI-NATURAL—PROPORTIONS OF THE SEXES—NATURE A CONFIRMER OF REVELATION—IRRATIONAL—WOMAN'S POSITION THE TEST OF PROGRESS—CHILDREN'S DEPENDENCE ON THEIR MOTHERS—WIVES' INFLUENCE OVER HUSBANDS—HISTORY AND DESTINY OF RACES—DIFFERENT LAWS OF MARRIAGE—UNMARRIED PROPHETS—INFERIOR RACES MOST PROLIFIC—"POLYGAMY A PREVENTIVE OF PROSTITUTION" EXAMINED—ANTI-MORMON—REVELATIONS—POPULATION OF UTAH, . . 284

CHAPTER XIII.

THE SUPPRESSION OF MORMONISM.

MORMONISM AS A CIVIL POLITY AND AS A RELIGION—CAUSES OF MORMON PERSECUTIONS AT MISSOURI AND NAUVOO—J. SMITH A CANDIDATE FOR THE PRESIDENCY OF THE UNITED STATES—SMITH A MOHAMMED—BRIGHAM SUCCESSOR TO HIS DESIGNS AS WELL AS OFFICE—HIS MANAGEMENT—FAMINE *v.* AMBITION—THE CAUSES OF HIS FUTURE FALL—MORMON POLITICS—THE OBJECTS TO BE ACCOMPLISHED WITH REGARD TO THEM—SUPPRESSION OF POLYGAMY—DUTY OF THE GOVERNMENT IN THE PREMISES—BENEFITS OF ANNEXATION TO THE MEN AND WOMEN—MAJORITY OF THE MORMONS FOREIGNERS—THE EFFECTS OF MERELY APPOINTING A GOVERNOR AND SENDING TROOPS—MORMONISM AS A RELIGIOUS EVIL—MEANS OF UPROOTING IT—DUTY OF SECEDERS AND OF CHRISTIANS—ITS FUNDAMENTAL ERRORS AND WEAK POINTS, . 306

LETTER ADDRESSED TO BRIGHAM YOUNG, ... 331

MORMONISM, ITS LEADERS AND DESIGNS.

CHAPTER I.

THE AUTHOR.

Mormonism in England and America—Embraces Mormonism—Is ordained and preaches—Goes as a missionary to France—Leaves England for America—Visits Carthage and Nauvoo—The Smiths—Icariens—The plains—Indians—Arrives at Salt Lake—Initiated into the Mormon mysteries—Efforts to leave Salt Lake City—Appointed a missionary to the Sandwich Islands—Leaves for California—Doubts and difficulties—Pacific ocean—Arrives at Sandwich Islands—Renounces Mormonism—Brigham's certificate—Motive for active conduct of the Church toward him.

Books require to be instructive and credible. These qualities altogether depend on the opportunities of the author to obtain corrrect information, and the purity of his motives in imparting it. To have been a Mormon, is to be an object of suspicion. To be an apostate, is to be regarded with distrust. To be an apostate Mormon, is to be doubly suspected. As the weight of testimony entirely depends on the credibility of the witness, I therefore commence my evidence with a statement as to myself. Who I am, how I became what I am, and why I write, are questions every one should ask. I endeavor to reply. Mormonism in England and Mormonism in Utah are two very different systems. In England all its objectionable principles were not only ignored, but denied.

Its Apostles and Elders not only uttered negative but also positive falsehoods, in order to induce belief. They not only denied many things that were true, but stated many things that were utterly false. As a sample of their falsehoods, I will instance polygamy. This was practiced by Smith in 1838, and the Mormon Apostles *knew it.* Yet, when the Church was charged with its adoption, Parley P. Pratt, in Manchester, England, before the general conference of the European churches, and in the *Millennial Star* of 1846, thus publicly denounced it: "Such a doctrine is not held, known, or practiced as a principle of the Latter-day Saints. *It is but another name for whoredom;* and is as foreign from the real principles of the Church, *as the devil is from God;* or as sectarianism is from Christianity" (*Millennial Star*, vol. vi., p. 22). And yet this man knew that Smith and others had children living who *were the offspring of this very practice!* John Taylor, another Mormon Apostle, in a discussion held at Boulogne, France, in July 1850, was charged with the belief of this doctrine, to which accusation he thus replied: "We are accused here of polygamy and actions the most indelicate, obscene and disgusting, such as none but a corrupt heart could have conceived. These things are too outrageous to be believed; therefore I shall content myself with reading our views of chastity and marriage, from a work published by us, containing some of the articles of our faith." He read in the Book of Smith's Revelations, p. 330, the marriage covenant: "You both mutually agree to be each other's companion, husband and wife; observing all the legal rights belonging to this condition; that is, keeping yourselves *wholly for each other, and from all others during your lives!"* And on p. 331: "Inasmuch as this Church of Jesus Christ has been reproached with the crime of *fornication and polygamy*, we declare that we believe that *one man should have one wife, and one woman but one husband*, except in case of death, when either is at liberty to marry again!" And again, on p. 124: "Thou shalt love thy wife with all thy heart, and *shall cleave unto her, and none else;* and he that looketh on a woman to lust after her, shall deny the faith, and not have the spirit, and be cast out." "There," exclaimed Elder Taylor, triumphantly, "that is our doctrine on this subject" (Taylor's Discussion at Boulogne, p. 8). And this man *had four wives wrangling and quarreling at Utah, and was paying attentions to a girl at Jersey, Channel Islands,* at the very moment he uttered these willful, intentional falsehoods!

The illustrious examples of such pseudo-inspired Apostles were industriously imitated by similarly inspired Elders. Where the former were content with mere affirmation or denial, the latter blasphemously called on God to attest their veracity; and challenged the Almighty to disprove their statements. Some of them denounced their accusers with bitter curses, and threatened them with all kinds of spiritual horrors. From the lips of such men, and others who had been deceived by such men, did my father and myself first hear of Mormonism. The character of Smith, his many mighty miracles, his profound sagacity, his inspired teachings, the love of the Saints, the purity of their Zion, their frequent tribulations and sufferings, their uncomplaining submission and uncompromising virtue, came forth resplendent from their testimonies. Such statements, repeated constantly, and by different individuals, accompanied by vigorous attacks on the divisions, dissensions, and acrimony exhibited in too many sectaries, spiced by the empty bombast and cant of all pretended moral, political, and religious reformers, apparently sustained by positive practice; added to these incentives, a bewildering method of using, and an extensive acquaintance with passages of Scripture; novel dogmas sincerely believed and enthusiastically taught, for which they claimed special revelation as their origin; all this, heightened by the most barefaced assertions of predictions accomplished, of singular healings certainly performed, of positive promises of conviction following obedience, of the ancient signs, and of the old priesthood—all this uttered by men who hesitated at almost no falsehood "which should convert a soul," could not but arrest our attention. "To doubt is to be damned already," said Paul; and he was right. Into this whirlpool of enthusiasm we, with many others, were insensibly borne. Very little attention was paid to the subject by the conservators of religious truth. Despised, it was neglected; and because neglected, it continued to grow. With little or no contradiction, and the little that was made, readily silenced by these men, they made themselves believed. All that was known of Mormonism was known from their statements; positively thinking it something holier, purer and truer, it was embraced by hundreds. To fervently *embrace* a delusion, is to more sincerely *believe* it. They clothed it in the drapery of warm emotions; and good men, in their desires for something more exalted and God-like, viewed it through the distorted medium of their own wishes; not knowing it as it was, they thought it was what they hoped it to be. When they began to see the difference between their conception and the reality, many were too enmeshed to forsake it. Men always strive to make that appear true which they conceive it their interest to be true; because they like to have for their actions the sanction of their own consciences. Nor is this mental process very difficult; and it easily and satisfactorily accounts for glaring absurdities, and yet actual sincerity. It is thus with many of the Mormons. They were sincere in embracing Mormonism; and when their minds began to doubt, if they ever had sense enough to doubt, the weight of interest crushed down the resistance of conscience; and, although ceasing to be true to themselves, they became true to their system. The dread of being called inconsistent induced sincere consistency to their religion, while sacrificing the only real consistency, that of man with himself.

I had an ideal of what religion and the worship of God might be; I imagined that this system, as I then heard it expounded, realized that ideal; and, in the love of that ideal, I embraced it and was accordingly baptized, on the 4th of September, 1848, being then a boy of fifteen years. Since proving that that ideal religion is fallacious, and that the reality of Mormonism is depraving, I have abandoned it.

That I was sincere in my faith and conscientious in my conduct, I believe no one will attempt to dispute. In the December of the same year, I was ordained a Priest, and commenced to preach Mormonism as I had received, and then believed it to be. This I continued to do in various places in England till, in June, 1851, I was appointed to join the French mission, as it was called, and then under the direction of Elder John Taylor, who had, in 1850, left Salt Lake, expressly to commence preaching Mormonism in that country.

On the 1st of August, 1851, I was ordained, as the following certificate shows, to be "one of the Seventies," an office of equal power but inferior jurisdiction to that of "one of the Twelve."

CERTIFICATE.

To All to whom these Presents shall come:

This certifies that JOHN HYDE has been received into the CHURCH OF JESUS CHRIST OF LATTER-DAY SAINTS, organized on the SIXTH DAY OF APRIL, 1830, and was ORDAINED into the EIGHTH QUORUM of SEVENTIES, the First day of August, 1851, and by virtue of his OFFICE he is authorized to PREACH THE GOSPEL, and officiate in all the ordinances thereof, in all the world, agreeable to the authority of the HOLY PRIESTHOOD vested in him; we, therefore, in the name, and by the authority of this CHURCH, grant unto this our BROTHER this LETTER OF COMMENDATION unto all persons wherever his lot may be cast, as a proof of our esteem, praying for his prosperity in the Redeemer's cause.

GIVEN under our hands at Great Salt Lake City, this Fifteenth day of June, 1854.

JOS. YOUNG, President.

ROBERT CAMPBELL, Clerk.

I remained engaged in the French mission till January,

1853 : a portion of which time I was in the Channel Islands, and a portion I spent at Havre-de-Grace.

On February 5th, 1853, I sailed from Liverpool, in company with nearly four hundred passengers for New Orleans. The passengers were exclusively Mormons, and all bound to the Great Salt Lake Valley; indulging high hopes of there realizing all that is desirable in holiness, purity, and brotherhood. We were organized in the Mormon fashion, with a President and his two Councilors, one of which I was chosen to be. After an ordinary passage to New Orleans, we ascended the magnificent Mississippi, to Keokuk, Iowa. From Keokuk, I paid a visit to Nauvoo, in company with an estimable and talented gentleman, then a Mormon, but whom a view of Salt Lake doings has since caused to apostatize and return to England. The Temple that the Mormons had built and completed in 1845, was in ruins, a savage specimen of modern Vandalism. (See *engraving.*)

I spent several days conversing with J. Smith's mother, wife, and family, and heard many charges against Brigham and his associates for actions in which, according to the Smiths, they had disobeyed the injunctions, contradicted the teachings, and maligned the memory of their late Prophet.

From this place I visited the Carthage jail, where J. Smith and his brother, Hiram, were assassinated in cold blood; and the wall against which he was placed, and barbarously shot at, after his death. (See *engraving.*)

The camp was thronging with life, there being nearly two thousand five hundred Mormons preparing to start for the plains. It presented a very pleasing view, and was delightfully situated on a hill overlooking the thriving city of Keokuk on the one side, and the majestic Mississippi on the other.

On June 1st, the company with which I traveled left for Council Bluffs City, crossed the river Missouri, on the 12th, saw the last civilized habitations that we were to see for months, and were fairly *en route* for Salt Lake. The scenery on the road, the incidents of camp life, with stampedes of cattle, toiling along by day, uncomfortable watchings by night, bad roads to mend, bridges to build, the sense of freedom exciting the mind, till the monotony becomes tedious and wearisome; all this has been so ably and so often described, as to be familiar to every one. We met a large party of Pawnee-Loups, on the Platte. They had just come from a battle with the Sioux; they were decked in all the glory of Indian war-paint, were well mounted and armed, and with their ferociously-daubed faces, heads shaved bare except the feathered scalp-lock, their threatening gestures, screaming tones, and insolent conduct, were very formidable fellows. We made them a large present of flour and other edibles for their "hungry *papooses*," or, strictly speaking, they levied the tax, and we paid it.

We arrived at Salt Lake City, in October, just in time for the Fall Conference. I married a young lady to whom I had been engaged in London, and began to teach school. Of course I was not long at Salt Lake before discovering the difference between what I had been taught to expect and what I saw. It may be asked why did I not immediately leave Salt Lake, and forsake Mormonism? Convictions received in boyhood, and that have been maturing and deepening with one's development, are not to be overturned by one disappointment or by one discovery. Inconsistency and contradiction do much to destroy belief; but these inconsistencies might be imaginary. Every tie that could bind any one to any system, united me to Mormonism. It had been the religion that my youth had loved and preached; it was the faith of my parents; of my wife and her relatives; my mind had been toned with its views, and my life associated with its ministers. I knew little or nothing of any other faith, and I clung with desperate energy to the system, although I repudiated the practices.

On Friday, February 10, 1854, I was initiated into the mysteries of the "Mormon endowment." What was the nature of those mysteries, none, before initiation, could have an idea. To understand, it was necessary to receive them. His is a strong mind over whom a mass of ceremonies could have no influence, in which representations of the most august beings are made to move and talk, and which included the most solemn oaths, accompanied by frightful penalties. The obligations of Free-masonry and Odd-fellowship exercise no small influence over the initiated; nor am I surprised that a superstitious terror, in many instances, enchains these endowed Mormons, at Salt Lake, in complete subjection to their Prophet Brigham, and his coadjutors.

In the spring of 1854, I determined to leave Salt Lake for California, but had not, neither could I obtain the means to do so. I candidly wrote and stated my views, however, to Orson Pratt, one of the Twelve Apostles, with whom I was intimate, and we frequently conversed on the subject. I had then resolved to leave in 1855, if possible, but was still prevented by poverty. At the conference held in April, 1856, I was publicly appointed, without any previous intimation, to go on a mission to the Sandwich Isles, and was instructed to leave by the May following. I accepted the appointment. I thought that perhaps, as I was told, I had "grown rusty;" that my waning faith was the result of inaction; that to be actively employed in the ministry might waken up my old confidence; that in the effort to convince others, I might succeed in reconvincing myself. The religion of my youth was still so enwrapped around my habits of thought, that I was desirous rather to prove it *true*, than demonstrate it to be *false*. I tried hard to believe it true, endeavored to act as though I did believe it, in the hope of producing conviction. In renouncing it, I have done so in spite of my prejudices.

In May, accordingly, I left Salt Lake City for the Sandwich Islands, having been chosen as president over the missionaries destined for that location. None of the missionaries to the Sandwich Islands were allowed to take their wives; this and other reasons compelled me to leave Mrs. Hyde with her relatives at Salt Lake. Besides this, my mind was at sea, floating in darkness and indecision. Ignorant of my real position, I knew not whither I should go if I were to turn; I therefore went straight on. I had to leave, for to remain was to abjure Mormonism; and I was not fully prepared for final and permanent apostacy. "I had seen Rome, was disgusted with Rome, and still tried to disconnect Romanism from Rome;" and as it was with another, to some extent it was with me, it needed time, it needed thought, it needed *collat-*

ing my recollections, that I might feel the force of their sum. The opportunity for this thought and collation could not be obtained at Salt Lake City, nor in the business of crossing the plains. I endeavored to view Mormonism *objectively*, for theoretically it assumes to be the religion of human progress, apart from Mormonism *subjectively*, as it was then existing. I tried and failed. On the Pacific ocean, in communion with God and my own soul, the darkness of doubt that had blinded my eyes, and the mists of indecision that had paralyzed my energies, left me, and I resolved not only to renounce Mormonism, but also to tell the world freely, fully, and fearlessly, as well my reasons, as my experience.

To this end I have labored in the Sandwich Isles, California, and elsewhere; and to this object do I determine to devote myself. If Mormonism as it is be true, the better it is understood the better will it be for the world. If it be false, it is the duty of every man to endeavor to manifest its errors. To deter persons from embracing delusion, and to rescue from complete self-sacrifice any who have already embraced it are my only motives for adopting my course.

My opportunities for knowing Mormonism as it is, will not, I think, be disputed by any of its believers. My motives for revealing that knowledge are open to God and the world. Ever since my first connection with the Church, honors and authority have been heaped upon me. Increased and increasing honors were before me when I abandoned it. I could not have been actuated by *disappointed ambition*, therefore, because they never gave me any neglect to avenge. Nor could it have been from personal pique, as I know of no antipathy felt toward me. That my secession was entirely voluntary, and my reputation unquestioned, the subjoined document, handed to me immediately previous to leaving Salt Lake, will prove.

The tone adopted by the Mormon authorities toward me, subsequent to my secession, may be judged by the following extract from a sermon, preached by H. C. Kimball, at Salt Lake City, January 11, 1857:

"There is a little matter of business that we want to lay before this congregation in regard to John Hyde, who went to the Sandwich Islands on a mission. There are a couple of letters that the brethren have received; we shall read a little from them, and give you to understand the course he is taking. (The letters were read.) You hear the letters and the testimony of our brethren in regard to John Hyde. Such matters, many times, have passed along, and we have not noticed them, but have let men deny the faith, speaking against it, and deliver lectures through the world. Many times we have let them run at large, but the time is now passed for such a course of things. By the consent of my brethren, I shall move that John Hyde be cut off from the Church of Jesus Christ of Latter-day Saints, and I will put the motion in full; that is, that he be cut off, root and branch; that means pertaining to himself. When this motion is put, I want you to vote, every one of you, either for or against, for there is no sympathy to be shown unto such a man. Br. Wells has seconded the motion I have made. All that are in favor that John Hyde be cut off from the Church of Jesus Christ of Latter-day Saints, and that he be delivered over to Satan to be buffeted in the flesh, will raise their right hands. (All hands were raised.)

A motion has been put, and unanimously carried, that

ELDER'S CERTIFICATE.

To All Persons to whom this Letter shall Come:

This certifies that the bearer, Elder JOHN HYDE, Jun., is in full faith and fellowship with the CHURCH OF JESUS CHRIST OF LATTER-DAY SAINTS, and by the General Authorities of said Church, has been duly appointed a MISSION to SANDWICH ISLES to PREACH THE GOSPEL, and administer in all the ordinances thereof pertaining to his office.

And we invite all men to give heed to his teachings and counsels as a man of GOD, sent to open to them the door of life and salvation—and assist him in his travels, in whatsoever things he may need.

And we pray GOD the ETERNAL FATHER to bless Elder HYDE, and all who receive him, and minister to his comfort, with the blessings of heaven and earth, for time and for all eternity, in the name of JESUS CHRIST. Amen.

Signed at Great Salt Lake City, TERRITORY OF UTAH, April 10th, 1856, in behalf of said Church.

Brigham Young

Heber C. Kimball

J. M. Grant,

FIRST PRESIDENCY.

John Hyde be cut off root and branch; that is, himself, and all the roots and branches that are within him. This has no allusion to his family. He has taken a course by which he has lost his family, and forfeited his priesthood; he has forfeited his membership. The limb is cut off, but the priesthood takes the fruit that was attached to the limb and saves it, if it will be saved. Do you understand me? His wife is not cut off from this Church, but she is free from him; she is just as free from him as though she never had belonged to him. The limb she was connected to is cut off, and she must again be grafted into the tree, if she wishes to be saved; that is all about it."—*Deseret News, January 21st*, 1857.

Not only was I not influenced by prejudice, pique or disappointment in my secession from the Mormon Church; but, in spite of all prejudices, at the sacrifice of all friendships, at the hazard of breaking every tie that united me to happiness and the world, and at the risk of life itself, I have acted as I have. That I have done right I am convinced. God knows I have done it in the love of right. To be able, in how slight degree soever, to expose error and yet to remain silent is to connive at and share the responsibility of that error. While deploring that my best years for improvement have been squandered in delusion, it is a duty I owe to others similiarly circumstanced, to endeavor to convince them of their true position. Less than this is less than right. For as the subject is of paramount importance to the world if true, and to the Mormons themselves if false, so its correct exposure must therefore be equally important, and consequently, so far obligatory.

If in the succeeding pages I may have been guilty of ex

aggeration, I am not aware of it; I certainly do not intend it. Mormonism licenses too much corruption under the name of religion, to need any exaggeration to make it atrocious. The Mormons are guilty of too many crimes to need any addition to them to render them abominable.

CHAPTER II.

SALT LAKE CITY.

"The big mountain"—Emigration kanyon—The benches—Great Salt Lake—The city wall—The city—The inhabitants—The houses of the leading men near Temple block—Kimball's city property—Brigham's Lion house—The Mansion and White House—Mormon theater and dancing hall—Public buildings—Tithing office and system of tithing—Communism and consecration—Public lands—Temple block—Tabernacle and Sabbath services—Endowment house and Temple—The soil—Capacity to support increased population—Starvation—Manufactories—Liquor making and consuming—Iron and coal for the Pacific railroad—Minerals—Weapon manufactories—The Mormon census and lying—Mormon prosperity and purity.

Between the western border of the States on the Atlantic side, and the Pacific States of this great continent, there are vast prairies, dreary and treeless, sand-hills, mud flats, rocky mountains, and rapid rivers. Sixteen hundred and sixty-seven miles of travel from St. Louis, Mo., *viâ* Council Bluffs City, brings one to the Valley of the Great Salt Lake. A journey through tortuous mountain defiles, crossing creeks with precipitous banks, over roads that terrify even expert Jehus; wearied with a monotony more fatiguing than a sea voyage, any valley would seem lovely, and any respite would be hailed as a paradise. This fact accounts for the joy with which travelers hail the first glimpse of the barren and bare-valleyed home of the Saints. Will the reader make the tour with me?

We have just climbed up a steep, rocky hill. Three or

four teams to each wagon have at last dragged them all safely to the summit of the "big mountain." The cattle are panting and puffing and lying down for a rest, while we gaze at a very imposing scene. We are now standing on an eminence of the Wahsatch mountains, over eight thousand feet above the level of the ocean, surrounded by peaks that rise majestically above our heads, and in the deep nooks of which continually glitters the eternal snow; beneath this, fringed and shaded by dark masses of balsam, fir, and pine. Behind us are receding ranges of hills, streams sparkling like silver threads, the trembling foliage of the quaking aspen, and narrow gorges looming like abysses in the distance. Before us, mountains growing lower, till a strip of valley relieves the sight, in the south-west. This is the first glimpse of the Valley of the Great Salt Lake. Mormons fall on their knees and pray; some shout hosannas and hallelujahs; many weep; husbands kiss their wives, and parents their children, in their paroxysm of joy, and the very faithful declare they feel the Spirit of God *pervading the very atmosphere*, and they enthusiastically declare that all their toils are repaid, for they have at length come home, where the "wicked cease from troubling and the weary are at rest." Poor people—poor deluded people!

We are not so overcome, and prepare to descend the "big mountain;" glad to remember only 18 miles now separate us from rest and society. We neither break our necks nor our wagon axles, and wind up a very pretty "kanyon"—a mountain defile. We are met by many a team and wagon crawling up toward the big mountain, for fire-wood. We cross another mountain ridge, and are in a most delightfully picturesque gorge, "the emigration kanyon." Admiring the beauties of its rocky heights, the slopes covered with shrubbery and painted by the sun in all sorts of rich colors, as though a rainbow had been wrecked on the hill side and had left its beautiful shades on the grass and ferns; forgetting every thing but the scene around us, we suddenly turn an abrupt point, and the valley is stretched before us. To our right and left is the continuous range of hills from which we have just emerged. We are on the rolling brow of a slight decline, and observe that for several hundred feet above our heads, there are long, level lines of ridges, which are deeply and evenly indented on the mountains, as far as our sight can reach. We notice also that there are other such before us till they form a narrow flat surface through which a river flows, and that the ground rises similarly up the mountains before us, 30 miles away. These are called "benches;" they extend throughout the entire range of valleys, are plainly visible, exactly level, and are the ancient shores of the Great Salt Lake. Like a blue tinted mirror reflecting the sunshine, we remark the lake about 35 miles to the north-west. It is now about 70 miles long, from north to south, and 30 miles wide, from east to west. It once filled, and most probably formed the entire "Great Basin," as it is termed, extending 500 miles from north to south, and 350 miles from east to west, hemmed in by the Sierra Madre mountains on the east, and the Goose Creek and Humboldt ranges on the west. Mountains were then jagged islands, ravines the straits, sweeping hollows the gulfs and shores of this vast and silent sea. It has shrunk away to its present dimensions, and is the immense reservoir into which all the streams and rivers of the "Basin" pour their melted snows.

It has no apparent outlet, although gradually diminishing apparently more rapidly than can be accounted for by mere evaporation. Many flats of black mud with an incrustation of dazzling salt crystals, were covered with water when the Mormons first went there; and their flat-boat was pushed easily over long stretches of now baking and cracked soil. Its bottom is very flat, however, and a very slight increase of water would again submerge miles of now exposed surface. The density of the water varies necessarily in different seasons from the quantities of fresh water pouring down into it. It averages from 1.16 to 1.18 of sp. gr. It is the strongest natural brine in the world, holding in solution over 22 per cent. of different salts.

Its dark sluggish waves forcibly recall the Dead Sea to the mind of the gazer, and were it not that this is 4,200 feet *above*, and that lies 1,000 feet *below* the level of the ocean; and that *this* is completely locked in by abrupt and surrounding mountains, while *that* rolls over the "cities of the plain," it would be easy to fancy one self away in Palestine, and on that scene of human corruption and divine vengeance. The water is extremely buoyant, and it occasions a singular feeling to be unable to sink in, and very difficult to swim through it. Its water produces immediate strangulation, excessive smarting in the eyes, nostrils, and ears, and on coming out converts even negroes into *crystallized white men.*

Numerous salt boileries are erected on the shores; from

four gallons of water they obtain nearly one gallon of clear dry salt. Nature, in her great laboratory, however, produces thousands of bushels of coarse crystals, and deposits them on the shore. Teams and wagons come from the cities and shovel it up, and it sells often as low as 50 cents per 100 lbs. From an analysis of the water, made by Dr. Gale, it was determined to contain by weight 22.422 per cent. of solid substances, in the proportions of 20.196 chloride of sodium, common salt; 1.834 of sulphate of soda; 0.252 of chloride of magnesium, and a trace of chloride of calcium.

We turn our eyes from the Salt Lake back to the city, which is just peeping from under the hill. We are stopped by a mud wall 12 feet high, 6 feet wide at the base, 2½ feet on top; in front of it, is a wide, deep ditch, and it is defended by semi-bastions at half-musket range. These are pierced with loop-holes to afford a front and flank fire in case of attack. It was pretendedly built to keep out Indians, but as it encompasses the city, which covers an area of *six* square miles, all its male population could not thoroughly defend it. The hills rise abruptly round it, and there are abundance of eminences where a rifleman could kill persons in the city, and the wall be but as a thread paper beneath him. It was built in 1854; its design was to give the people something to do, as to keep the mind and hands occupied is the best means to prevent impertinent inquiry and leave no time for rebellion.

We enter at a gate of the wall, and are in the city. We remark that it is divided into blocks, of ten 10 acres each, intersected at right angles by streets, running due north and south, and east and west, 130 feet wide; that the roads in them in wet weather, are almost impassable; that there are very few houses in the suburbs, although they grow closer toward the center; that here they are mud hovels, with dirt roofs, or mere log shanties. We observe, too, that the sidewalks are 20 feet wide, and they have a stream of water at times flowing down each sidewalk: that on some of these streams, cotton wood, and other rapidly-growing trees are planted; that the houses are all built on the edges of blocks, leaving well-cultivated fields and gardens in the center. We notice that every thing bears the impress of work, and when one looks back at the bleak mountains, and forward at the barren valley, without spontaneous vegetation higher than a willow bush, we realize that it must have been hard work.

There are about 15,000 inhabitants at Salt Lake City. They consist of a very few Americans, and the large majority English and Scotch; very many Welsh, and numerous Danes. I think certainly not one third of the whole would embrace all the Americans in the city, and not one fourth of the whole in the entire Territory. These are principally from the western borders of the States. They have all the power in their hands, fill all the offices, ecclesiastical and civil, and receive all the emoluments. They are almost without exception polygamists, and are singularly full of prejudice, intolerance, and boasted fidelity to Mormonism.

Here we are at the Temple Block, in the center of the city. We have come up a street full of stores. There are some very excellent business premises here, and enormous stocks of merchandise are yearly imported across the plains, in huge ox-drawn wagons. The merchants make money very rapidly, profits on some articles amounting from 150 to 600 per cent. We remark that all the stores, etc., are built of adobé, sun-dried bricks; and from their slate-white color, make the streets very lively in appearance. On these streets there are some good houses. A very pretty house on the east side, was occupied by the late J. M. Grant and his five wives. A large barrack-like house on the corner, is tenanted by Ezra T. Benson and his four ladies. A large, but mean-looking house to the west, was inhabited by the late Parley P. Pratt and his nine wives. In that long, dirty row of single rooms, half-hidden by a very beautiful orchard and garden, lived Dr. Richard and his eleven wives. Wilford Woodruff and five wives reside in another large house still further west. O. Pratt and some four or five wives occupy an adjacent building. All these are "Apostles;" they are well known among the people, and their names are inseparable from Mormon history.

Looking toward the north, we espy a whole block covered with houses, barns, gardens, and orchards. In these dwell H. C. Kimball and his eighteen or twenty wives, their families, and dependants. Strange scenes disturb the serenity of this Mormon Paradise. Walking toward the east, we pass three or four low cottages. In that seraglio D. H. Wells has some six of his "feminines" installed. Passing these, we arrive at Brigham's Lion House. This is of stone to the first story, on the ridge of which, in front, is a very excellently sculptured lion, "resting, but watchful." It is a tangible compliment to Brigham, he being called "the Lion of the Lord." The peaked gable, narrow pointed garret windows projecting from the steep roof, attract our notice. That house is occupied by some seventeen or eighteen of Brigham Young's wives (see chapter on Brigham at Home). This house cost him over $30,000, and would have cost more but for his method of building it. It was completed and ready for shingling in 1845. The shingles were ready and waiting. At a Sunday meeting in the Tabernacle, Brigham announced that he had a mission for all the carpenters, and demanded if they would accept it. They raised their hands, and were then coolly commanded to "shingle the Lion House in the name of the Lord, and by the authority of the holy priesthood." So Brigham's Lion House was shingled, for although the carpenters grumbled still they obeyed. A range of neat offices next please the eye, and speak well of Mormon architectural taste; and we arrive at Brigham's mansion. This is a large, handsome adobé building, excellently plastered, and dazzlingly white. It is balconied from ground to roof; on the top is an observatory, and surmounting all is a bee-hive, the Mormon symbol of industry. This cost over $65,000, and is the best edifice in the Territory. It is occupied by Brigham's senior wife and her family. Orchards and gardens lie behind and around it. On the hill to our right is the "White House," formerly Brigham's. This and its adjoining grounds he lately sold to a rich Englishman for $25,500 in English sovereigns, and presented the money to liquidate an old Church debt, due for money borrowed in emigrating the poor Saints to Salt Lake City from Europe.

Struck with the fact that all the eligible property appears

to be in the hands of "the authorities," we continue our walk to the Social Hall. This is an adobé building, 73 × 33 feet. In it is performed dramatic representations, from Shakspeare's tragedies to Colman's farces, by a company of unpaid Mormon amateurs. James Ferguson, *one of the stars*, says "they excel any thing he ever saw in Europe." Faith works wonders! In it, too, Brigham and the other leaders "teach the young idea" to dance. Cotilions, contra-dances, and reels are in vogue. They repudiate waltzes, mazourkas, schottisches, etc., because disliking to see their wives and daughters so "intimate with other men." A Mormon genius has invented a "double cotilion," giving two ladies to each gentleman, something of which kind is necessary, too, as I once counted over three and a half females to each male in a ball-room.

The Council House, a two storied building, 45 feet square, attracts our notice. It is used as the printing-office, and thence issues the Mormon weekly and *weakly* paper called the "Deseret News." The Court House, a large adobé structure, is pointed out to us from the roof of this one, into an observatory on the top of which we mount to get a good view. The Arsenal, on the north hill overlooking the city, also arrests the eye in its passing glance. On the north-east corner is the Tithing-office, a large spacious building, with cellars, store-rooms, and offices attached. Each person on entering the Mormon Church is required to pay the tenth part of his or her property to the Lord's servants for "building up temples, or otherwise beautifying and adorning Zion, as they may be directed from on high." Having tithed their property, they must tithe their yearly increase for the same purpose. This tenth part is really a fifth part; for each man is required to work every tenth day on the Temple, or hire a substitute, and as well pay the tenth of the increase on the other nine days' labor. It is even more than this in many cases, amounting nearly to fifty per cent., as the ladies pay the tenth part of their fowls, then a tenth part of the eggs, and then a tenth part of the chickens that may be hatched, irrespective of loss. This law of tithing, however, is only the "milk of the gospel;" and was the preparative to a more rigid system of property-holding. Smith, in the beginning of the Church, attempted to establish Communism, each giving their all to the Bishop, and only drawing out of the office sufficient to live upon. This, however, was not more practicable for Smith than for Fourier or Cabet, and it was silently permitted to glide into the payment of tithing. In 1854, however, Brigham attempted to revive the old law in an improved shape. He commanded the people to consecrate by legal transfer all right and title to all personal property. A law was passed through the Legislature making such transfers strictly valid; quit claim deeds were drawn up, and from their land to their wearing apparel, the majority of the people transferred every thing to Brigham, or his successor, as trustee in trust for the Church of Latter-day Saints; and some, in the exuberance of enthusiasm, threw in their wives and families. The property of each is retained by each person only at the option of Brigham Young. He can eject any person who has thus "consecrated," for he becomes strictly a trespasser by toleration on Church property. Each is permitted to enjoy the fruits of his labors on condition of his paying a net tithe for immediate purposes, and to be ready to give up ALL should it be required in any emergency. Thus in fact Brigham is the positive owner of almost all the property in the Territory, and is one of the wealthiest men in the world, holding all at his unconditioned will.

He frankly stated the object of this policy at the conference. It was to prevent Gentiles from purchasing any property without ecclesiastical sanction; to hinder departing apostates from taking any property from the Territory; to make it the *interest* of every man to be submissive, and thus to more completely rule the people. Said he, "Men love riches, and can't leave without means; now, *if you tie up the calf the cow will stay.*" Some distressing circumstances have already resulted from the operation of this law. Brigham was in earnest at its devisal, and will be in earnest as to enforcing its execution. He thinks of re-establishing Smith's system of ecclesiastical communism by degrees, and by using the mace of the priesthood, to drub refractory individuals into the practice of obedience. The tithing contributed by the people is paid to the employees of the "Public Works;" and, as the authorities are engaged on public duty, of course they have the first selection, the tithing clerks posting an open account between them and the Lord. Favoritism the most glaring is exhibited in the distribution of the articles. They pretend to pay very large wages to artizans, and salaries to the clerks, but charge equally exorbitantly for articles paid; and while the leading clerks, etc., have an abundance, the poor artizan is half starved, half clad, wretchedly housed, almost insulted on applying for any thing; and, by a singular system of book-keeping, are always found *heavily in debt*, should they wish to quit and find other employment. I can give instances of these things *by dozens*. It is universally known at Utah, and almost universally reproached. I have seen many tears, heard many groans and curses on D. H. Wells, the Superintendent of the Public Works, general business man, third President of the Church, and a prophet, seer, and revelator forsooth, for the misery endured by the suffering "hands." In some cases such pretended balances of account have been collected by law with monstrous officers' fees, from persons who were disgusted with Mormonism, and who were leaving Utah.

But here is the Temple Block. This is a square containing ten acres; it is surrounded by a ten-foot wall, with four gates, around which are planted some handsome shade-trees. We enter at the south gate, and to the west is the Tabernacle. This is an adobé structure, 126 feet long, and 64 feet wide. It has the inside shape of an elliptic arch, the width being its span. Here Brigham and the other leaders give the word of the Lord every Sabbath to the people. It will seat over 2,000 persons, and is generally well attended. They have an instrumental band that plays marches, and even polkas to enliven the feelings of the people, and get up the spirit; besides a choir, who sing from original Mormon songs in the tnue of "Old Dan Tucker," to Bach's chants and Handel's oratorios. They pretend to give to their meetings a religious form, always commencing by singing and prayer, but discourse on adobé-making, clothes-washing, house-cleaning, ditch-digging, and other kindred subjects; advertise letters, appoint labor days for the wards; get up pleasure excursions, organize relief companies to meet the arriving emigration, etc., etc. It is no more worship than any thing else they do, as they open their theatrical performances with public prayer, and dismiss the actors, *and some of them very intoxicated too*, with a benediction. This plan is also adopted in their balls, Brigham not only praying for a blessing on the dancing, but often stopping the ball to give the people a preachment; when, by the inspiration of dancing, he had got under the influence of his prophetic afflatus.

North of the Tabernacle is a frame erection, called "The Bowery," and is used for conference meetings, being capable of accommodating 8,000 persons. It is a singular scene to witness it crowded full of decently dressed people, and sitting under the ringing voice and fluent "talk" of Young, the nonsensical trash of Kimball, the enthusiastic declamation of Hyde, the calm reasoning of P. Pratt, or the abstractions of his brother Orson, swayed by every thought, and eagerly gulping all down as gospel inspiration to this wicked age, if they did but know it.

In the north-west corner of this block is the Endowment house, where is administered the secret ordinances of Mormonism (see chapter on Mormon Mysteries). On the eastern side of this square are the foundations for the famous Temple. They are now nearly level with the ground, and are 16 feet deep, and as much wide. They are of solid rock, and, with the wall, have already cost over $1,000,000, in material and labor, more than the whole of the Nauvoo Temple when complete. The proportions of the proposed building are very

Temple Building at Salt Lake City.

imposing. It is in shape a parallelogram, 193 feet long from E. to W., and 105 feet wide, having an octagonal tower, 40 feet in diameter on each corner. The main building is to be nearly 100 feet high to the ridge of the roof. It is intended to build it of cut stone, and the Mormons for the last three years have been unsuccessfully digging at a canal along the benches to boat instead of carting the stone. Its architecture is symbolic and original. On some buttresses will be representations of globes in all positions, on others the sun in its various phases. On others Saturn, with its rings and satellites, and in the pompous Mormon style, "every stone has its moral lesson, and all point to the celestial world." Its entrance will be on the east side, and will consist of another tower. Surmounted by pinnacles, it will "point upward continually." It was intended to build it of adobé from the first story upward; but they have now determined on erecting it entirely of cut stone. It is going to be the *chef d'œuvre* of all human architecture, and is expected to survive the conflagration that will some day enwrap the world. The accompanying view is accurate, being the copy of the extended drawing at Salt Lake. Its designer, Mr. William Ward, who was also the sculptor of the Lion on Brigham's house, has seceded from the Mormon faith, and left Utah. This will probably occasion some delay and changes in its erection.

All the ground has to be irrigated very extensively, in order to produce even cereals. As the water privileges are very limited, there is consequently but little cultivated soil, and often very slight crops. Along the benches there is a strip of alluvion, and by using the mountain creeks for irrigation, the people can avail themselves of this narrow strip. Hence, all their settlements are on the western inclines of the mountain ridges. The vast portion of Utah is sandy and alkaline deserts, dry dust in summer, impassable swamps in winter. Much interest attaches to the question of its capability of sustaining a large increase of population. There are now about 50,000 inhabitants, at the outside, in the Territory; and they are perhaps, with the exception of 500 persons, exclusively Mormons. Their pursuits are chiefly agriculture and stock-raising. The unwatered ranges during the spring, and mountain gorges in the fall, supply excellent pasture for their stock. This strip of alluvion affords all their tillable land. They have not, however, sufficient water, even now, for irrigating all they attempt to cultivate; and there is more quarreling and positive fighting about the water than all other subjects. With the assistance of more engineering capacity than at present possessed, however, canals might be dug, and they would treble the quantity of available soil by affording more water. One difficulty, however, they labor under, which can not be obviated. Timber is very scarce and uncome-at-able. It requires two days for mule teams to fetch a load of fire-wood from the mountains, and, with the increased consumption, grows necessarily daily scarcer and dearer. Cutting down the timber, by exposing the soil, dries up the springs, which materially lessens the creeks, and this diminishes the water supply, while the increasing population demands a greater abundance. This inevitably dries up the ground, and makes stock-feed very scarce and expensive.

which augments the price of fire-wood in the ratio of time and expense. Although they have discovered coal in the southern portion of the Territory, the badness of the roads and distance to Salt Lake City, make it cost $30 per ton; it is only used by blacksmiths for forge purposes. The scarcity of wood for fuel and building purposes tries the patience and perseverance of the Saints excessively.

Another disagreeable consequence of thus stripping the mountains of their fringes is painfully felt. While the summers are a continual drought, the winters have deep snows and violent storms. The trees used to retain much on the hills, which, melting gradually in the spring, produced full creeks. It is now blown in clouds into the valleys, burying up feed and killing off stock frightfully. Hence it is that at every succeeding winter they have increasingly deep snow. In that of 1854-'55, many thousands of animals perished with hunger and frost, the snow being four to six feet deep. It was naturally followed by very little water in the streams in the spring, because the snow had been deposited in the valleys instead of on the mountains. Last winter the snow was still deeper, and this spring there is still less water in the creeks. Add to this, for the last three seasons the crops have been eaten up by grasshoppers and blue worms, or filled with smut. The harvests have been light, and many starving persons were compelled to subsist on wild roots during the winter. The future promises nothing better; but with the continual influx of population, they must either constantly find new valleys to settle, or starvation and removal will be inevitable. The Mormons, in selecting Salt Lake, chose it as a place where no others would wish to come; and where no others would remain if they did come. Their desire was only to get out of the world: for their object, their selection was good. They have fiercely battled with obstacles thus far in their strife with nature. I think that even Mormon energy and hardihood will not be able to maintain the unequal combat much longer. A few more seasons such as their last three will effectually starve them out; and to judge physical probabilities by appearances, there is little else before them.

The Mormons are an extremely industrious people. Remembering the short length of time they have been at Utah, their utter poverty when they arrived, their many difficulties since, and then viewing their present condition, all must admit their steady industry. They have various manufactories. Wool-carding machines, cloth and blanket factories, tanneries, a pottery for coarse brown-ware, machine-shops, iron and brass founderies, beside all the ordinary avocations. In 1853 they brought some machinery for the manufacture of sugar from beet-root. It is now in the hands of the Church. They have not yet been able to produce any sugar, through incompetent management; for in Utah as elsewhere, personal friendship, far more than proper capacity, induces many appointments, and principal of the sugar works is not an exception from the general rule. The whole affair has almost been useless, except to afford the Saints something to boast about. I forgot, however, one very important operation it produced. In 1854 some hundreds of gallons of syrup were spoiled by the charcoal through which they were endeavoring to refine it. It was, of course, very wicked, according to Mormon economy, to destroy so much property. A luminous thought struck Brigham in 1856. It could not be converted into sugar, it could not be used as molasses, *he would distill it into* RUM. Accordingly, this bad molasses was converted into worse liquor; and, after coloring it with *burnt sugar* and flavoring it with *green tea*, the delicious compound was sold by Brigham's adopted son, W. C. Staines, at the very reasonable price of *eight dollars* per gallon. By this ingenious operation quite a little sum was clearly gained, and it was slyly hinted that the proceeds were expended in helping to build the Temple. If it be true, and I confess I doubt it, it was cementing the walls of the Lord's house with human drunkenness and human degradation!

Nor was this by any means the only distillery in Salt Lake City, although, in order that the Church might regulate such matters, and perhaps to *prevent competition*, all the other distilleries were prohibited from making any liquor during the above saintly speculation. A Dr. Clinton had a distillery producing the most infamous decoction of wheat. He was sent on a mission, and the *Church* purchased his distillery from his wives for its own private working. A Hugh Moon has quite an extensive one in operation at Salt Lake. During the life of Dr. Richards, a prophet, seer, revelator, and editor, his little cart used to make *daily* visits to Moon's distillery, and take thence from a quart to a gallon of liquor; and J. D. Ross, now preaching in England, was sent away from Salt Lake as a missionary, almost entirely because he was overbold in asserting that Moon made the spirit that inspired the leaders in the "Deseret News." There is also another distillery in the city, and several in other parts of the Territory. Brigham has a city named after himself, on Box-elder creek, sixty miles north of Salt Lake City. Even in this holy place, a man named Clarke produces a liquid he calls and the people buy for whisky. At Ogden City there is another such distillery ; another at Provo, and so on throughout the whole Territory. Added to the hogsheads of wash produced at these Mormon factories, each of the merchants imports hundreds of gallons every year, and, as a general rule, although not arriving till June, all is sold out by Christmas. Besides these, there were seven breweries in active operation at Salt Lake alone ; and hundreds of gallons of something called beer was consumed weekly. Of course, the other cities of Utah could not be behind their elder brother of Salt Lake in the necessity that demanded, or in the skill that supplied these delectable compounds ; and "cakes and beer" stared us full in the face, go wherever we might, through the cities of the Saints.

The Church, however, has several times endeavored to prevent the sale of these things. Stringent city ordinances were passed by the Council, prohibiting all sale except by order of the mayor. Still all who so applied succeeded in obtaining these orders, and all who could make, made ; and all who had, sold. In 1854, that was attempted, but the "Church" getting out of supplies, the ban was taken off from Moon's distillery and he produced some "just for the Church." In 1855, it was again resuscitated, preached about, and enforced. Several poor brewers were fined, their utensils destroyed, themselves threatened, etc., etc. A. Mr. Nixon boldly said that it was a shame to punish the poor beer makers only, when there were far more important men equally transgressing; for which manly and honorable speech he was mulcted in fine to a considerable amount. Messrs. Williams & Hooper, an extensive business firm, had a large quantity of liquors the same season, and they obediently refused to sell any, but as it would have much afflicted the authorities to have so much money lost, Brigham got possession of it for a mere trifle, and himself and his adopted son, W. C. Staines, entered into partnership. Staines took the liquor home and sold it *very discreetly*. They, however, watered it down till it was very weak and charged a very high price for it, so that it was difficult for the people to purchase it and almost useless, for intoxicating purposes, when they did obtain it, and thus they appeased their consciences. Of course, some unbelievers dared to suggest that this was profitable as well as expedient, and were astonished the city ordinances about sale of liquor were not enforced in their case. Perhaps the evil did not last long enough, for, although watery, weak, expensive, and only to be bought with cash, it was all sold in an incredible short space of time. A similarly discreet disposition was made in another case of some more liquor. Its owners were forbidden selling it, but the Church made the purchase of it, early in 1856, and Joseph Kaine, one of Brigham's pets, was permitted to vend it. Some scandalous persons said that water came in at the back, as fast as liquor went out of the front door; and hinted that the liquor was only a *little less* inebriating by passing through the saintly hands of Mr. Kaine, but the money was in Church coffers, and that made all the difference.

There are vast mineral resources in Utah, which, had the

Mormons more skill, might be made productive of great wealth. Two hundred miles south of the city is Iron county. Iron in almost inexhaustible quantities, together with abundant coal, is found there. The Mormons have been long laboring to get up furnaces, but want of correct chemical information has much retarded their progress. Should the great Pacific railroad pass through or near Salt Lake, iron and coal for a third of the route might be obtained there. Among other minerals, they have found silver, at Los Vegas, and some lead. It is said that the Church know where there is gold, near the Valley, although I am disinclined to believe it. They have vast quantities of sulphur, alum, borax, and saleratus. They have laid down saltpetre-beds and have commenced the manufacture of gunpowder. Swords, Colt's revolvers, rifles, lances, and guns are made in great abundance, and every man is compelled to have a weapon, to be well supplied with ammunition, to enlist in a military company, and regularly drill.

There are some very singular springs in Utah Territory; chalybeate, sulphur, salt; boiling hot, and very cold; deep sink holes, rivers losing themselves in the sand, small cataracts, remarkable rocks, and other natural curiosities. The atmosphere is astonishingly clear. Optical illusions are very remarkable, and often lead to ridiculous mistakes. Mirages and deceptive distances puzzle many a new comer.

It is reported by the Mormons that there are over 76,000 inhabitants in the Territory. This I know to be a palpable falsehood. Caché valley, with only a dozen Church herdsmen, at most, is given a census population of over 700 persons. *They named the oxen and cows.* In Battle creek returns they report many whom I know to be dead, some who died before leaving England, many who are still in England, but who purpose coming to Utah *when they can;* and, in some cases, all the children that courting couples might expect to have, if they were married, and if they should have offspring; and all that old married people ought to have had in the estimation of the census agents. These outrageous falsehoods were sworn to by the different agents. The object of the whole affair was to present a more imposing appearance at Congress on demanding admission into the Union as an independent State. They publicly defend lying for expediency, believing the end justifies the means. To be unwilling to approve such "evil that good may come," is to them a sign of sectarianism, and Gentilish. This practice they pursued with regard to polygamy for fourteen years, and with regard to other dogmas they still pursue it, contending there is no evil, *per se*, and that the intention of the act and its results only determine its goodness. How much reliance can be placed on the statements of such men, is evident, when mental reservation is advocated; equivocal expressions constantly being employed in all their preaching; they intending to convey an erroneous impression by the use of terms, that, strictly construed, are not in themselves a lie. Jesuit casuistry is not more ingenious in the "deceiving by truth" than are some of the Mormon Elders; but who knows not that the most outrageous falsehoods can be communicated, and yet the words in a different sense be true?

The Mormons have labored diligently, and are therefore

prosperous. It is the only policy by which they could be kept together, and be made contented and happy. When they begin to feel less contented, and less happy, Brigham only makes them work all the harder. To give no time for thought prevents thought; and by making them *merry* when not laboring, helps them to make them satisfied. Hence, the Mormons are a jovial people, hospitable, dance and song, and dram-loving. Their kindness to strangers, their general affection for each other, their devoted obedience to the authorities, their bitter animosity to all Gentiles, their rigid adherence to ceremonies, their lax code of morals, and yet precise restriction to that established code, arrests the attention of all observers.

One thing must be also remarked. There is less *public* drunkenness, no houses of ill fame, no public bad women, less *monstrous* crime among the Mormons than in any other community of equal size. These are the inevitable results of their system, as will be shown. They were far worse at Nauvoo than they are at Salt Lake, were worse at Missouri than at Nauvoo; but compared with another deluded, isolated sect, the Shakers, they are far inferior in every thing good. The Mormon community must not be compared with any *irreligious* community; composed exclusively of Saints, up to the standard of their own selection and boasting must they be brought. Their crimes and their degradation assume other shapes and hues than that of the rest of the world. Their sins are toned with the peculiarities of their religion. They are essentially Mormonic, but while vaunting the absence of other atrocious species of crime from among them, they must be reminded of the flagrance of their own.

CHAPTER III.

PRACTICAL POLYGAMY.

Family arrangements—Favorites—The men—Domestic happiness—Sleeping alone—Making tabernacles—Mormon salvation—Wife hunting—Mothers and daughters married to one man—Half sister—The women—First wives—Whisky—Termagents—Adultery—Jealousy—Fanaticism—Brigham on connubialities—Single girls—Proportion of the sexes—Arguments used to induce young girls to marry polygamists in preference to young men—Why they do not leave—The children—Mortality—Barrenness—Boys—Girls—Early marriages—Divorce—Mrs. M'Lean and Parley Pratt—Mrs. Cobb and Brigham Young—Utah marriages.

THE only correct method of judging a cause, is by the effects that result from its operation. The most confounding argument against the Mormon doctrine of polygamy, is the Mormon practice of polygamy. The Mormons ever endeavor to conceal the real workings of their system from outside inspection. They must feel great confidence before allowing any one to grow intimate. One must be very intimate, before being competent to correctly describe their "family arrangements."

The intention of marriage was to increase personal happiness, to propagate a healthy offspring, and to secure to those children protectors, instructors, and support. What are the effects of polygamy on these objects?

The Mormon polygamist has no HOME. Some have their wives lotted off by pairs in small disconnected houses, like a row of out-houses. Some have long low houses, and on taking a new wife build a new room on to them, so that their rooms look like rows of stalls in a cow-barn! Some have but one house and crowd them all together, outraging all decency, and not leaving even an affectation of convenience. Many often remain thus, until some petty strife about division of labor, children's quarrels, difference of taste, or jealousy of attention kindles a flame, only to be smothered by separation. When they live in different houses, they generally have different tables, and the husband has to give each house its turn to cook for him, and honor their tables with his presence in rotation. The evenings at his disposal, his constant distribution of himself among them, has to be by rule. Jealousies the most bitter, reproaches the most galling and disgusting, scenes without number, and acrimony without end, are the inevitable consequences of the slightest partiality. It is impossible for any man to equally love several different women; it is quite possible, however, for him to be equally indifferent about any number. The nature most in unison with his own, will most attract him. The most affectionate will be certainly preferred to the least affectionate. I am acquainted with scores of polygamists, and they all have *favorites*, and show partiality. To feel partiality, and not to exhibit it, is unnatural. To exhibit it, and for it to pass unnoticed by a jealous women, is impossible. For it to be noticed, is for it to be reproached.

The Mormon polygamist, therefore, has to maintain a constant guard over himself. Any husband might feel to kiss his wife gladly: to go round a table and kiss half a dozen, is no joke. It is so in every thing with him. With a dozen eyes to notice at what time he retires to rest, or arises on any one occasion, and half a dozen mouths to talk about it, he must be perfectly governed by rule. Every look, every word, every action has to be weighed, or else there is jealousy, vituperation, quarreling, bitterness. For this reason, the idea of obtaining domestic felicity is ridiculed. Brigham is the model, and he to some extent adopts the dogma of the Quietists, "Repose is the only perfect happiness." He acts as though he felt, and wished others to feel, that man was the frigid *master*, performing every act of kindness, not as springing from his heart, but because he had *reasoned it out*, to be an act of duty. Warmth of feelings, tenderness of attachment, devotedness of attention to a woman, is there called, by that worst of Mormon epithets, "Gentilish." "Man must value his wife no more than any thing else he has got committed to him, and be ready to give her up at any time the Lord calls him," said Brigham one Sunday afternoon; and J. M. Grant followed the remark by saying, "*If God, through his prophet, wants to give my women to any more worthy man than I am, there they are on the altar of sacrifice; he can have them, and do what he pleases with them!*"

They carry this same coldness of affection into all their connubial relations. Brigham always sleeps by himself, in a little chamber behind his office. I have heard the leading men publicly advocate the adoption of this practice. They quote the animals as an argument in favor of polygamy, and adopt their instincts as models for practice. Marriage is stripped of every sentiment that makes it holy, innocent, and pure. With them it is nothing more than the means of obtaining families; and children are only desired as a means of increasing glory in the next world; for they believe that every man will reign over his children, who will constitute his "kingdom;" and, therefore, the more *children*, the more *glory!* Said Brigham, September 20th, 1856, speaking on this subject:

"It is the duty of every righteous man and every woman to prepare tabernacles for all the spirits they can; hence if my women leave, I will go and search up others who will abide the celestial law, and let all I now have go where they please; though I will send the gospel to them."—*Deseret News, October* 1, 1856.

Marriage, consequently, is only an addition to man's monster *selfishness.* Not only do they admit, but they even advocate openly, that salvation is altogether a selfish matter; and Lorenzo Snow, an Apostle (!) publicly contended that "God was the most intensely selfish being in existence." To sacrifice one's self, to the most trivial extent, for a wife, is therefore esteemed as beneath manly dignity. To love home, or seek to make it your rest and heaven, is called "squeamishness;" and men bedin your ears to "take another wife, and that will cure you," and they are right. The first effect of polygamy on the Mormons was to force them to deny the doctrine, and disavow their families. For many years after they practiced it, did the leading men indignantly deny it. Its next effect was to make them heartless. It first made them liars, and then brutes!

"If it does not increase their happiness, and it certainly does their care and expense, why practice it?" Mormonism teaches that all salvation is *material;* that men's positions here determine their stations hereafter, and as a man can only rule over his family, then, no wife, no family; many wives, much family; much family, much glory; therefore, many wives, much glory, and as the selfish desire for glory is the only incentive of Mormon action, so, therefore, he tries to get as many wives as he can. They quote Paul's words, "Woman is the glory of man," and argue, the more women, the more glory; no women, no glory at all! Full of this thought, I have seen old men with white hair and wrinkled faces, go hunting after young girls, deceiving them with all sorts of professions and promises, using the terrors of Brigham's name and threatening the penalty of excommunication and consequent perdition, in order to induce them to marry them, and then to leave them, despoiled and degraded, either to the obloquy of a divorce, or to the incurable sorrows of a grieved and a wrung heart. I could mention the names of a dozen such, who ought to be thinking of God and their graves, who instead, visit arriving trains and pester the girls with all the ardor and far more impudence than the young men.

The utmost latitude of choice is permitted to the faithful, in their selection of wives. It is very common for one man to marry two sisters; Brigham advises, indeed, that they both be married on the same day, "for that will prevent any quarreling about who is first or second!" A R. Sharkey has married *three* sisters, one of whom was married to, and divorced from another man. A George B. Wallace left a wife at Salt Lake and went to England to *preach*. He made the acquaintance of a very worthy man named Davis, who had three fine-looking girls. Mr. Davis and family were persuaded to embrace Mormonism. When Wallace returned, as he occupied a high position in the Mormon Church, he appropriated Church moneys for the emigration of Mr. Davis and family to Salt Lake City. Poor, and under obligation to this man, and, by "counsel" of Brigham, Davis gave him his three daughters, to all of whom he was married; and, when I arrived at Salt Lake, were all living with Mrs. Wallace, proper, in a little two-roomed house. Wallace kept a butcher's shop, and it was currently reported that he was engaged with others stealing cattle and selling the meat on his premises. A Curtis E. Bolton is married to a woman and her daughter. A Captain Brown is married to a woman and two daughters and lives with them all. When their children's children are born it will be bewildering to trace out their exact degrees of relationship.

This may appear disgusting enough, and prove degradation enough. A G. D. Watt has excelled either of them. He brought from Scotland his half sister to Salt Lake City: took her to Brigham, and wished to be married to her for his second wife. Brigham objected, but Watt urged that Abraham took his half sister and "reckoned he had just as much right as Abraham." The point was knotty and difficult. If Abraham's example justified polygamy then it must equally justify this action. "God blessed Abraham although he did it," say the Mormons, "and ought to bless me if I do it too." The girl happened to be good-looking, though, and so, to cut this gordian knot he could not untie, Brigham took her himself. So far so well. But she was not contented, or Brigham had reconsidered the matter, or from some cause, after a few weeks he told Watt that, after all, there was force in his argument, that it was just as lawful in him as in Abraham, and, accordingly, G. D. Watt accepted his half sister to wife from the arms of Brother Brigham! This piece of complaisance recommended him to the favorable attention of the "authorities;" as a good illustration of the childlike simplicity and implicit obedience of which they so constantly preach.

What the brutalizing effects of such marriages are on the men's minds, can easily be conceived. With small houses and several wives, more than one often sleeping in each apartment, men must soon lose all decency or self-respect, and degenerate into gross and disgusting animals. Many of them frequently sleep with two of their wives in the same bed. Indeed so evident are the effects, that Heber C. Kimball does not scruple to speak of his wives, on a Sabbath, in the Tabernacle, and before an audience of over two thousand persons, as "my cows!!" This he has done on more than one occasion and the people laughed at him as at

"A fellow of infinite jest."

As the Mormons are taught to believe that all their honor and "glory" in the kingdom of God, depends on the number of their wives, all their anxiety is, therefore, to obtain a large number. Irrespective of their ability to provide, careless too about any incongruity in disposition, careless about every thing but obtaining them, they spend their time in courting. If they be poor, it is expected that the woman ought to be able to do enough to support herself. If their temper be incongruous, the Mormons boast "great powers of government," and expect to "break them in, like horses, to the harness." This last is a common and favorite expression among them.

Whether they are on missions, away from their wives, or present with them, their care is to induce more girls to marry them. Many do not do this at Salt Lake, but their faith is considered weak; for unless they entangle themselves inextricably, so that the interests of Mormonism become necessarily their interests, but little attention, and no honor is paid them. As future salvation is made to depend on the size of the family, almost all present reputation is made to depend on the same cause.

Such are the results of this practice on the men. What are its effects on the women?

The females are divided into two classes, first wives, and those taken subsequently. We will view them separately.

I will narrate a few instances as to the first wives. I intend mentioning names, not only to convince the reader of the correctness of my statements, but because I think men who act thus ought to be named and known. Mrs. S. W. Richards is an interesting and intelligent lady at Salt Lake City. She accompanied her husband among the early emigrants. In 1852, he went to England as a Mormon missionary, and was absent several years. During his absence, in the love of her husband, she labored for her own support and that of his children. He returned, and to prove to her his appreciation of her fidelity and affection, he took three other wives! One was his cousin and a mere girl; and one was a lady who ran away from the arms and heart of her father, in Liverpool, and whose attentions, during his stay in that city, had often consoled him for his absence from home. Mr. Richards took his wife round to her share of the balls, theaters, and other amusements; but no one could help remarking, in the wasted and sallow wreck of a woman, all the withering effects of an anguished heart, wounded in its keenest susceptibility, and sinking unloved, unpitied, and with its griefs untold.

> "She never told her grief,
> But let concealment, like a worm i' the bud,
> Feed on her damask cheek."

Mr. G. P. Dykes accompanied the Mormon Battalion to Mexico, leaving his family at Council Bluffs, Iowa. On returning through Salt Lake, he was appointed to go to Europe as a missionary, which he did. During his residence in Europe, Mrs. Dykes and family toiled their way to Salt Lake, so as not to be burdensome on her husband on his return. They sustained themselves, and made some little provision for the future, hoping and expecting to welcome him on his coming home. He returned, accompanied by a lady who had run away from her husband in England. He was married to this person at Council Bluffs City, and amid the first greetings between himself and his first wife, at Salt Lake City, was, of course, an introduction to the woman who had supplanted her in his affections! The first wife was neglected, till her wrung heart demanded a divorce, which was readily accorded. It was an easy thing to sacrifice the wife of his youth and the mother of his children for the paramour of his affections.

A Mr. Batie was married to an amiable person, and they had a very interesting family. He desired another wife, had seen and loved a young person and courted her. Mrs. Batie, however, for a long time, had refused her consent, and had weepingly told him if he married this girl it would break her heart. To yield to her affection was to submit to be controlled. To consider her feelings was to be "ruled by petticoats." As she would not consent, he was married without her consent, and without her knowledge. Is there any man or woman who can fail to conceive her feelings?

A Mr. Eldredge had a very handsome lady for a wife. She had shared her husband's sufferings and privations. Together they had toiled, happily and affectionately. They had amassed some property around them, and were very comfortable, too comfortable for Salt Lake City. On their dream of peace Brigham Young rudely broke by a command that "Brother Horace must take another wife!" Disobedience would be contumacy, contumacy is to be cut off, and that is taught to be perdition. He chose to obey. He married a second, who was inferior in every thing except in age, to Mrs. Eldredge. She, however, speedily weaned her husband's affection from the first wife, whom he soon after turned out of the apartments she had toiled to furnish, and installed his second wife therein. The feelings of Mrs. Eldredge can be imagined, it is impossible that they be described. I could quote a score of similar cases.

The real effects of polygamy on the first wives can be imagined, when they force Brigham Young to use this language from the pulpit, September 21, 1856 :

"Now for my proposition; it is more particularly for my sisters, as it is frequently happening that women say that they are unhappy. Men will say, 'My wife, though a most excellent women, has not seen a happy day since I took my second wife;' 'No, not a happy day for a year,' says one; and another has not seen a happy day for five years. It is said that women are tied down and abused; that they are misused and have not the liberty that they ought to have; that many of them are wading through a perfect flood of tears, because of the conduct of some men, together with their own folly.

"I wish my own women to understand that what I am going to say is for them as well as others, and I want those who are here to tell their sisters, yes, all the women of this community, and then write it back to the States, and do as you please with it. I am going to give you from this time to the 6th day of October next, for reflection, that you may determine whether you wish to stay with your husbands or not, and then I am going to set every woman at liberty and say to them, Now go your way, my women with the rest, go your way. And my wives have got to do one of two things, either round up their shoulders to endure the afflictions of this world and live their religion, or they may leave, for I will not have them about me. *I will go into heaven alone, rather than have scratching and fighting around me.* I will set all at liberty. 'What, first wife too?' Yes, I will liberate you all.

"I know what my women will say; they will say, 'You can have as many women as you please, Brigham.' But I want to go somewhere and do something to get rid of the whiners."—*Deseret News, October* 1, 1856.

Even in Brigham's family, and that is the best-managed in Utah, there is still "scratching and fighting."

From all I have seen of Salt Lake polygamy, I can assert the almost universal rule—a man does not marry a second wife, until he finds somebody he prefers to the first; and when he is married, it is not long before he exhibits the preference. It is pretended that the consent of the first wife is obtained to such subsequent marriages. That consent is asked by the husband, and who knows not the thousand petty tyrannies that a husband can use toward his wife to extort or compel acquiescence? If the consent be given, she is willing to contribute to his glory, and the ceremony is performed. If she do not consent, women must not be an impediment either in doing one's duty, or obtaining one's salvation; so, therefore, the ceremony is performed just the same, whether she consent or no, whether she like the girl or no; for her husband to will it, is for the Lord to will it, and nothing is left to her but to bend and groan. Polygamy, however, does not thus affect all the first wives at Salt Lake. That which will crush one woman into the grave, *and I know more than one such case,* will sink another into depravity, arouse another to desperation, incite another to retaliation, and by others will be regarded with the most stoical indifference. I can name a dozen families where the men and women have sunk into the most complete and disgusting brutishness. They fulfill the definition of man, "food-cooking animal," and that is almost their only distinction. If superior to the animals at all, it is only in adding disgusting talk to disgusting deeds; in aggravating the instincts of nature with the excitement of meditation; deceiving simple girls, and appeasing their own consciences by disguising their practices with the name of religion. There are many women in Utah who drink whisky to a very great extent. To drown thought, is to kill feeling. Many women who will not become depraved, try to be indifferent. I asked a lady once at Salt Lake, why she never appeared jealous of her husband's attention to his three wives? Her reply struck me painfully, "Mr. Hyde, my husband married me when we were both very young in England; O! I was very fond, and very proud of him. We came out here, and he took another wife. It made me very wretched, Mr. Hyde, but I am not jealous now, *for I cease to care any thing about him!*" When love dies, jealousy ceases. Nothing makes people more indifferent than does liquor; not only indifferent as to others, but also callous as to one's self. Many Utah women seeking this callous state of heart, drink very extensively. Of this no resident of Salt Lake can be ignorant. Some, however, become termagants, fiercely jealous, and furiously violent. The quarrels resulting from such matters often cause merriment in the gossiping circles of Utah. The constant policy of the "authorities," however, is to train the mass of the people to despise such proceedings, and to view with contempt any such woman. By this means they crush the voice of nature under the weight of their public opinion. Instead of such a course eliciting sympathy, if it be felt, it falls still-born and unexpressed; and the poor woman, goaded till she is mad, has to stand alone. To stand up under the pressure of public vituperation; to endure the coarse crimination of the Tabernacle platform, where on Sundays Brigham and Kimball will refer most minutely to the persons, and sometimes even name them before the whole congregation, needs a stronger mind than possessed by most women. If she be discontented, there is the divorce alternative; but to be divorced is to lose her children. If she decline divorce, she must submit. Broken and crushed, she must submit!

There is yet another class of first wives. These, finding their jealousy only increases neglect, and their reproaches only serving to drive their husbands from them to others and more affectionate of their wives, fall a step lower. Neglect breeds anger; anger engenders hatred; hatred meditates revenge. They are powerless to retain their husband's affection, *but they can retaliate his infidelity.* The penalty of adultery is death, unsparing and bloody. It has been inflicted, is being inflicted, and yet they can not arrest the commission of the sin. Startling and frequent have been the disclosures. Brigham, in his public sermons asserts, that even in his own family, he can not preserve his own honor. For that reason, among others, he said, "he wanted to get them all in one house, under his own eye," because he "could trust no one else, and not even them." Just previous to my leaving Salt Lake City, a very flagrant case got into the public mouth about one of the wives of P. H. Young, Brigham's brother. While he was with his other wives, a young man in their employ, was consoling her for his neglect. The women are very poor; many of them almost entirely destitute. Their husbands and fathers, burdened with debts, they can not pay, and with families they can not support, are often unable to buy clothes enough for them to be decent, to say nothing of being respectable. The love of dress is just as strong there, as anywhere else; and to obtain clothes, leads to the same conduct there as anywhere else. Many of the missionaries have to leave their families in penury. No assistance is given such families, in many instances, till they are almost perishing for want. Neglected by absent husbands; knowing that in all probability they will bring home other and better-loved wives when they return; surrounded by suffering children; tempted by flattery and allured by money, it is not unnatural for them to fall; it would almost be supernatural for them not to fall. I could name several such.

It is this fact that makes the Mormons so averse to any outside inspection of their "peculiar institution." Men who are giving constant reasons to be suspected, are the most suspicious of all persons. The Mormons, who are continually wringing their wives' hearts with jealousy, are the most tyrannically jealous. The most rigid watch is maintained; and a look, passing word, a visit, above all when it is repeated, is tortured into

"Proof strong as holy writ."

Heber C. Kimball refused to allow one of his wives to correspond with her friends, lest improper use might be made of the liberty. On the slightest occasion of distrust he will mount the rostrum on a Sabbath, and publicly tongue-lash his wives; and it is a common jest at Salt Lake, that his reason for doing so at such a time and place, is because "they can not reply!" Coercive measures never produce virtue. To constantly suspect, is often to suggest crime. To bitterly accuse, is frequently to instigate. These are unfailing truths, and they are as unfailing at Salt Lake as elsewhere. Were it not for the great counteracting influence of a strong religious fanaticism, Utah would be a perfect pandemonium of debauchery.

How can they permit it at all? The whole secret lies in that one word, fanaticism. The women are all sincere: their sufferings and their sacrifices prove that. They are taught that polygamy is a heaven-ordained institution; that it was countenanced by God anciently and is commanded by God now; that the instincts of their nature which rebel against it are the results of false education and tradition; their pride is flattered to think that the exaltation of man depends on them; they learn to sacrifice themselves to elevate, as they think, their husbands. The desire to be eternally glorious, is made to overcome the wish to be temporarily happy. The ambition to excel their neighbors is also used to induce them to submit patiently to privation and misery. What will not weak minded persons endure from a feeling of rivalry? Where wealth is regarded as the *summum bonum*, any sacrifice will be made to give wealth to their husbands. In Utah, women are esteemed that *summum bonum*, and therefore many sacrifice all personal feeling, and give other women to their husbands. The fanaticism that prompts it is old; it is only this peculiar development of fanaticism that is new. It is common that people be fanatical; it is growing to be too common that they should choose Mormonism as their style of exhibiting it. Some women in Utah seem contented enough. The most enthusiastic arguments in favor of polygamy are used by some of the women. That, however, is natural enough. If polygamy be not commanded by God, as they believe it is, then they would feel their fate as others see it. For them to see themselves deceived, is to know themselves dishonored. To maintain their own self-respect, they must maintain their own self-deception. Who knows not what an easy thing it is to find force in weak arguments that justify our position, and not to feel very strong ones that condemn our actions. It is necessary that these poor deluded and degraded women should debate the questions very often, for they very often feel the necessity to out-clamor the voices of their own hearts.

> "Oh that some gude God would gie 'em
> To see themselves as others see 'em."

The extent of this infatuation is very extraordinary. Mrs. Joseph K——e was the only wife of her husband, whose position was very comfortable; he having considerable property as well as a profitable situation in the post-office. She was very desirous to obtain a second wife for Mr. K., thereby to increase his glory, and as she could only shine by reflecting his light, thus increase her own glory too. Accordingly, when the new emigrants arrived from the plains, she visited their camps and invited several good-looking single young persons to come and remain with her during the winter. She treated them with all hospitality and kindness; contrived excellent opportunities for her husband to plead his suit, and, as he was a little backward, often plead his cause for him. Unfortunately for her wishes, however, her efforts had failed, and she was, when I left, condemned to be the sole satellite of her planet-master. One of Brigham's wives affords a still stronger proof of this singular infatuation. An uneducated English girl saw Brigham and loved him. She read in the Old Testament that Jacob served seven years to get a wife; and as the New Testament says, that in the last days, "old things shall pass away and all things shall become new," she interpreted that to mean, a reversal of matters; and, consequently, determined to reverse the case of Jacob. She offered her seven years' service to Mrs. Young, only demanding as her hire, the right to marry Brigham. He was consulted as to this novel method of getting a husband, and, of course, had no objections to offer. Eliza served faithfully, demanded her wages, the thirtieth share of Brother Brigham. She was married, and I saw Brigham fondle her child, and call him his "English boy." It was an attachment on her part worthy a better object.

A Mrs. Howard is an intelligent person, but madly infatuated with Mormonism. Her husband saw a young lady and admired her; got acquainted with and fond of her. He told his wife of the affair, and desired her to call on this young lady and request her to marry him. The wife wept bitterly at this singular command; she had lost her power to longer please; another had supplanted her in the affections of the man whom she devotedly loved, and to whom she had borne four children: she felt as a woman in such a position only can feel, but Mormonism was stronger in her soul than her nature itself. She went and asked this girl, who directly refused. She informed her husband of the result, and this MAN bitterly reproached his madly-devoted wife for not succeeding in persuading her, attributing the failure to his wife's jealousy. Mrs. Howard did not murmur, but only wept; while he blubbered like a boy, told her how much he loved this young woman, how miserable he must ever be without her. I believe he induced this heart-wrung woman to visit and again make this offer, but was again refused. With these women Mormonism is inwound in their hearts, every hope is centered in it; out of it they fancy there is nothing but despair. They are taught to think that God has re-established a priesthood on this earth; that this priesthood is almost immaculate and quite infallible, as a priesthood; and brought to this standpoint, they blindly believe and as blindly obey all they are commanded. Degraded into slavery by this Mormon step-back into barbarism, they are almost as submissive and as miserable as the Indian squaws around them.

The engine of Mormon power is not brute force; not attempted or threatened violence, but the lever of a skillfully-combined and ably-handled system of religious machinery, operating on duped and bewildered fanatics. They feel its force, are not able to explain or investigate and discern its reality, but supinely obey its impulses.

"While it is not very surprising that the first wife should submit, or be compelled to submit, how is it that the single girls themselves marry old men with several wives, in preference to young men with no wives?" This is more surprising from the fact of there being, in Utah, so many single men. By the census returns of 1851, made by the Mormons themselves, the remarkable fact is proven, that there were seven hundred and ten more males than females in Utah. That is, there were nearly a thousand more marriagable men than women; and as some of the authorities monopolize from thirty to five wives each, and as there are a great number of others with two and three wives each, there must have been a very large proportion of the males compelled to be single, because there were no wives to be had. This proportion is materially reduced, since that time, from several causes. Many young men have left the Church and Utah; many have been sent to the States and Europe and commanded to be sure and bring back wives; many of the married Elders who have been sent out have been counseled "to bring in as many ewe-lambs as they could into the sheep-fold; though not to *appropriate any till they got home.*" (H. C. Kimball.) There are also a larger number of females than males who emigrate to Utah. Yet, notwithstanding these causes being in operation, there is not a large plurality of females, and there are still hundreds of young men in Utah unable to get wives: and many of the new-coming ladies marry old polygamists in preference.

While nothing proves more plainly their fanaticism than this, nothing proves more plainly their sincerity. Men, who, by a long course of fidelity, have "proven themselves" receive as a reward for their merit, certain mysterious ordinances; pass by secret rites into a sacred order and are finally "sealed up against all sin to salvation, except the sin against the Holy Ghost, which is denying the faith, exposing the mysteries, and shedding innocent blood." These men, who are thus sealed, think that they can not be lost; nor their wives, nor their little ones, nor any who shall "cling to them." Having, they believe, accomplished their own salvation, they are able, like Jesus, "to save to the uttermost all who shall come unto them." To be married to such a man, it is taught to these confiding neophytes, is to "secure eternal salvation with a high degree of glory." They have been previously made to believe that woman can not obtain any kind of salvation but through the man. "Eve led Adam out of Eden and he must lead her back again!" As her future position will be regulated by that of her husband, and as she is taught that to obtain a high position ought to be the only object of her existence, hence she is induced to desire to marry a man who has been thus sealed.

Mormon women go to Utah, zealous in their religion; they go there for its sake; they have made great sacrifices already, and are prepared to make still greater for it; they are firmly convinced that these atrocious dogmas are the precious truths of heaven, and that these men are God's vicegerents; they swallow the gilded bait, marry, and when they wake up to the temporal miseries of their positions, console themselves in more dogmatically believing their fanaticism and their creed.

Not only the prospect of securing their own salvation is held out to these misguided beings, but that of entailing salvation on their children. The Mormons believe that the pure seed of the house of Jacob can not be lost: they are "children of the covenant made to Abraham." It is also believed that Brigham's children can not be lost: they are "children of the covenant made to Brigham!" It is thus with all those who have been "sealed up to eternal life." Every woman has a strong love for her children, even when they are only prospective. It is a chord that can be played upon, that will send out deep vibrations. The Mormons play on that delicate fiber of the female heart. The woman is told that by marriage with this young man, he may apostatize and be lost; she would share his fall and ruin; her children, assimilating, not to her, but to his character, would be lost too, and that thus she would barter eternal loss for a little passing pleasure. To marry this old, well-proven, and sealed man, would not only secure her own salvation but that of her children; and if not to enjoy all the temporal happiness she might with the young man, she should enjoy more of the Spirit of God and secure eternal gain by suffering a present loss.

If this be not enough to persuade the deluded victim, previously confounded by bad argument, as to the scripturality of the practice, and bewildered by pretensions to infallibility by the Prophet; then they use another and more powerful appeal. Who knows not the love that clings around the sacred memories of the dead? If these men can perform such works of supererogation as to save children yet unborn, they can also save people who are dead. This is inevitable, and hence the Mormons claim to be "saviours to the dead." The rationale they adopt is this: Mormonism is the gospel; not to have heard Mormonism is not to have received the gospel, and that is not to be saved: but the dead can hear the gospel in spirit, and their friends at Zion can receive the ordinances for them as proxies or agents. This then, say they, will be your privilege, if you take this man. Salvation for yourself, for your unborn generations, and for your dead kindred. They went there for the sake of their faith, and on the shrine of their faith, with the devotion of eastern idolatry, they immolate themselves. The sincerity of their hearts or their purity of motives, can not be questioned; whatever is said must be as to their credulity.

"But they must awaken as wives and as mothers, why do they not leave?"

Fanaticism may be strong; self-love is stronger. Many do awaken, and weep bitterly. Many would fly, but they are mothers, they would be forced to desert their children. The mother's love often overcomes the woman's shame. Besides they are dishonored, betrayed; however innocently on their part, they are still degraded. To lose self-respect is to lose the energy of a motive. They are poor, entirely dependent, and could not leave if they would. They are a thousand miles from civilization. To solicit the protection of a company would be to subject herself to the vilest slanders from the Mormon authorities, and, perhaps, death; some shame and much curiosity from the company; and would certainly subject her protectors to arrest for abduction; a suit in a Mormon court for monstrous damages; extortionate fees for officers, and the property of the offender would be sold at auction, for almost nothing; as well as, in all probability, *a pistol-ball through his head for daring to interfere in a Mormon's domestic arrangements.*

Not only this, but having all her few friends at Utah; seeing polygamy constantly practiced, and hearing submission constantly preached; no adverse public sentiment to support, or sympathy to console, and no one to protect her; alone and wavering in mind, she sinks, and to sink is to be lost. Besides, virtue deferred is virtue lost; for the practice of vice is like the waters of a fabled river, it soon petrifies the heart.

What are the effects of polygamy upon the children?

It is urged that polygamy is beneficial to increase of population. "It is not the question," shrewdly observes Paley, "whether one man will have more children by five wives, but whether those five women would not have more children, if they had each a husband?" That Brigham has more children by his large number of wives, is certain; but whether there are as many children in the world as there would have been had each of his wives been married to a separate husband, and whether those children of Brigham are any better developed, physically or mentally, is an important question. Nature, as shown in the proportion of the sexes (see chapter on Theoretical Polygamy), points to monogamy, and she will punish any infringement of her law. This is plainly shown in Utah. The proportion of female to male births, is very much in favor of the female sex. In monogamic countries, the surplus is on the male side. In polygamic countries, as in Utah, it is the reverse of this. Were the inhabitants of Utah, therefore, to grow up, intermarry without any mixture from other incoming people, and practice polygamy as they now practice it, the male race in a few generations would become extinct. I have observed, very frequently, that the more wives a man has, the greater the proportion of female to male children he has This might have been predicted not only from facts observable in all polygamic countries, but also from well-known physiological laws. If the Mormons were to adopt the old Arab custom of burying female children alive, when they had more than one or two, hundreds of babes would be murdered in Utah. Not only is there this disproportion, but there is a fearful mortality among the Mormon children. I think I can say, more children die in Salt Lake City, notwithstanding the salubrity of its climate, than in any other city of its size in the Union. According to their own census, the mortality of Utah is next to that of Louisiana, and the large proportion is children. Salt Lake City is therefore nearly as unhealthy as New Orleans.

This mortality, too, is particularly noticed in the families of polygamists. Brigham Young, considering the number of his wives, has but a very small family, something over thirty children. Quite a number of his wives are sterile; many others have had large families, but who have all died in infancy. His houses are filled with his women, but their children are in their graves. Joseph Smith had many wives; no one but himself knows the number, and many of them had children, but with one or two exceptions they are all dead; and well for them, poor little ones. Many of the Mormon leading men have many wives, but their children are not proportionably many. Facts like these are not confined to Utah. Mohammed had many wives and concubines, some say twenty-five; he had but one son. Fatima, the only one of his children who survived her father, died soon after, and Mohammed's direct line was extinct. There are many barren women in Utah, and as this is regarded as a signal curse, it has led, to my knowledge, to more than one case of adultery. A Mr. Hawkins was absent on a mission to the Sandwich Islands; he had left behind him a wife, who had never had any family. Boarding at her house was a Mr. Dunn, whose wife was on the road to Salt Lake, coming to join her husband. Mrs. Hawkins was, however, found to be *enceinte* by this man, and the affair was patched up by a precipitate marriage between them; although her husband was away preaching Mormonism to the "Kanakas." When Mrs. Dunn arrived, her feelings may be imagined. Many expected that Hawkins would shoot Dunn on his return; but Brigham hushed the matter very quietly, and Mrs. Hawkins Dunn now fondles her two children.

If polygamy be inimical to the physical, it is still more so to the moral and mental developments of the children. Parents owe other duties to children than merely to beget them. Many men marry wives, quite indifferent about their means of sustaining them. It is notorious at Salt Lake City, that men have been walking about, doing nothing, and making their wives support them by taking in washing. I could name several such. With all their toil it is as much as most of these men can do to supply their physical wants. Food and clothing, and both scanty and poor, exhaust their purses and energies. They have no time, and if time, no disposition to attend to the mental culture of their children. There are always too many domestic quarrels to adjust; some old wife to scold, or some new wife to court. What they have not time to attend to themselves, they have no money to pay others for. The Salt Lake system of schools is merely a farce and a name (see chapter on Schools). Their children are impatiently turned over to their mother and their *aunts*, as they call them, who drive them out of their little crowded houses. They companionize with children bigger than themselves; go with them to herd cattle; become early inured to vice, and accustomed to foul thoughts and words; premature observers of the brute creation; practicing, many of them, the worst vices, and making the most sacredly private matters of their families a jest for their playmates. As soon as they can crack a whip or use a hoe, they have to work to help support their brothers and sisters. Education is neglected, and consequently despised. The habits of men are contracted at the age of boyhood. Many of their parents, themselves born in the backwoods, encourage their precocity. Their cheating the confiding, is called smart trading; mischievous cruelty, evidences of spirit; pompous bravado, manly talk; reckless riding, fearless courage; and if they out-talk their father, outwit their companions, whip their school-teacher, or out-curse a Gentile, they are thought to be promising greatness, and are praised accordingly. Every visitor of Salt Lake will recognize the portrait, for every visitor proclaims them to be the most whisky-loving, tobacco-chewing, saucy and precocious children he ever saw. It is true, however, that the Mormons have been driven from place to place; and to some extent this has prevented much attention being directed to the education of their children. This will account, perhaps, for the ignorance of the older boys; but this ignorance is almost universally the case, and indeed could not be otherwise. Large families of young children, and many wives, with frequent female ailments, are all dependant on the toil of one man, where most persons are agriculturists, and where they can not raise even cereals without irrigating the land several times. All are obliged to work as soon as able, women and children as well as men, in the fields and gardens. Add to all this bad school regulations, incompetent instructors, and the leaders fiercely declaiming against the Gentiles and their education; ignorance, wickedness, and corruption among the boys is inevitable.

With the girls, the routine, though different, produces nearly the same result. There is a weekly meeting at Salt Lake Tabernacle attended exclusively by women; it is called the "Council of Health," its object, to discuss the most in delicate subjects. It is presided over by an old man named Richards, whose ordinary topics of conversation make even Mormons blush. It is attended frequently by H. C. Kimball, from whom I have heard the most disgustingly filthy talk before eighty or a hundred men and women. The subject-matters of this Board of Health form staple for conversation during the week. Marriages and births in detail are the *morceaux choisies.* The presence of young girls, instead of repressing, excites their garrulity. "To blush at truth," says Kimball, "is from the devil." These women copy their prophet; mock the blush of half shame and half horror; and laugh at the look of childish wonder. The consequences are certain. Children from hearing learn to repeat; from repeating, learn to understand; from realizing, *learn to act!* The sore begins to bloat with corruption; and as the climax of abomination, the authorities now advocate early marriages!

With snow constantly in sight, they urge the example of tropical nations. They expect to obtain the hardy bodies and sound minds of northern Saxons from the worst practices of effeminate Asiatics. The fact is, some remedy has to be adopted. Passions precociously developed will be precociously gratified. If not licensed, they will be gratified illicitly. "Boys should marry at fourteen and fifteen, and girls at thirteen and fourteen," says Kimball. "Boys should be married," teaches Brigham, "and still live under their fathers' direction." Accordingly both these men had their boys married and living at home. But as to the offspring of these marriages? "The sins of the fathers shall descend upon the children, unto the third or fourth generation." Men can not transgress nature's laws with impunity. To infringe her ordinances, is to secure her penalties.

Where marriage is thus prostituted to gratify licentiousness, either there must be a great facility of divorce, or else there must be an unmitigated hell. Jesus said, Matt., xix. 9, "Whosoever putteth away his wife, except it be for fornication, and shall marry another, committeth adultery; and whoso marrieth her which is put away, committeth adultery." The Mormons are wiser than the Saviour on this subject, as well as on many others. The most trivial imaginable cause justifies and obtains a divorce at Salt Lake. Nor is any scruple made to re-marrying such a divorcee. One woman in Salt Lake has been married six times; four of her previous husbands are, I believe, still in Utah. Several cases occurred where people were divorced a day or two after their marriage; several cases where divorcees were married a few days after being divorced. So common did the applications for divorce become, that in 1854, Brigham had to impose a price to be paid in cash (*then very scarce*) upon all "bills." He charged ten dollars if married for time; fifty dollars if sealed for eternity. The money went mostly to the clerk. Not a few amusing scenes occurred, where parties who came for divorce had to return and live together, because they could not raise money enough between them to pay for the "bill." It had the desired effect: it decreased the applications.

One peculiarity of the Mormon Churches outside Utah, can not but be observed, and that is the number of *mis-matches* that become Mormons. Motives of interest, advice of friends, thoughtless indifference, or an act of jealousy, have united many men and women. Mormonism to them offers peculiar charms: a divorce to be had for the asking, and a free choice afterward. There are also at Utah many women who have deserted their husbands for the sake of some of the Elders. Some very distressing circumstances have occurred in consequence of this feature. One particularly is very painful. Mrs. M'Lean was married, and had several children. She embraced Mormonism in San Francisco, where she afterward saw P. P. Pratt, one of the Mormon Apostles, and admired, believed, obeyed, and loved him. She several times endeavored to abscond with her children from her husband; he, who loved her and them very devotedly, prevented her taking his children. The children were finally sent from San Francisco to Louisiana, to their grandparents. Mrs. M'Lean went to Salt Lake and married this man Pratt, where I saw her in 1855. She came with him from Salt Lake in 1856, went to her parents' house, pretended repentance and regret, promised amendment, and accused the Mormons. She obtained their confidence, and then stole the children from their refuge; leaving the grandparents and their father nearly distracted. Mr. M'Lean has subsequently shot Pratt in Arkansas, U. S. I much regret his desperate action, however deeply I sympathize with his misfortunes. I made the acquaintance of Mr. M'Lean in California, where he was universally respected and esteemed as an honorable and an upright man; deeply devoted to his wife, and tenderly attached to his children. Another of this Pratt's wives, I understand, was a similar case, but not so far prosecuted by the husband.

Nor is this Parley P. Pratt the only one of the authorities who has acted in this manner. Both Joseph Smith and Brigham Young may be cited as examples. A Mrs. Cobb saw and loved Brigham at Boston, Mass. She embraced Mormonism, and absconded from her husband, taking with her her daughter Charlotte. She got to Salt Lake, and was married to Brigham. Charlotte is still there; she is considered the *belle* of Salt Lake; and if Brigham does not take a notion to marry her himself, will most likely be "sealed" to one of his sons.

Marriage with the Mormons is regarded peculiarly as a religious rite, to be performed by the priesthood, wholly irrespective of any civil authority. "Any High Priest, Bishop, Elder, or Priest," can perform it; and as almost all the Mormons hold one of these offices, almost every man has the right to unite a couple. In this way a great many marriages are performed that are only lawful in Utah. Outside Mormondom they would be regarded as concubinage. This is an artful means of keeping people in subjection, and of retaining them at Salt Lake.

Thus far we have reviewed the immediate effects of polygamy. The Mormons have, however, another system of marriage, in the carrying out of which there is still more of the atrocious and corrupt. This is what they term "the sealing for eternity," and will require a separate chapter.

Orson Pratt.

CHAPTER IV.

MORMON MYSTERIES.

Sealing for eternity—Women married to one and sealed to another husband—Spiritual wives—Smith's death—Smith's widows—"Proxy doctrine"—Marriage and sealing for the dead—The endowment—Washing—Anointing—Creation—First degree of Aaronic priesthood—Second degree of Aaronic priesthood—First degree of Melchisedec priesthood—Second degree of Melchisedec priesthood—"Behind the vail"—Obedience—Examples—Murders—Sealing at the altar—Initiative lectures—Sealing to Indian squaws—Adoption—Selling their daughters.

THE married relationship, say the Mormons, was intended as eternal. As marriage is a religious ceremony more than a civil institution, they urge, therefore, it must be performed by an ecclesiastical dignitary. All other marriages are mere contracts sanctioned by law, but dissolvable at the option of both contracting parties. As marriage, ordinarily administered, is only "till death;" it is perfectly null and void for any period after death. As they believe that unless married, the saved will not enjoy any "glory" in the next world; and if not married on earth, can not be married afterward, therefore they "*marry for eternity*."

This power is vested in Brigham only. He can, however, transfer it at option to any other Apostle. Heber C. Kimball usually performs the ceremony. These marriages are always performed in their sacred and secret Temple, in a singular manner—of which hereafter—and are termed sealings. People, according to Mormon technology, are *married* for time, but *sealed* for eternity.

It is impossible to state all the licentiousness, under the name of religion, that these sealing ordinances have occasioned. A woman has been married to a man she does not like. She comes to Salt Lake and sees some one whom she does like. The man's position, however, is such that she does not wish to leave her husband, but only desires to secure another for an *eternal husband.* She can be sealed to this other man and still remain with her first husband; and the Mormons believe that all her children will belong to the man to whom she is "sealed." "No marriage is valid till physically consummated," is a maxim of all human and divine law. These marriages or sealings are therefore consummated to make them valid. But the husband may know of the sealing ordinance, and desire to get his wife sealed to him. To tell him the real facts might make him apostatize; convert a warm adherent into a devoted enemy; and, therefore, the Mormons will perform a "mock ceremony," contending that it is better one man be deceived, rather than the whole Church should suffer. In this way no man, unless his position be so high as to make it impolitic, is certain of his dearest wife's virtue, or his warmest friend's honor. Suspicion and jealousy are the inevitable results.

There is a Mrs. Dibble living in Utah, who has a fine son She was sealed, among others, to Joseph Smith, although living with her present husband before and since. On the head of her son, Smith predicted the most startling prophesies about wielding the sword of Laban, revealing the hidden Book of Mormon, and translating the sealed part of the records. There is not a person at Salt Lake who doubts the fact of that boy being Smith's own child.

It is these wives, who, married to one man and sealed to another, are the "*spiritual wives*" of those to whom they are sealed. Joseph Smith lost his life entirely through attempting to persuade a Mrs. Dr. Foster, at Nauvoo, that it was the will of God, she should become his "spiritual wife;" not to the exclusion of her husband, Dr. Foster, but only to become his in *time* for *eternity!* This nefarious offer she confessed to her husband. Some others of a similar nature were discovered, and Dr. Foster, William Law, and others began to expose Smith. Their paper was burned, type and press demolished, for which Smith was arrested and afterward shot, by Missourians, at Carthage, Ill. Of course, all this is denied by the Mormons, but the same men denied that Smith practiced polygamy at all. One of their denials is proven to be a falsehood; may not the other be equally false? Not only did they deny the action, but also the principle involved in the action. Not only have they subsequently acknowledged polygamy, but they now admit the principle; but still persist in denying this action of Smith. Two of the facts being admitted, when all three were previously denied, makes the third very probable. It is certain Mrs. Dr. Foster knew of the *principle*, else she could not have told her husband. It is also certain that she would not have known it had Smith not revealed it to her. It is, therefore, strongly presumptive that as Smith certainly did reveal to her the *principle*, that he did so for the *object* she states: and I think that her testimony, which is very positive, is irrefutable in the matter.

The Mormons do not *now* seek to deny the fact that women married to one, may be sealed to another husband; only asserting that such marriages *go no further*. But as they contend that no marriage is valid till consummated, and insist that these marriages are valid, either they destroy their own system, or else there is licentiousness and corruption. There would be only one choice in the mind of any believing Mormon. When a woman sinks low enough to prefer another man for her *pseudo* eternal husband, she is certainly sunk low enough to sin in *deed* as well as *thought*. When the promptings of affection are sanctioned by religion and legalized by precedent, few persons would hesitate at indulgence.

As a man's "kingdom" depends solely on the size of his family; and as all the children that the woman may have belong to her sealed husband, whether by him begotten or not; and as if the *husband dies*, all his anticipated glory seems to be arrested; the "Saints" have, therefore, adopted the plan of appointing brethren as their *agents* to continue their "*glorifying*," after their decease. Alexander McRae, an old Mormon and companion of Joseph Smith, but not a polygamist, was called on abruptly, at Fillmore, in 1855, to "increase the kingdom" of a dead brother by taking his widow; she having seen, liked, and wanted him, and having gone to President Kimball and solicited to have him *counsel*

McRae to take her. Kimball gave McRae the "word of the Lord," and, although it very much displeased him, he had to submit. Many of the widows of Joseph Smith, who could not find other husbands, were taken by Brigham, who has been endeavoring to perpetuate his kingdom on earth. Not only is it deemed proper to take the widows of some good brother, but also to take *fresh wives* for your dead brother. There was a lady named P———, in Salt Lake, in 1854, who had heard of and loved Smith. He had been dead for ten years, but that is nothing to the wings of Mormon faith. She was desirous to be sealed to him, although, I believe, she had a husband still living in the States. Brigham consented to act as proxy or agent for Joseph Smith, and accordingly the interesting ceremony was performed. Mrs. P——— good soul, gave up all her property to the Church, faithfully believing she had joined the numerous army of the Smiths in general, under the especial banner of the Prophet, Joseph.

A still more atrocious, but natural result of his sensual salvation remains. As a man's family constitutes his glory, to go on a mission for several years, leaving from two to a dozen wives at home, necessarily causes some loss of family, and consequently, according to Mormon notions, much sacrifice of salvation. This difficulty is however obviated by the appointment of an agent or proxy, who shall stand to themward in their husband's stead. Many and many a little child has been thus issued into the Mormon world. This is one of the secret principles that as yet is only privately talked of in select circles, and darkly hinted at from their pulpits and in their works. They argue that the old Mosaic law of a "brother raising up seed to his dead brother" is now in force; and as death is only a temporary absence, so they contend a temporary absence is equivalent to death; and if in the case of death, it is not only no crime, but proper; so also in this case it is equally lawful and extremely advantageous! This practice, commended by such sophistry, and commanded by such a Prophet, was adopted as early as at Nauvoo.

Much scandal was caused by others than Smith attempting to carry out this doctrine. Several, who thought what was good for the Prophet should be good for the people, were crushed down by Smith's heavy hand. Several of those have spoken out to the practices of the "Saints." Much discussion occurred at Salt Lake as to the advisability of revealing the doctrine of polygamy in 1852, and that has caused Brigham to defer the public enunciation of this "proxy doctrine," as it is familiarly called. Many have expected it repeatedly at the late conferences. Reasoning their premises out to their natural and necessary consequences, this licentious and infamous dogma is their inevitable result.

Another result of their doctrines is another excuse for licentious indulgence. The Mormons believe, as before stated, in the possibility of man's administering salvation to the dead. Hundreds of devout, strangely devout and fanatically sincere people are immersed on the behalf of their dead relations; males for men, females for women. But the salvation of the dead, say they, has to be consummated in the same manner as that of the living. "They will be nowhere," says Kimball, "unless they have wives:" and these immersed people are therefore *married* for their dead. But as marriage is only a transient affair, they have to be also "*sealed*" for the dead. And as a marriage ceremony is not valid till *completed*, there is practiced in consequence more abomination. For as the glory of the dead, as well as the living, depends entirely on the size of their families, these accommodating proxies *raise children for the dead too!*

That these practices should be indulged, is not surprising. That they should be vailed under the garb of sanctity, and excused on the grounds of religion, is infamous. Mormonism is ingenious in finding excuses for licentiousness; it is a bitter and a burning satire on human purity and progress; a disgusting but a palpable proof of human depravity.

Much has been said of the Mormon endowment. It has been extolled by its recipients until the bewildered minds of their hearers have thought it something sublime. Men, who proud that they had a secret, and desirous that every one should know that they had it, uttered dark hints. They exhibited a singular kind of an under-garment which they constantly wore. This was fantastically marked and given them in the Temple. They promised this endowment to their awe-struck disciples, as the full fruition of the blessing of heaven, etc., etc., etc. As to what it really was, all was perfectly hidden; as all who received the initiation were bound by the most fearful penalties not to reveal any thing of the matter. Oaths were exacted, obliging the person who took them, to agree to undergo a violent and cruel death on revealing the "mystery." I am about to make a statement, as nearly as I can remember, of what the ceremonies, etc., were. I am induced to this violation of my oaths, from five reasons. *First*, As no on knew what were the oaths previous to hearing them; and as no one on hearing could refuse to make them, they are not binding in justice. *Second,* As the obligations also involved other acts of obedience as well as secrecy; and as I do not intend to obey those other obligations, it can be no more improper to break the oath of secrecy than the oath of unlimited obedience. *Third,* As the obligations involve treason against the confederacy of the United States; and therefore illegal *ab initio;* and as the law makes the misprision or concealment of treason, treason itself, it becomes a duty to expose them. *Fourth,* As the promise of endowment is one of the great inducements held out to deluded Mormons, to persuade to emigration to Salt Lake, it is right that they should know the value of their anticipated blessing; and *Fifth,* It is better to violate a bad oath than keep it: as it would have been better for Herod to have forfeited his promise, than to kill John the Baptist. As to the penalties I incur, I have but one duty to God and the world; and to God and the world I confide my safety.

On Friday, February 10, 1854, pursuant to notice I had received, with no other instructions than to wear a clean shirt, myself and wife went to the Council House, Salt Lake City, at about seven o'clock in the morning. About thirty persons were previously waiting there, who were to be "endowed from on high" that day. Our names, with full particulars of birth, marriage, etc., were all registered in a record; our tithing-office receipts examined, because, before hearing the music, it is first necessary to "pay the piper." All those who had not been previously *sealed* to their wives, were then sealed by Heber C. Kimball, who has under his peculiar direction the giving of the endowment, and we were ushered into a long room which was divided into many little compartments by white screens. All was solemn and hushed. Our shoes had to be removed in the outer register office, those who were officiating were in slippers, and the few words spoken in giving directions were only in a dim murmur. The women were sent to one portion of the place, the men to another. All was still; the simmer of the wood in the stove made quite a painful impression on the nerves. The novelty of the situation, the uncertainty and expectation of what was to follow, the perfect stillness heightened by the murmuring whispers, the dull splash of water, the listening and serious faces, the white screens themselves, every thing was calculated to excite the superstitious in any one. One by one the men were beckoned out till it was my turn. I was told to undress, and was then laid down in an ordinary tin bath, which I remember was painted inside and out; a Dr. Sprague—who, in passing, is one of the filthiest-minded men I ever met—was officiating as "washer," which ceremony consisted of washing one all over in tepid water, and blessing each member as he proceeded, from the head downward: "brain to be strong, ears to be quick to hear the words of God's servants, eyes to be sharp to perceive," nose, mouth, arms, hands, breasts, with the peculiar blessing appropriate to each, down to the "feet to be swift to run in the ways of righteousness." Washed, and pronounced "clean from the blood of this generation," I was handed over to Parley P. Pratt, who was seated in a corner, and appointed to give to each "clean man" a "new name, whereby he should be known in the celestial kingdom of God." He called me "Enoch," and I passed on back to our waiting-room, where each in turn was seated on a stool, and some strongly scented oil was ladled out of a mahogany vessel in the shape of a cow's horn, by means of a little mahogany dipper, and poured on his head. This unctuous compound was rubbed into eyes, nose, ears, and mouth, sodden in the hair, and stroked down the person till one felt very greasy and smelt very odorous. This ordinance, performed by Elders Taylor and Cummings, was accompanied by a formula of blessing similar to the "washing," and was "the anointing," administered preparatory to being ordained a "king and priest unto God and the Lamb," which ordination, however, can only be performed in the real Temple. Greased and blessed, we had then to put on the "garments," a dress made of muslin or linen, and worn next to the skin, reaching from the neck to the ankles and wrists, and in shape like a little child's sleeping garment. Over this was put a shirt, then a robe made of linen, crossing and gathered up in pleats on one shoulder, and reaching the ground before and behind, and tied round the waist. Over this was fastened a small square apron, similar in size and shape to masonic aprons, generally made of white linen or silk with imitation fig-leaves painted or worked upon it. A cap, made from a square yard of linen, and gathered into a band to fit the head, socks, and white linen or cotton shoes, completed the equipment. While thus dressing ourselves, a farce was being performed in the next compartment. The creation of the world was being enacted. Eloheim, J. M. Grant, was counseling with Jehovah, Jesus, and Michael (Adam), W. C. Staines, about making and peopling the earth. He sends these three down to take a look and bring him back word as to what are the prospects. They pretend to go, examine, and return to report. The first chapter of Genesis is then performed, Eloheim taking the "and God said" part; the three pretending to go and accomplish the command, and return and make report, using "and it is so." The mind was struck with the wild blasphemy of the whole affair. When they came down to the creation of man, the three, Jehovah, Jesus, and Michael, came into our compartment, and by stroking each of us separately, pretended to form; and by blowing into our faces, pretended to vivify us. We were then supposed to be as Adam, newly made and perfectly ductile in the hands of our makers (an allegory to be terribly carried out). But we were alone; a little more farce, and our wives were introduced, who were similarly arrayed, and had been similarly conducted toward as ourselves, their officiaries of course being women, Miss E. R. Snow, and some others. We were made to shut our eyes as if asleep, commanded to arise and see, and our wives were severally given to us. Joy of course filled our hearts, and we filed off by twos to the compartment where we had heard the voice of Eloheim. This compartment, by the aid of some dwarf mountain pines in boxes, (now paintings), was made to looking something like a garden. W. C. Staines, as Adam, and Miss Snow as Eve, were our "fuglemen;" we did what they did. Some raisins were hanging on one shrub, and W. W. Phelps, in the character of the devil, *which he plays admirably* (!), endeavored to entice us to eat of them. Of course, "the woman tempted me and I did eat." We were then cursed by Eloheim, who came to see us: the devil was driven out, and this erudite astronomer and Apostle (!) wriggled, squealed, and crept away on his hands and knees.

We were then supposed to be in a cursed condition, and here commences the terrible intention of this otherwise ridiculous buffoonery. We were now helpless without the intervention of *a higher power*, and the establishment of *a higher law.* Any law that could apply to *the body* was of small consequence; any power that could control *the body* was of no moment. Thus lost and fallen, God establishes the *priesthood*, and endows them with the necessary jurisdiction; their power unlimited, their commands indisputable, their decisions final, and their authority transcending every other. They were to act as God, with God's authority, in God's place. Oaths of inviolate secrecy, of obedience to and dependence on the priesthood, especially not to "touch any woman, unless given by this priesthood, through the President" were then administered to the intimidated and awed neophytes. A sign, a grip, and a key word were communicated and impressed by practice on us, and the third degree of the Mormon endowment, or *first degree of the Aaronic priesthood*, was conferred. Man, continues the allegory, goes out into life, having one law of purity, one key of truth, and one power of priesthood. With these he goes forth into the world, where light is made darkness and darkness light. He is lost in doubt as to where the truth is. He is, in the next room, supposed to be in the midst of the sects of the present day.

Several imitations of the common styles of Quakers, Methodists, and others are performed. The devil, W. W. Phelps, meets and accosts each of them with "Good-morning, brother Methodist," etc., "I love you all," "You're my friends," etc., etc. Three Apostles, Peter (P. P. Pratt), James (J. Taylor), John (E. Snow), entered, and after a little badinage between the devil and them, Peter commands him to depart in the name of the Lord Jesus Christ, and by the authority of the holy priesthood, and that makes him foam, hiss, and rush out. These Apostles then begin to examine us as to our position; and new instructions are given to us, not only as to priesthood in general, as an *abstract idea*, but to the Mormon dignitaries as the only representatives of this idea of priesthood. The intention of this step is, that Peter, James, and John came down to Joseph Smith, and conferred on him this priesthood, which has descended to Brigham Young; that all the reverence that Christ in them could induce, was now to be paid to *this Mormon* priesthood; immediate, implicit, and unquestioning obedience; to be, as Kimball said, "*like a tallowed rag in the hands of Brigham Young.*" Now, pre sumed this allegory, we were advancing toward the kingdom of God. The man Adam, lost by reason of his fall, the great original sin; doubly lost by the addition of his personal sins, has received powers and blessings, and wandered away from the truth. As it was the priesthood who took him up in his fall, gave him the promise of a Redeemer, so it must be this priesthood that must be the instruments of accomplishing his redemption. God has now taken pity on the world wandering in darkness, and revealed his gospel to Smith, be stowed upon him this priesthood, and is now demanding entire obedience to him and his successors.

An oath, with the penalty of throat-cutting, was the condition of the first; heart being plucked out, etc., etc., dragged into agonizing details, is the penalty of the second oath. New secrecy is impressed, and the second degree of Aaronic priesthood, with signs, grip, and key word, is bestowed.

This farce, heightening into a fearful reality, is continued. The allegory presumes man to be now in a partially saved state. He is ushered into a room with an altar in the center of it. Undying fidelity to the brethren is here inculcated. "Never to speak evil of the Lord's anointed," or, in other words, to shut your mouth on all iniquity; to see and not to speak. Not only to think with their thoughts; to come to them as mediators between Christ and man, as Christ is their Mediator between them and God; to feel as they feel, and act as they act; to render implicit obedience to any requisition however treasonable, however criminal, however unnatural, however impious it might be; not only all this, but never to "speak evil of the Lord's anointed." To have the "Church" the first thing in your mind, and filling the only place in your affections; to be ready to sacrifice to its *dictum* or its interests the warmest friend, the nearest relation, the dearest wife, or even life itself; to hold no trust as sacred, no duty obligatory, no promise or oath binding that militates or infringes the interests of the Church. On this oath being taken, the penalty, on either breaking or revealing it, being that you shall have your navel ripped across, and your bowels gush out, etc., etc., in all sorts of disgusting and horrifying details, another sign, key word, and grip is communicated, and the first degree of the *Melchisedec* priesthood is conferred.

Stupefied and weary; bowing under a sense of fearful and unnatural responsibility; excited by a species of apprehension as to what would come next, we were ushered into another room. An altar was in the center; on it the Bible, Book of Mormon and Book of Smith's Revelations. Man and woman, we were ranged around the place; Kimball in the same, and Brigham in the next room looking on; Parley Pratt officiating, and the fourth oath was administered. The allegory presumed that man, now in a fair and certain way to salvation, had a great temporal duty to perform, not an *abstract theory* of obedience, nor obedience in *abstract things*, but a great positive, present, immediate duty. We were, therefore, sworn to cherish constant enmity toward the United States government for not avenging the death of Smith, or righting the persecutions of the Saints; to do all that we could toward destroying, tearing down, or overturning that government; to endeavor to baffle its designs and frustrate its intentions; to renounce all allegiance and refuse all submission. If unable to do any thing ourselves toward the accomplishment of these objects, to teach it to our children from the nursery; impress it upon them from the death-bed; entail it upon them as a legacy. To make it the one leading idea and sacred duty of their lives; so that "the kingdom of God and his Christ" (the Mormon Church and its priesthood) "might subdue all other kingdoms and fill the whole earth." Curses the most frightful, penalties the most barbarous, were threatened and combined in the obligation either on failing to abide or in daring to reveal these covenants. A new sign, a new key-word, a new grip, and the second degree of Melchisedec priesthood was administered. We were now acceptable to God, and could approach him as children, but had to learn how to pray. We were now told that our robes were on the wrong shoulder and as a sign of our entire dependence on the priesthood in spiritual things, they set them right. In order to impart a deeper religious tone to these proceedings, and to feed the flame here kindled, a new method of praying was shown to us. All the endowees were to stand in a circle; silently to repeat all the signs with their formula, and then to be united by a fantastic intertwining of hands and arms. While in this position one who is previously chosen to be "mouth-piece," kneels on his right knee, takes hold of the hand of one of the standing brethren, thus completing the "circle," and prays slowly; all repeating his words after him.

Thus to meet in circle, to solemnize our thoughts by assuming the garb, to refresh our memories and realize our obligations by repeating all the formula of sign, token, key-words and penalties; and then to pray standing in a mysterious position, using abracadabratic terms, is thought to call down from heaven an immediate answer to prayer, because, finding peculiar favor in the eyes of God. These circles meet every week, and Brigham and the Twelve Apostles often meet every day in this manner and for this object. Standing thus, Parley P. Pratt prayed, and we slowly repeated his words, calling on God to bless or curse as we obeyed or neglected the covenants we had made. We were now brethren, members of the holy orders of God's priesthood;

admitted to the full participation in the privileges of the fraternity; recognizing each other readily; constantly wearing a garment as a protector and remembrancer; bound to each other by tremendous secrets; chained to the priesthood by fearful oaths.

We were now to pass through the Vail, a thin partition of linen, through which all the whole formula had to be repeated; certain marks on the bosom and front of the shirt are cut with a pair of scissors; another name is whispered very softly and very quickly, too soft and fast to be distinguished; and we were ushered into the Celestial Kingdom of God, having passed "behind the Vail!" The men then turn round and admit their wives, who have to repeat the whole affair once more, and the door is opened and they are let through. In the "Celestial Kingdom" we found Brigham, and many others waiting to hear the "Endowment Lecture" which is delivered on every initiation day. We were then allowed to dress, retaining our under-garments; got a hurried lunch, it being nearly four o'clock, and returned to the "Celestial Kingdom" to hear the lecture. This was by H. C. Kimball, explaining the allegory and enforcing the seriousness of the affair; repeating the different signs with formulas of recognition; giving some pointed warnings and uttering some tremendous threats; and about six o'clock we returned to the office, resumed our boots and shoes, and the affair was ended.

There are very few minds, of the caliber usually converted and seduced into Mormonism, that can readily shake off the benumbing effect of such a day as that above described.

Free-masonry, Odd-fellowship, and other kindred ceremonies sway very mightily the minds subject to their influence, and initiated into their secrets. The mysteries of sacred orders paralyzed strong energies, inflamed cold hearts, and inflated hard minds of ancients. It is not astonishing that these ceremonies stimulate the terror and excite the supersitions of their initiated too. It is not surprising that thus bound; thinking that the whole is a revelation; hurried along; seeing Brigham Young just as infatuated as any of them, firmly convinced that this is the kingdom; this, the age; this, the means; and themselves the people, that they should suffer and act as they do. It may show them in a state of frail human nature, but it does not show them at all unnatural.

That there is much genius shown—if genius be shown in the adaptation of means to ends—in these Mormon mysteries, none can dispute. They are admirably fitted to sternly imprint and superstitiously to enweave themselves in the hearts of their recipients. It is hard to concieve of a better means to soften prejudices, almost to amuse, by an apparent triviality, till leading one gradually and unsuspiciously along, making every word an iron bar, and every bar a step to the grand finale, till the farce deepens into the real, and the real is sublimed into the tragic.

There is one thing that is utterly ridiculous, the pretending to claim inspiration as its source. Its signs, tokens, marks and ideas are plagiarized from masonry. The whole affair is being constantly amended and corrected, and Kimball often says, "We will get it perfect by-and-by." The giving the "new name" is optional with the namer, and he has no rule.

The inspiration of the moment is the inspiration of God. Many have the same name, but as they are not known by any but one's self, and he to whom they are uttered at the Vail, that does not make the slightest difference. One man forgot his name in the mass of excitement, and Pratt could not remember what name he gave him, and so, to settle the difficulty, he gave him another, and he passed through the Vail, and that did just as well. From first to last, the intention of the mystery is to teach unlimited obedience to Brigham, and treason against the country. However infatuated, they all see this plainly; and the stronger their infatuation, the prompter their obedience.

To many strange extremes do they carry this obedience. Mr. Eldredge had a daughter, handsome, intelligent, and amiable. She loved a young man, and he her. Brigham's nephew, Joseph W. Young, saw and liked, but was disliked by her. He spoke to Brigham, who told Eldredge "that he had to marry his girl to Joseph W., that it was his 'counsel,' and that every man must be master of his household." Her wrung heart, her crushed love, her blasted hopes, and her stifled aversion yielded at the shrine of this monster superstition, and she married Joseph W. Young. Bishop Hoagland had a daughter, Emily. A Mr. J. C. Little was married and not desirous to become a polygamist. Kimball commanded him to take this girl, commanded Bishop Hoagland to give her, and commanded Emily to have Mr. Little. Indifference was overcome, the warm hopes of a girl's heart for a fond young husband, torn up like weeds, and she married, and she wept! Z. Snow had been one of the Utah judges, was a

Mormon, kept a store, offended Brigham, who cursed him most fearfully; reproached, rebuked, charged, threatened him, and finally commanded him to go on a mission to Australia, for at least three years. Z. Snow was a man of education, a lawyer, had fought his way to the bench, a man of money and business, had struggled with the world and had conquered; but yet, like a child, he bowed his head to Brigham's withering rebukes, fearful criminations, merciless anathemas; left his family, gave up his business, said nothing, accepted the appointment, and is now in Australia, preaching Mormonism! I could name a score of such evidences of the cruelest tyranny and the most superstitious obedience. Mormonism, at Salt Lake, is a whirlpool; once get into the stream, and you must either be sucked down into its vortex, or else be cast out bruised and broken.

While men will themselves thus suffer unrepining, and never think of resistance, it is not at all astonishing that they should inflict suffering on others, and never dream of any thing but doing their duty. What is still more singular, men who have been employed in the commission of positive crimes, never think of taking any extra freedom on that account, but show and actually feel all the same veneration for their Prophet. Second Zeids giving up women to a second Mohammed, could not evince more superstition and more obedience. When the Mormons talk so much of death as a penalty, it is not the idle threat of imaginary killing, but the strong word of merciless men. They never threaten what they will not perform, and fear of risking the penalty withholds many from apostacy.

That the Church has instigated many murders there can be no question. Not only do they not deny, but even publicly preach its propriety, as a means of salvation. As soon as the news of the murder of Squire Babbett and party reached Salt Lake, the impression grew strong in the minds of the people, that it had been done by the instruction of the Church; as Babbett was very troublesome, was feared, had often been threatened, was a "covenant-breaker," and, consequently, by Mormon law, ought to die. The desire prompted the suspicion, and the more closely that the circumstances were scrutinized, the stronger these suspicions became. Some weak-minded people, however, did not approve of such bloody measures, and Brigham, to effectually quiet their scruples, preached this strange doctrine on Sabbath afternoon, September 21, 1856:

"There are sins that men commit for which they can not receive forgiveness in this world, or in that which is to come, and if they had their eyes open to see their true condition, they would be perfectly willing to have their blood spilt upon the ground, that the smoke thereof might ascend to heaven as an offering for their sins; and the smoking incense would atone for their sins, whereas, if such is not the case, they will stick to them and remain upon them in the spirit world.

"I know, when you hear my brethren telling about cutting people off from the earth, that you consider it is strong doctrine; but it is to save them, not to destroy them. I will say further; I have had men come to me and offer their lives to atone for their sins.

"It is true that the blood of the Son of God was shed for

sins through the fall and those committed by man, yet men can commit sins which it can never remit. As it was in ancient days, so it is in our day; and though the principles are taught publicly from this stand, still the people do not understand them; yet the law is precisely the same. There are sins that can be atoned for by an offering upon an altar as in ancient days; and there are sins that the blood of a lamb, of a calf, or of turtle doves, can not remit, but they must be atoned for by the blood of the man. That is the reason why men talk to you as they do from this stand; they understand the doctrine, and throw out a few words about it."—*Deseret News, October* 1, 1856.

When the citizens of Carroll and Davis counties, Mo., began to threaten the Mormons with expulsion in 1838, a "death society" was organized, under the direction of Sidney Rigdon, and with the sanction of Smith. Its first captain was Captain "Fearnot," alias David Patten, an Apostle. Its object was the punishment of the obnoxious. Some time elapsed before finding a suitable name. They desired one that should seem to combine spiritual authority, with a suitable sound. Micah, iv. 13, furnished the first name, "Arise, and thresh, O! daughter of Zion; for I will make thy horn iron, and thy hoofs brass; and thou shalt beat in pieces many people; and I will consecrate their gain unto the Lord, and their substance unto the Lord of the whole earth." This furnished them with a pretext; it accurately described their intentions, and they called themselves the "Daughters of Zion.' Some ridicule was made at these bearded and bloody "daughters," and the name did not sit easily. "Destroying Angels" came next; the "Big Fan" of the thresher that "should thoroughly purge the floor," was tried and dropped. Genesis, xlix. 17, furnished the name that they finally assumed. The verse is quite significant: "Dan shall be a serpent by the way, an adder in the path, that biteth the horse's heels, so that his rider shall fall backward." The "Sons of Dan" was the style they adopted; and many have been the times that they have been *adders in the path, and many a man has fallen backward, and has been seen no more.* At Salt Lake, among themselves, they ferociously exult in these things, rather than seek to deny or extenuate them.

Some of the leading spirits of that band are still in Salt Lake City. Although they do not maintain their organization, being generally merged into "Brigham's Life Guards," yet without the same name, they have performed the same deeds. O. P. Rockwell, the attempted assassin of Governor Boggs, and who was instructed by Smith to commit the deed, Brigham has had into the pulpit to address the meetings! A W. Hickman, against whom many indictments are out in Iowa, and who is publicly known as an "avenger of blood," is one of Brigham's most particular intimates. It is no secret at Salt Lake that several men have disappeared after being last in the company of this man, and no question is raised as to the matter there. This man was one with three other such who left Salt Lake without any ostensible reasons for their journey, traveled near to the spot where Messrs. Margetts and Cowdy were said to have been murdered, and returned bearing the news of their murder. This circumstance is still more significant, remembering that Margetts and Cowdy were both "covenant-breaking" apostates; that they were returning to their native country; that they could make many terrible disclosures, and do Mormonism much injury in England; that it was Mormon law that they should die, and Mormon interest to kill them; that these men had no other motives for traveling more than a thousand miles; that they returned as soon as they had got near the spot where these unfortunate men and their families were murdered; that the excitement at Salt Lake on hearing the news was so great that it needed Brigham to preach the above discourse in order to allay it; and that in this discourse, instead of endeavoring to deny the suspicion or extenuate the act, he defends such means as the only remaining method of insuring their salvation. It is, say they, a portion of the penalty they invoke on themselves, and therefore *secure* to themselves. Whether Brigham be guilty of the murder of these men, can not, perhaps, be known till "the great day." I can not but feel that it appears strongly suspicious; although one of them being my own cousin, perhaps incapacitates me from correct and impartial judgment. What is for the salvation of a saint, must, of course, be the very best means of securing the salvation of a "Gentile, and heathen without the gate." Men who are sworn not to hesitate at the sacrifice of themselves, will not be very chary at the sacrifice of others. Nor have they been; several Missourians, well known and well hated as enemies, have been put under the ground. When a man is missing at Salt Lake, it is a common expression, "He has met the Indians." Colonel Peltro and Mr. Tobin, with their servants, were severely wounded by Mormons, who attacked them in the night, on Santa Clara river, 370 miles south of Salt Lake. They lost six horses, worth at least one thousand dollars, and were compelled to abandon their baggage, which was perfectly riddled with shot. The object of their enmity and this attempted assassination was Mr. Tobin. He went with Captain Stansbury to Salt Lake in 1851; then met Brigham, and admired his daughter Alice; was engaged to her, and left Salt Lake on business. He returned in 1856, and renewed his engagement with Miss Alice; although she was at the same time under a *written* engagement to a Mr. W. Wright, whom Brigham sent off to the Sandwich Islands, to get him out of the way. Mr. Tobin told me in California that he had the most convincing proof that Miss Young had sacrificed her honor, and accordingly refused to marry her. For this, Mormon hated; for the influence he might exert abroad, Mormon feared; and because both hated and feared, he was nearly Mormon murdered.

Elder Willard Snow, while sitting as a justice of the peace, in the trial of Mr. John Galvin, for striking a Mormon, said to him, "If you ever lay your hands on another Saint, I will have your head cut off before you leave the city. I thank God that the time is not far distant, and I shall rejoice when it comes, that I shall have the authority to pass sentence of life and death on the Gentiles, and I will have their heads snatched off like chickens in the door-yard." The threat was not vain, and the opinion is very commonly entertained. Mr. George Grant, then deputy sheriff, on the same occasion, said to the same individual, "If I had my way, I would drown you in the Jordan river."

Such are not only the sentiments of Brigham, haranguing the people, but the large majority of the Mormon people, expressing their sentiments through Brigham.

The penalty of adultery is death. Dr. Vaughan was shot by a Mr. Hamilton, on suspicion. James Monroe was murdered by a Howard Egan, for the same reason. Should an endowed Mormon commit adultery he must die for his salvation. If a Gentile, he must die for atonement.

The endowment they are now giving at Salt Lake, is viewed but as a temporary affair, in force only till a Temple is built, where it will all have to be repeated, with increased performances. Since I went through the ceremonies, they have built an "Endowment House," in which they have added a sealing ordinance. This endowment is essential, say they, to salvation. No man but an endowee can have a wife! "From him that hath not, shall be taken what he seemeth to have; and to him that hath, shall be given more abundantly," is their generous reading of the promise. To have a wife you must be "sealed at the altar." Unless previously endowed, one never sees the altar, nor knows what it means. Accompanied by my wife, I went to the "Endowment House." We assumed our robes, aprons, caps, etc., and, looking like a mongrel of half Hebrew half Brahmin, went to the "altar room." It is well carpeted; its altar is a kind of solid table, nicely cushioned, with a cushioned ledge to kneel on. I, kneeling on one, and my wife kneeling on the other side of the altar between us, grasping each other's hands across its cushioned top, with the "patriarchal grip," Kimball demanded the usual questions as to willingness, and pronounced us "man and wife for time and for all eternity, by the power and authority of the holy priesthood invested in me, and I seal upon your head the blessings of Abraham, Isaac, and Jacob, for time and for all eternity, in the name of the Father, Son, and Holy Ghost. Amen. Kiss your wife." Such was the formula; Kimball had so often repeated it, that he gabbled it off without stops or pauses; running "kiss your wife" into the amen, like some clerks of courts administering oaths to witnesses.

In the lectures, which used to be always delivered after the initiations, the most disgusting language I ever heard in my life is reveled in by Kimball. He boasts, "you are under oath, and you can 't tell it." Comparisons and expressions that would disgrace a prostitute are luxuriously mouthed over, before a congregation of sixty to a hundred men and women. He speaks them as though he wished them to dwell on his tongue, the same as they dwell in his thoughts. Duties the most secret and sacred are not only plainly but filthily spoken of by him, as though the essence of nastiness had been distilled and his heart lay festering in it. I have heard him, in these meetings, avow "that a little drunken spree, if quite in secret and among a few good fellows, was no great sin."

So sunk are they in infatuated and fanatical licentiousness, that the white women at Utah do not content them. Although Smith, speaking of the Indians, in his Book of Mormon, p. 66, says, "Cursed shall be the seed of him that mixeth with their seed: for they shall be cursed with the same cursing," Brigham now teaches that "the way God has revealed for the purification of the Indians, and making them 'a white and delightsome people,' as Joseph prophesied, is by us taking the Indian squaws for wives!!" Accordingly several of these tawny beauties have been already "sealed" to some of the Mormon authorities.

Another method of "increasing their kingdom," is by *adoption* for eternity. "Children," say they, "born out of the 'covenant of sealing,' are only bastards; they have the claim of paternity on their father, but he has no eternal right to them." As their "glory" depends on their family, much wish is felt to get some of these children to adopt. The son must share the father's "glory;" and, therefore, the more glorious the father, the more elevated the child. Many young men give themselves over to the leading men as "eternal sons," in the hope of sharing the honor of their adopted parents. Both Brigham and Kimball have many such adopted sons. A W. C. Staines is as well known to be Brigham's son, as a D. Candland is to be Kimball's.

Brigham Young, and others of the authorities, have discovered another novel method of extending their kingdoms, by trafficking for sons. Woman adds to man's "glory," say they, only as a wife. If he can not marry her, she is a burden. Unmarried daughters, therefore, do not lead very happy lives. They are poor and valueless property to any but their husbands. Brigham, however, has turned his to some account, by compelling the man who wants to marry one, to be first adopted to him. "If," says he, "you won't help to glorify me, she sha'n't help to glorify you!"

His daughter Alice, mentioned above, in connection with

Mr. Tobin, was for some time and to some extent "kept in the market" at these terms. When Mr. Tobin left, she was *very quickly* married to H. B. Clawson, notwithstanding Brigham had promised her to W. B. Wright, who was preaching in the Islands.

When persons give themselves up, blindly and enthusiastically, to the directions of other and designing men; imagine they are invested with God-given powers, and endowed with a God-given sagacity, it is inevitable that they run into the wildest vagaries that lunatics could rhapsodise, or fanatics believe. Nor is it surprising that men, by a gradual system of rigid self-training, should positively be sincere in their folly and their faith. Nor can it be astonishing that this sincere exaltation should be cunning in forging chains and artful in imposing them on the minds of other equally deluded, but less gifted believers. While this fanaticism can wield such a mighty influence over the female heart, crushing into the dust the tenderest susceptibilities, the dearest hopes, the voices of the heart, and the instincts of nature; binding together tempers the most antagonistic, opinions the most diverse, nationalities the most jealous; grinding woman to degradation and misery, and almost freezing her tears and stifling her groans, it is not singular that it sways the men.

Religious fanaticism is almost epidemic. Like black and fetid pools that lie stagnating under the sun, noisome with miasms and feculent with contagion, are the reservoirs of delusion. From slimy depths breathes out this moral and mental malaria, and while men are wondering if such things can be, thousands are swimming in lasciviousness; and by surrounding it with a few ridiculous rules, teaching it with an affected sanctity, decking it in tinsel gew-gaws, flimsy trappings and trickery of the stage; defending it with a few specious sophistries, and obeying it with devout buffoonery, it can be made respectable in the eyes of the men, sacred in the eyes of the women, infallible in the eyes of future generations. It is thus with Mormonism. Designs the most treasonable, utopias the most impracticable, dogmas the most ridiculous, and pretensions the most ill-sustained; visionary projects and outrageous tyranny, self-abnegation and disgusting sycophancy, the very worst of practices under the very best of assumptions, and the whole greedily swallowed and enthusiastically taught. Thus it comes robed in the ægis of religious prerogative which enhances its deformity, while it disarms much opposition. Mormonism in the old is ridiculous and distressing; but these are still bound by old ties to old friends, and old homes. Mormonism in the young is frightful; they know no sense of right but their Prophet's word, no standard of evidence but the Prophet's opinion, no aspirations but for the festering bathos of their impious creed, and no duty but implicit obedience to their conspirator leaders. Taught to regard all the world as their enemies, their country as their oppressors, and their duty to destroy it; taught, too, that in the accomplishment of this object, all means are honorable, every weapon an especial providence, and every advantage a prestige of victory, they are being trained for desperate ends; and I fear, finally, to be subdued alone by desperate measures.

Mormonism has some principles of power in it, else like

bloated and corrupt fruit it would burst and fall. Their laws allow male *licentiousness*, however it may be cloaked under pretense of religion, but it is only found in certain channels, and it is retained there. Under the enslaving shackles of religious fanaticism, they are strongly united; not with the cords of reason, or the garland-strings of love, but by the heavy fetters of infatuation.

While this gags their press, cleaves down their liberties, and makes of men and women moral and mental slaves, it still accomplishes some little good; and viewing that little good, at the same time ignoring all the evil, the Mormons really believe that Utah is the best place in the world. It compels them to work hard, and that builds up cities and manufactories. It certainly does away with prostitution, and that is a prominent argument urged by the Mormons in its favor (see its refutation in chapter on Theoretical Polygamy). It prevents all disastrous difference of opinion, by *coercing* all to believe alike; and this makes intelligence *stagnate.* There are less robberies, murders, arsons, rapes at Utah, than in any other place of equal population in the world. While the bad is remembered, it ought not to exclude the good. These are the natural consequences of their system of government, but in order to produce these results a gross superstition with licentiousness peculiar to itself; belief in, and fear of ridiculous pretensions of religious authority and universal degradation, has to be adopted. Imitating Mohammed in polity of government, the Mormons obtain some of the results of Moslem rule. All know that there is not so much crime among Mussulmans as among Christians, still but few Anglo-Saxons, from that cause, would be willing to become Turks. Under the goad and lash of a barbarous overseer, slaves work hard, produce wealth; neither murder, rob or rape, and yet few would infer that therefore this overseer was a benefit to the country, or an institution of God. To secure to man the liberty of progressing in powers of intellect, in discovery of principles or their application, in freedom of thought, speech, and action, without also giving him greater liberty to commit crime, if he so will, is impossible. Opportunities of elevation and degradation must be equal. Nations renowned for their great and good, have also become infamous for their bad men. The Hebrew nation itself, when its opportunities and its greater light is considered, were the most wicked people on the earth. Other people have arisen, and lit by the star-glimmers of their vague intuitions, have culminated to their meridian, and then sank into the silence and obscurity of an eternal night; while the Hebrews, whom God has endeavored especially to direct and bless, have only left an equally checkered history, bright with illustrious characters, and black with outrageous sins. At either side of the broad line of mediocrity there is an infinite; and the only means by which the one side can be trodden over, is by leaving the other equally free. The system, therefore, that degrades all men to one miserable level of fanaticism and mental debasement is fallacious, however successful it may be in the suppression of a few of the worst crimes. To repair a *partial* evil, the remedy is too *universally* applied. To preserve *a few* from sinking too low, *all* have to be prevented from rising at all.

CHAPTER V.

EDUCATION.

Working men—School systems—Braggadocio—School teachers—Three months' term, and nine months' vacation—Evening schools—Dancing schools—O. Pratt and Brigham Young—H. C. Kimball—Pratt's mathematical class—Grammar schools—Cultivated female society—Home education—Female lions—Literary institutions—Novel reading—Deseret alphabet—Newspapers—Book of Mormon—Doctrines and covenants—New translation of Bible—Book of Abraham—Key to Apocalypse—Prophecy of Enoch—Gospel of Adam—*Lex ora*, v. *lex scripta*—Controversial works.

THE moral and mental health of a community can safely be predicated from their system of education. The physical system is relaxed or invigorated according to the nature of the food we eat, and so, also, the mental system relies on its aliments for present power and future hope. On the education of the boys of to-day depends the nature of the men of to-morrow. Thinking men discover principles of nature, working men apply them to the purposes of art. Brigham Young keeps the people of Salt Lake, as before remarked, constantly at work. He aims at making them *working* men and women, and has succeeded. In the attention bestowed on physical education, the mental and moral training is neglected. It is true that outside of Utah they boast, and in Utah they *talk*, of the school systems. Orson Pratt, in a sermon delivered at

Salt Lake Tabernacle, February 10, 1856, very aptly remarked on this subject:

"Have we had a high school here? Not in this Valley. But, says one, we have had a parent school, and that is what we consider a high school. Yes, we have had a great many things in name, but mere name is not what is wanted. We have had a university *in name, but as yet we have had no such university.*

"Have we colleges? I believe none, even in name. Have we had academies? I believe not. If we have, they have been very inferior to those in the eastern States. Go to the schools in the New England States and see the order that is kept in them, see the improvement of the youth who are taught in them, and then come back to our common schools and you will see that the common schools of the East will far surpass any that we have yet had in our Territory."—*Deseret News, May* 14, 1856.

The "authorities" at Salt Lake send out reports of university boards, literary and scientific institutes, etc.; dub men with names of offices, and send regents, professors, lecturers, etc., out into the world; but, as Pratt himself is forced to acknowledge, they are only *names.*

Their system of education is eminently practical, but, unfortunately, any thing but eminently beneficial. They have in Salt Lake City, nineteen school-houses, one in each ward. It is only during the three winter months, however, that a boys' school is ever attempted to be kept. During the other nine months, at three or four of their school-houses, they have endeavored to employ a female teacher, who has great difficulty in obtaining a class of little children, some being too poor to afford to send their children; some being too idle to get them ready; some being too careless whether they go or not, and the generality regarding it as only one mode of *getting their children out of the way!* No respect is felt for a school-teacher; he can only obtain a small salary; experiences the greatest difficulty in procuring it after it becomes due; is forced to take as "pay," the poorest and commonest articles, at the most exorbitant prices, often obliged to take "trade" he does not need at all, and rely on bartering with it for some other commodity that he may require, or perhaps trade off again, and even after all this "trucking and trading" can never obtain more than one half or two thirds his due. This is so well known in Utah that it has become a common expression when a man can get no other employment, "O you had better turn school-teacher!" or when a debt is extremely bad, and its recovery almost hopeless, "O it is just like a school debt." From these reasons, men who could at all teach, never attempt it, unless compelled by poverty, and, as generally, if they be sufficiently intelligent to teach, they are sufficiently intelligent to obtain some other livelihood, consequently Mormon school-teachers are usually very ignorant themselves.

The boys' schools continuing only for three months, with an interval of nine months, they return to their schools in the winter nearly as ignorant as when they left the preceding spring. All the work of education has to be nearly recommenced under a different tutor, each one having his own peculiar style of instruction, and very peculiar those styles are too; confidence has to be established, obedience exacted, and attention enforced, and the struggle between the large scholars and their teachers frequently ends in the triumph of the former and in the grieved feelings of the disgusted and insulted teacher, who often resigns before his term of three months has expired, and reproaches himself with the folly of attempting to "teach a school."

In most instances these men would be the most efficient; men of some sense and of some sensibility, who are neither boxers nor wrestlers, and who value their own dignity too highly to fight with their pupils, and prove their superiority *vi et armis.* I could mention names of wards in which such exhibitions have occurred. Mr. Pugh, who for many years was the principal of a large academy in Shropshire, England, heard, believed, and embraced Mormonism; emigrated to Salt Lake with his family in 1853; and was persuaded to accept the teachership of the fourteenth ward school, the best and largest in the city. The trustees promised him a salary of $50 per month, where provisions are dearer than in California! When his three months' term had expired, he wasted as much time in trying to collect the sums due from the parents of each scholar, and in 1856 had not been able to obtain more than two thirds of the amount.

The same winter, the trustees of the thirteenth ward, the wealthiest in Utah, refused to pay over $30 per month to their teacher, and Brigham eventually discharged a clerk from his office, Mr. Corey, in order to compel him to teach the school, because Corey was qualified, and Brigham wanted to send his children there! In the winter of 1852–'53, a Mr. E. B. Kelsey endeavored to establish a superior kind of a school.

Among other pupils were the children of the Presidents. One of Brigham's sons was very unruly, and refused obedience. Kindness being inadequate, Mr. Kelsey tried the ferule, intending to compel the submission he could not induce. The boy left the school and complained. Instead of sustaining the tutor in his authority, J. M. Grant, on a Sabbath forenoon, before several thousand persons, laid down this singular doctrine: "Some children are bass-wood and may be bent, but these are hickory saplings, and they can't be bent or whipped into submission." Protected by the "authorities" in their insubordination, the result was inevitable. Mr. Kelsey threw up his school and wisely turned farmer. In the winter of 1854–'55, W. Eddington, a school-teacher from Portsmouth, England, attempted to establish a similar institution. He was nearly reduced to starvation, as, having no assistance, he had to be at the school-house. If he attended the school, he had no time to collect his fees; if he neglected school, they refused to pay; if he sent an agent, they either ignored the debt or plead a hundred excuses. From instructing the young he turned to be a small peddler in every thing, on the principle of universal barter. The consequences are unmistakable. Those who could teach, will not. Those who attempt to teach, can not! The young, therefore, do the best they know how, and that is always the very worst possible.

There is yet another drawback on schools. The Mormons love dancing. Almost every third man is a fiddler, and every one must learn to dance. This is old, too, for Smith used to delight some beer-shop loafers at Nauvoo with scraping on catgut. A fiddling Prophet! School-houses occupied by the classes during the day, are turned into dancing academies in the evening. There are many who can afford only to pay one tutor. Their children *ought* to learn to read, but they *must* learn to dance. The children themselves urge this view very strenuously. The dancing-master must be paid in advance, and either the day-school is neglected, or else the teacher is defrauded of his remuneration. In the winter of 1854–'55, there were dancing-schools in almost every one of the nineteen school-houses, and necessarily so much more attention to dancing involved so much less attention to study. Just so much less education, and just so much more injury.

Many abortive attempts have been made to institute an evening adult school. Every such endeavor has been discontinued after a few evenings, with the gloomy announcement that receipts did not pay for fuel and candles. The instigators of the effort have been forced to turn to other occupations in order to maintain themselves from hunger and destitution. Many a sigh and groan have been breathed over the spade-handle and ax-helve by blister-handed men; who, had their talents been employed and encouraged, would have benefited the Mormon community. Many of the people express satisfaction in seeing these "better-dressed fellers" obliged to "nigger it" as well as themselves; and some of them will come and slap such on the shoulder; laugh at their awkwardness, while they say encouragingly, "Wall, bruther, ye're gwine through the mill now, for sarten—ye're a cummin down from yer high horse to be one on us; yer'll soon be perfec' now!" This is by no means a rare occurrence.

But what is the conduct of the "authorities" in this respect. They ought not to be accounted responsible for the many foolish things said or done, especially considering the many foolish things of their own they have to answer for. Brigham is a very ignorant man. By his position as Prophet and President, he considers himself the only proper person to commence any work, originate any principle, and turn on the "gas" for the listening multitude. For another to assume this privilege, is to usurp his prerogative, and that is to illumine his ire, and to awaken his power of prophetic rebuke. One Sunday afternoon, in the Bowery of Salt Lake, before 3000 persons, during the summer of 1855, O. Pratt was addressing the people on the necessity of studying from books. Said he,

"Suppose that you and I were deprived of all books, and that we had faith to get revelation, and no disposition to understand that which has been sought out, understood, and recorded in books, what would be our condition? It would require an indefinite period in which to make any great progress in the knowledge that is even now extant."

Brigham arose, his dignity hurt, his temper ruffled; and he administered to Pratt, the presumptuous offender, the most outrageous tongue-lashing I ever conceived of. He said,

"The professor has told you that there are many books in the world, and I tell you there are many people in the world; he says there is something in all these books; I say each one of these persons has a name; he says it would do you good to learn that something, and I say it would do you just as much good to learn these somebodies' names. Were I to live to the age of Methusaleh, and every hour of my life learn something new out of some one of these books, and remember every particle I had acquired, five minutes' revelation would teach me more truth and more right than all this pack of nonsense that I should have packed into my unlucky brains."

Orson Pratt hung his head, while the very faithful exulted in this defeat of Brigham's favorite antagonist. This celebrated speech was much talked of by the people. It was thought best not to publish it, however, and as it had irritated the public mind, and weakened rather than increased Brigham's influence, he, on the following Sunday morning, paid Professor Pratt a high compliment, and called on him to deliver "*a lecture on astronomy*," instead of preach a sermon; which accordingly O. Pratt did. Some extolled Brigham's magnanimity; others slyly laughed at his astuteness; and a very few made a memorandum in their journals of the event, and asked, What next?

Brigham is the model and standard of every thing. It is thought that as the keys of the kingdom give all knowledge, to require any knowledge but that which comes through the holder of these keys is apostacy. His *fiat* revokes all science and destroys all demonstration. Now, Brigham not being an educated man, to commence to educate the people would be compelled to ask advice. To ask advice is to exhibit inferiority; to betray inferiority would be to destroy confidence in himself, as far as that inferiority extended. To betray inferiority, is also to elevate some other to a higher position than he would occupy, to the extent of that other's acknowledged superiority. To sacrifice, for a moment, the people's *unbounded* confidence, is to peril it on other points. Teach the people to doubt his unlimited authority, is to teach them to compare; to excite remark; weaken his influence and destroy Mormonism. Hence Brigham can not be *active* in education measures. He can only talk to the shallow extent of his own superficiality. He *talks* about it, but it almost stops there.

Heber C. Kimball, the second man in the Mormon triad, not only does not possess, but openly ridicules education. It is a remarkable fact that all educated men apostatize from the Mormon Church; and this is, therefore, a remarkable argument against education. To retain slaves, they must keep them ignorant. The mode of reasoning adopted by these men is peculiar, and ridiculously sophistical. Mormonism, say they, is the plan of salvation instituted by God. Fidelity to it is, therefore, the greatest blessing; infidelity to it, the greatest curse. Any thing which increases faith in, or induces obedience to it is a good; any thing which inclines to doubt is an evil. Now, Gentilish education only leads its possessors to dispute the wisdom of the authorities, to criticise their sayings and scruple at their deeds. This weakens their own faith and that of other persons; consequently, they conclude, Gentile education is a positive evil. Kimball elaborated this idea once in his very remarkable style. Said he:

"Here are some edicated men, jest under my nose. They come here and they think they know more than I do, and then they git the big-head, and it swells and swells till it gits like the old woman's squash; you go to touch it and it goes ker-smash, and when you go to look for the man, why, he ain't thar. They 're jest like so many pots in a furnace—yer know I've been a potter, in my time—almighty thin and almighty big, and when they 're sot up, the heat makes 'em smoke a little, and then they collapse and tumble in, and they ain't no whar."

These coarse but forcible comparisons form the staple of Heber C. Kimball's ordinary discourses.

In the fall of 1855, O. Pratt volunteered to instruct a class in the higher branches of arithmetic, algebra, and mathematics; proposing to charge only enough to pay for lights. He advertised and received one or two applications. He then offered, by advertisement, to provide the candles, fuel, and room; and to teach the class *gratis*, if he could obtain twenty scholars, of any age or either sex. Not content with this, as he was desirous to induce the young to such studies, he agreed to suit his evenings to the convenience of the largest number of the scholars; only stipulating their regular attendance if they promised to come. One of the last questions I put to Orson Pratt, before leaving Salt Lake City was, "How many applications did you receive?" To this he replied, "Only three or four!" The class was never organized. I have heard some of the "very faithful" predict the final apostacy of this learned and talented, though grievously mistaken gentleman, in consequence, they say, of his education. "It will lift him up, till he topples over."

Several have essayed to establish grammar schools. Strange have been the remarks they caused; bringing both sexes together, they have occasioned many a suspicious husband to be jealous of his wife. The attendance has dwindled down to one or two, the most disgusting jokes perpetrated in them, and their entire utility questioned. One man, who stands high in authority, argued in this wise:

"The Sperit is a gwine to lead and to guide us into all truth, yer know. Now, if grammar is truth, why, the Sperit will jest lead us into it a kinder nateral like: and if it ain't truth, it 's no use, and I ain't a gwine to bother my brains and pay my money about it."

Even the editor of their paper, the "Deseret News," denies all originality of thought. Denying it, of course, he is never guilty of it in his newspaper.

A great incentive, perhaps the greatest incentive to education, is a cultivated class of females. The natural proclivity of one sex for the other maintains a constant action, and induces by rivalry, great efforts at personal improvement. Men always assimilate with the society kept, as certainly as those who walk constantly together adopt each other's gait and carriage. Intellectual female society, the great polisher of manners, sharpener of wit, purifier of sentiment, and refiner of expression is, at Salt Lake, entirely unknown. Not only is it unknown, but despised, and called "Gentilish affectation." To be esteemed by the people, all must be esteemed by the authorities. To obtain their approval, they must feign entire inferiority, by simulating entire reverence for them. This might not be difficult if their minds were cultivated or their habits even decent. Conversation the most filthy, obscene anecdotes, jests, and allusions form much capital in the stock of Brigham and Heber. Indeed I have often heard it said praisingly of Brigham, that he can "tell the dirtiest story in the dirtiest way." To stand well with them, all must sink to the level of their social habits; not to stand well with them is not to stand well in the estimation of the people, and that is to be suspected and annoyed.

So complete is this mental sycophancy, that however trivial or serious be the subject a party may be considering, if any one has heard Brigham or Heber express an opinion on the topic, all discussion is discontinued. I once listened in one of "the schools for the prophets" to some remarks from W. C. Dunbar, a more than ordinarily intelligent Mormon. He proved his position, I thought satisfactorily; an American Elder however told him, that "Brigham taught the contrary doctrine." Said this mental Colossus, "If he said so, he must be right, and I withdraw my argument!"

One very striking illustration of this mental abnegation occurred in the late Dr. Richards's office in 1854. Mr. Thomas Bullock, Mr. Leo Hawkins and some others were talking to Kimball about the resurrection. The Mormons believe in a literal physical resurrection, and were desirous to learn "Whether, when the body came forth from the grave, it would leave a visible hole in the ground?" "No," said Kimball, "not at all, the atoms will be reunited, and they won't leave no hole." He proceeded to explain his reasons for this opinion, and presently Brigham came in, when this important question was referred to him for his prophetic decision.

"Why, yes, certainly it will," was his verdict. "Christ is the pattern, you know; and he had to have the stone rolled away from the sepulchre, and that left the hole visible, for did not the soldiers see it?"

"Brother Brigham," immediately cried Kimball, "that is just my opinion!"

Orson Hyde, the President of the Twelve Apostles, has

endeavored to set a better example to the Saints. Himself and daughters assumed a more cultivated style, but it is the common significant remark, "The Elder was always a little Gentilish in his feelings."

The greatest of all education is "home education." Home education depends upon the mother. Where the woman is degraded, there is no home education.

"To teach girls to sow, and weave, and work in the garden, and cook, and be smart in the dairy, and neat about the house, is the best education," says Brigham; "stuff their heads with reading and they go to novels and romances, and such like trash, and neglect their duties, and they won't be obedient to their husbands and fathers. Teach them to work—teach them to work."

This is good practical philosophy, but it is only half the truth. There is but one step from neglect of, to contempt of education. It is so at Salt Lake. Women who are taught to believe that the "husband's power is absolute," and that all "their sins committed in obedience to their husband's commands, are borne by their husbands," care nothing for self-education, and as little for the instruction of their daughters. The few persons who go there, who are a little superior, are mocked. They are the "speckled sheep;" the hearts which still cling to "Gentile customs and notions of things." "They look back to the flesh-pots of Egypt." "The leaven of the gospel has only partially worked in them." Their apostacy is predicted, and any influence they might obtain, crushed out. Oases in a desert, a thousand hands heap sand upon them. Hence the women who endeavor to make a reputation for mind are the most rabidly fanatical. Miss Eliza R. Snow, the Mormon poetess, a very talented woman, but outrageously bigoted, and one or two kindred souls, are the *nuclei* for all the female intellect at Salt Lake. Let any recant from their creed, or oppose it, she and her band of second Amazons crush the intrepid one down. In the society of such women the Mormon youth stand abashed and terrified, like small children who, it is said, "ought to be seen but not heard."

Another element has been lately introduced into Utah society. Mormonism is too well known in America to attract any but the most ignorant to its standard. Mormonism in England, atrociously misrepresented, has attracted some rather better informed people. Among these are the printers of Utah, all Englishmen; these tried to organize a "Typographical Association," for the purpose of obtaining a library, hearing lectures, and procuring scientific apparatus, etc. They succeeded in getting up some *balls*, which was far more in unison with Mormon prejudices; drawing up a constitution, etc., etc., all in due form. They got their society very admirably on to *paper*, but could get it no further. A. Carrington advertised a lecture for their behalf, and could not obtain a sufficient number of persons to make an audience. Another institution arose, called "The Deseret Universal Scientific." Officers were elected, constitution framed, prospects and projects blazed forth in double capitals in their journal, but, like a choke-damp, made much noise, emitted much "gas," but settled down in smoke. Elder E. Snow, one of the Twelve Apostles, then organized another institution in 1855, and called it by a name that was new-coined for it by Phelps, the Mormon devil, "The Polysophical Society." Its birth quickened other mushroom children of this humid soil. The "Seventies' Variety Club" was organized among a class of Elders; dragged out its length over two meetings, and expired. The "Deseret Universal Scientific" was resuscitated, but only to die again. Brigham grew envious of these little pistolets, and resolved to assume his position, and lead in this as in all other things, and fired off his big gun. *He* founded an institution! Its officers were the chief dignitaries. Its object "universal truth." Its name "The Theological Institution." But Brigham found that his Elders could only preach "sermons" after the approved Mormon style. The people had enough of that on Sunday, and failed to attend the meetings, and so the "Theological" went out. The death of this was followed by the decease of all the rest. Some young men, however, tried again to bring an institution into life, and a "Deseret Literary and Musical Society" was commenced. I attended the organization meetings, and the great fear we all felt was, that perhaps Brigham and the authorities might *patronize the institution*, so it was agreed not to ask "counsel" on the subject, but let it stand or fall by its own merits. It was dreaded that Brigham might nurse this to death; and, without asking his consent, they commenced their meetings. It flourished pleasantly; but I observed that Brigham began to pet it last summer, and I presume it has followed the path of its defunct predecessors.

There are very few books in Utah. Very few persons are rich enough to carry libraries over the plains. There is a public library, however, for which Congress appropriated $20,000. It is tolerably well selected, but is necessarily small, and but very little used by the people. Sympathizing in Brigham's views as to the futility of acquiring knowledge out of books, of course they do not allow their *practice* to disprove their *faith.* He often tells the people, "When you come here, you have got to unlearn all you have ever learned, and begin to learn all again. The Gentiles put light for darkness, and darkness for light, and we've got to turn you right round." Consequently, many would rather not attempt to obtain any book-information, believing it *better not to be informed at all than to be incorrectly informed.*

While those works that could instruct or improve them are neglected, works of fiction are very ravenously sought for and devoured. The most trashy *feuilleton* is carefully preserved and constantly lent around. Over their lascivious and ridiculous pages the Mormon women pore and prose with extravagant zest, till Brigham's wholesale condemnation is deserved, "their reading only fills their head with trash and nonsense." While, however, this is their real practice, in their WORKS they endeavor to impress a contrary lesson. In Smith's Revelations there is an express command, "Get learning, even by study;" but almost side and side with this law, there is the command, "Thou shalt love thy wife with all thy heart, *and cleave unto her, and none else!*" How much respect the Mormons pay to the commands of their deity, is very apparent.

But still the Mormons have done something. One notable enterprise must be remembered. Brigham does not know how to spell, finds it very difficult indeed to spell, yet in his broad spirit of philanthropy, has endeavored to correct English orthography. With some very original emendations, he has adopted Pitman's system of phonographic spelling, as the basis of the "Deseret alphabet." Lines that would frighten Hogarth, and that would puzzle even Pitman's pliant hand to form, were adopted. This is nearly all the pretentious named "Board of Regents of the Deseret University" have accomplished since their organization; and this, like the other literary efforts of the Mormons, although blazoned forth, fonts of the new type made, and schools instituted to teach it, has resumed its proper level. It began in a flash and ended in smoke; "went up a rocket and came down a stick."

As to their own literature, they publish a weekly paper at Salt Lake, which is almost wholly filled with the autobiography of Smith, and sermons of the "First Presidency." It neither gives honest reports of speeches, nor correct statements of facts. Much talk has been made about getting up a separate paper, devoted to scientific and literary purposes; but its friends are afraid the Church might become so fond of it, as to hug it to death, as it has their literary institutions. They publish a weekly sheet at San Francisco, California. Its editor, workmen, and even devil, are all "on mission;" get nothing but food and raiment; but are "therewith content." Their sincerity can not be doubted, whatever be said of their intellect. The "Mormon" dribbles out its weekly quantum of saintly notice and opinion at New York. A "Luminary" hardly lit its own path into obscurity at St. Louis, Mo. At Liverpool they publish a "Millennial Star." By compelling the believing to take several copies, they say they have a circulation of over 16,000. At Paris they published "L'Etoile du Deseret," but the star has set. "Zion's Panier" floated at Hamburg: a month's wind blew it into shreds. They still publish periodicals in the Welsh and Danish languages.

Of their standard works, the Book of Mormon, although most mentioned, is not the principal. The Doctrines and Covenants, containing some of the Revelations that Smith pretended to obtain, is viewed as the "law of God to this generation." Its contents are very miscellaneous, comprising the organization of the Church; revelations as to priesthood, and cattle medicine; chewing tobacco, and sending out missionaries; "endowments from on high," and "building taverns;" "supplying all the wants of my servant Joseph;" and anathematizing apostates, etc., etc. Besides these, Smith attempted a new translation of the Old and New Testaments. This translation, however, is kept very secret, the people "not being able to bear it now." Some singular extracts from it have reached their presses, but the impression they created was not favorable. More than Jew ever read, or Christian ever conceived, and far more than Hebrew or Greek MS. ever contained, is to be seen in Smith's new translation of the Bible. While at Nauvoo Smith obtained four Egyptian mummies. In the bosom of one of them, a MS. was pretended to be found. Smith gave out that he made a "*translation*," and the result was, "A Book of Abraham." He announced it ("Times and Seasons," vol. iii., p. 704), "A Translation of some Ancient Records that have fallen into our hands from the catacombs of Egypt, purporting to be the writings of Abraham, while he was in Egypt, called the Book of Abraham, written by his own hand on papyrus." This was received with especial unction by the devout. Although evidently the work of the same hand as the Book of Mormon, Smith had somewhat improved himself in the use of words. It contains several singular engravings, a chart of astronomy, and is altogether quite unique. The Apocalypse of St. John occupied the attention of Smith, and he composed "A Key to the Book of Revelations." The Bible-student would be startled at some of its views. As Smith had to labor to sustain his reputation as a prophet, accordingly, in December, 1830, he issued a Revelation, pretending to contain a "prophecy of Enoch," "A revelation of the gospel to Adam after he was driven out of the Garden of Eden." These, which are of course *morceaux choisies* to the Church, have been collected and bound together into a little work called the "Pearl of Great Price."

But, happily for the Church, they are not at all limited to their *leges scriptæ*. O. Hyde, at Iowa, taught that "these books were only our school-books, and as boys put away their elementary books, so Saints should learn to put away and live above these." This is very convenient doctrine, as too close a scrutiny in their book of Smith's Revelations, proves him a very singular prophet; showing that Missouri was Zion; then Nauvoo was Zion; then Mormon salvation depended on building "Smith's Tavern," and as it was not built, all the Mormons must be damned, according to Smith! And now Missouri is not Zion, and Nauvoo is not Zion, although they were both to be "eternal habitations for my

Saints, saith the Lord," but Salt Lake is Zion, about which the "Book" says nothing. The great criteria and guide to the Church, however, is, *constant* and oral revelation.

"The words of our Prophet Brigham are as much more important to us than those of the Saviour and Apostles in the New Testament, as their words were to the people at that time more than those of Noah in the Old Testament."

This is the doctrine constantly urged, and believed; hence, Brigham's sermons are all revelations, and, consequently, standard works for the Church. It is rather amusing to notice how frequently those revelations of Brigham contradict themselves and all reason.

Of their standard controversial works, P. P. Pratt's "Voice of Warning" is the most popular. O. Pratt's works are the most able. A great spite is felt toward O. Pratt at Salt Lake, in consequence of his refusing to blindly submit to the mere *ipse dixit* of Young. He published the "Seer" at Washington; and although it was the production of *an inspired Apostle*, Brigham not only publicly ridiculed it and its author, but also wrote to the "Saints in England and elsewhere," that it contained "many falsehoods, and much incorrect doctrine; but that they might exercise their faith and discernment, he would not point out its errors." This letter was published in the "Millennial Star" at Liverpool by Brigham's direction. Orson Pratt's influence was great in England; he was a little contumacious at home, and it was thought "wisdom to somewhat break him down." O. Pratt is the only really able man they have among them, "but his head is always among the stars," his love and hobby being the study of astronomy.

The late Parley P. Pratt, something of a poet, something of a preacher, very much of a panderer, and a bad man, has written a singular work, "The Key to Theology," about which much expectation was excited, and much disappointment felt. Andrew Jackson Davis has contributed no little to its matter and style. The Mormons have other and less important works; an ephemeral effort of J. Taylor, "The Government of God," and several pamphlets.

The literature of the Mormons is like their preaching. What is lacked in ability, is made up in earnestness. The singular success their Elders have met in proselyting, abundantly proves that sincere enthusiasm is a very formidable weapon. It is a pity such earnestness and sincerity were not exercised in a better cause.

CHAPTER VI.

BRIGHAM YOUNG AT HOME.

His biography—Birth and education—Embraces Mormonism—Meets Smith the Prophet—Journey to Missouri—Is ordained an Apostle—Preaches—Appointed President of the Apostles—Flies for his life—Re-lays foundation of Temple in Jackson county, Mo.—Mission to England—Returns to Nauvoo—Brigham and Smith—Brigham and Sidney Rigdon—Builds up Nauvoo—Conducts emigration—Mormon Battalion—Salt Lake City—Brigham's leadership—Appointed President of Church—Quarrels with Judges and expels them—Colonel Steptoe—*Modus operandi*—Should he die, fate of the Church—Personal appearance—In council and in pulpit—Satellites to this planet—His manners—Style of oratory—As a writer—As a husband and father—Domesticities—His wives—His favorite Women—Courting the men—Occupation and property—Universal confidant and adviser—Administrative blunders—Secret of success.

Brigham Young, the President of the Mormon Church and Governor of Utah Territory, was born at Whittenham, Vermont, June 1, 1801, and is, consequently, now fifty-six years of age. His father was a farmer, and had been a soldier of the Revolution. The whole family moved to the State of New York in 1802. Brigham's youth was occupied by the ordinary pursuits of a farmer's son; familiarized with tools and accustomed to hard work.

In the year 1832, being then thirty-one years old, he heard

and embraced Mormonism. He was convinced by Elder Samuel H. Smith, brother to the Prophet, Joseph Smith, who has since apostatized, and was baptized by Eleazar Miller, now at Salt Lake. Brigham gathered with the Saints to Kirtland, Ohio, in September of the same year, and soon became intimate with Joseph Smith. He was ordained an Elder, and began preaching. His shrewd views of policy, and almost intuitive knowledge of character, soon attracted attention and favor among the small and despised Church. Illiterate, among the ignorant his lack of education passed unnoticed and unknown. He accompanied Smith, in 1834, from Ohio to Jackson county, Missouri, with the companies who "went for the relief of the Saints," who had just been driven out of that, into Clay county. He had become a marked and prominent man. Eminently practical and far-seeing, at a time too when practical ability of any kind was much needed to meet the exigences of the Church, then being driven, starving and naked, in the winter season, from their homes to suffer and several to die; he made his presence felt in the Church, and was regarded as one of the *men* of Mormonism. Accordingly, in 1835, on the 14th of February, at Kirtland, Ohio, Brigham Young, then thirty-four years of age, was ordained one of the newly-organized quorum of the Twelve Apostles; he having been previously designated by a special revelation, that Smith pretended to obtain. Under the hands of the three witnesses of the Book of Mormon, all of whom subsequently apostatized, Brigham was ordained and set apart to his office. The Twelve were sent from Kirtland, in March, to different parts of the States, and Brigham, firmly believing in the authority, and enthusiastically devoted to the person of Smith, as well as fully convinced of his being in reality an Apostle, and equal with Paul or John in the eyes of God, went out to preach. He traveled through the eastern States, and proselyted with much zeal and, therefore, with much success. Not only had he been ordained to the apostleship, but had subsequently received an especial blessing designed to peculiarly aid and comfort him in his travels at this particular time.

When the Kirtland Temple was completed, in 1836, we find Brigham's name as being present at its dedication. A great many of the Saints on that occasion, were seized, as the Irvingites, with an uncontrollable desire to utter unknown sounds, called "the gift of tongues." Brigham, among others, was thus favored, and this, more than ever, confirmed him in the faith and inspired him with renewed zeal to "bring many to the knowledge of the truth." He continued to labor ardently in the Mormon ministry.

In 1837, Smith's bank, "The Safety Society Bank of Kirtland," failed; his stores were seized, and goods sold, and himself (Smith) was forced to fly by night, to avoid arrest, and very likely being mobbed. Brigham Young accompanied this second Mohammed, in this second Hegira, and Missouri was the Medina that opened its gates to receive them. A new revelation was obtained, and Brigham was commanded to make his home in this State of Missouri.

Thomas B. Marsh, the President of the Twelve Apostles, had apostatized, finding Mormonism too bad a faith, or Smith too bad a Prophet. Brigham Young who, by having "preached in tongues" to the Saints, who did not understand him though, in 1836, and having abundantly proven his practical superiority, was appointed President of the Twelve Apostles in Marsh's stead.

Then came the dark days of Mormonism; days that proved Smith's tact and talent severely. Orson Hyde, the present "President of the Twelve," had apostatized, and testified against Smith. W. W. Phelps, the present Mormon devil, almanac maker, "Brigham's jester," etc., had made affidavits against the Church. The Pratts were wavering; Dr. Arvard, a prominent member of the Danite band, had exposed the hidden machinery of Mormonism. Almost alone, and discouraged, Smith was arrested. Brigham fled to save his life, on September 14, 1838. He reached Illinois in safety, met with the Twelve at Quincy, Ill., in council, transacted some "Church" business and returned to Far West, where, in company with several of the Apostles and "other brethren," he assisted to re-lay the foundation of the Temple at "The New Jerusalem" in Independence, Jackson Co., Mo. This was done at midnight on the 25th and 26th of March, 1839. In the darkness of a gloomy night, surrounded by enemies who had sworn to take their lives, who had previously driven them from their habitations, that lay in ruins silently around them, these men met to perform fantastic rites for a fanatic object. However much one may denounce their malpractices, or deplore their delusion, he can not but admire the stern intrepidity of these fearless and foolish men.

On 14th September, 1839, Brigham was appointed with others, by Joseph Smith, to go to "open England by preaching the gospel." They landed at Liverpool on 6th April, 1840, partook of the sacrament, and commenced preaching. As they were penniless, and depended entirely on the charity of their audiences, then very poor and very small, Brigham suffered much and often. He here superintended affairs, issued an edition of the Book of Mormon, and commenced the publication of the *Millennial Star*, a weekly periodical still living. He found that gullibility formed a strong ingredient in the characters of residents of the old as well as new countries. He shipped off, to Nauvoo, Ill., seven hundred and sixty-nine of the faithful who had been converted to Mormonism; and on April 20, 1841, Brigham sailed for New York, leaving behind him many Mormon Churches with organizations completed.

His value was felt and appreciated. Smith received him cordially at Nauvoo, in the July following, and all the Saints applauded him very warmly. Although it is, and always has been, Mormon policy that there should be but one head, and he the all in all of the Church; yet, in April, 1843, Brigham was possessed of influence sufficient to even grapple with Smith, as to the trustworthiness of the Twelve. Smith, who had trained Brigham, had to yield to the pupil he had educated.

The summers were spent by Brigham in preaching, in which his handsome face and pleasing manners obtained him much success; his winters, in attending to the necessities of his wives and children.

It was June, 1844. Smith was shot. The Twelve Apostles were scattered in different places. Nauvoo was threatened.

Ruins of the Temple at Nauvoo.

Illinoians were alarmed. The most absurd rumors were circulated. Troops were in arms, and their generals had lost their brains. Brigham was then in Boston, Mass. Sidney Rigdon, to whom the right of presidency belonged, according to Mormon law, assumed his authority and began to obtain revelations, confer endowments, institute new mysteries, and dictate *à la* Smith. Brigham came hurriedly to Nauvoo—and now came the tug of war—convinced of his right to lead the people. O how easy it is to be convinced of what is to one's interest! He called his quorum and the people together; ran Sidney Rigdon into the earth completely; broke up his organizations; denounced his revelations as from the devil; crushed his influence; cut off himself and adherents; cursed him; "handed him over to the buffetings of Satan for a thousand years," and was chosen President by an overwhelming majority. He did not stay to reason with the minority, but cut them all off at once. The Church was going to ruin; a thousand divisions threatened to tear it piecemeal. Four claimants to Smith's position appeared, and each had his followers among the people. Brigham aimed at the most prominent. His energy intimidated those whom it did not cut off. He saved the system, and achieved his own triumph.

One thing is certain, had Rigdon remained President, there would have been no Mormonism to-day. Brigham had given a strong proof of his administrative ability. The people obeyed him willingly, for people will always obey men who are able and determined to lead. Energy grew in him with its exercise. From pleading with the people, he began to teach them; from teaching, he dictated to them. Possessed of a far more powerful mind, more dogged pertinacity, clearer views, and more pointedness of means than Smith, he soon made Nauvoo show the firm hand of the helmsman. The Temple was completed, the Mansion was growing fast, Nauvoo was increasing rapidly, and, with these, his popularity and power.

Not only on the present did he keep his shrewd gaze. He felt the then position of the Saints was entirely a false one, and he was busy laboring to convince them of the necessity of moving from Nauvoo, even though it should be at the sacrifice of their all. They had reared their Temple in the munificence of their poverty; to leave it was like forsaking a child. Smith's promises and prophecies about Missouri had failed; those about Nauvoo were about to fail too; might not Brigham's predictions of the Rocky Mountains also fail? They hesitated, and they wept. Still Brigham's authority prevented further expression. The force of a strong will bent them before it; and his influence carried the measure through. The Temple was finished in 1845, and endowments were commenced. Thousands were hurried through. They were bound together and to him by oaths, which, while they made them shudder to remember, yet made them love him the more. Their tenderest attachments, their deepest superstition, their fiercest passions, and most sacred reverence were artfully enlisted, to make them more united, and more unitedly obedient. Loving Brigham as their brother, venerating him as their President, obeying him as their God, they left even their beautiful Nauvoo. They crossed the Mississippi on the ice, in February, 1846. Here Brigham proved himself a general as well as a commander. He directed every thing. Thousands were leaving; many destitute, and all poor; their future location was undecided and unknown, it being "somewhere in the Rocky Mountains," and all their property left behind them. Without confusion, without hurrying or even discord, their long trains rolled by him, while he comforted, inspirited, blessed, and counseled the weeping emigrants. Committees were left behind to sell the property of the Church; all business was arranged, and he left Nauvoo, for Winter Quarters, Iowa.

The same skill and energy directed the next movement of the Church. Their avowed intention of going to the Rocky Mountains, then Mexican country, was to establish an independent government. Disgusted with the institutions of a country that had allowed them to be expelled three times, they resolved to forsake it, and forever. In their style, they would "worship under their own vine and fig-tree, and none should make them afraid." But they were poor: money was needed to enable them to move. Their design they desired to cloak under a sham patriotism. The United States offered $20,000 bounty money, and Brigham recruited a regiment, persuaded, commanded them to leave their families, many of them perfectly destitute, and join General Scott's army, then in Mexico, and they obeyed. One hundred and forty-three men, with Brigham at their head, made the trip to Salt Lake, where they arrived July 24th, 1847; and leaving a few to commence farming operations, Brigham returned to Winter Quarters, Iowa, where the Church were suffering poverty and starvation; while the cholera, and fever and ague, were mowing them down in ranks.

A very serious step had now to be taken. The veneration of the people for the memory of Smith was very sensitive. No man could supplant him in their affections: few men could have dared to attempt occupying his position. A thousand reminiscences of him, that the people loved to cherish, were sanctified in their thoughts by his blood. Brigham was only ruling the people in his capacity of President of the Twelve Apostles. He needed greater influence; therefore, he coveted the higher authority of the President of the Church. Cromwell was content to be king in fact; Brigham demanded the name as well as the power. It was a bold step, but his feet were firm; he attempted it, and succeeded

The Church was reorganized at Council Bluffs, Iowa, on the 24th December, 1847. After the pattern of Smith, Brigham was chosen "President of the Church of Jesus Christ of Latter-day Saints in all the world." He appointed Heber Chase, Kimball, and Willard Richards, to be his Counselors. These three formed the "First Presidency." All this was subsequently confirmed at a conference held 6th of April, 1848, at the same place. Brigham was then the nominal as well as virtual "head of this strange community." A greater trial demanded his forethought. The whole of the Church had to be moved a distance of 1030 miles, through an almost unknown country, full of dangers and difficulties. Some ability is required to efficiently remove bodies of armed troops over such new and pioneering obstacles; well supplied, equipped and mounted, it taxes a commander's skill; but here were poor, unprovided, feeble men, women, and children, shaking with ague, pale with suffering, hollow and gaunt with recent hunger. Without strife, without discord, without almost a murmur, this heterogeneous mass moved off. Many groaned with anguish, but none with complaint. Brigham's energy inspired them all; his genius controlled them all. Marking their road with their grave-stones, they arrived at Salt Lake Valley, destitute and feeble, in 1848. The desert, to which they had come, was as cheerless as their past history. From cruel foes they had fled to as unfeeling a wilderness. Renewed difficulties demanded a renewed effort from Brigham. Every thing depended on him. Starvation and nakedness stared in the gloomy faces of the desponding people. Murmurs and complaints were uttered. He quelled every thing; scolded, plead, threatened, prophesied, and subdued them. With a restless but resistless energy he set them to work, and worked himself as their example. He directed their labors, controlled their domestic affairs, preached at them, to them, for them. He told foolish anecdotes to make them laugh; encouraged their dancing to make them merry; got up theatrical performances to distract their minds, and made them work hard, certain of that rendering them contented by-and-by. Feared with a stronger fear, venerated with a more rational veneration, but not loved with the same clinging tenderness that the people still felt for Joseph Smith, Brigham swayed them at his will. They learned to dread his iron hand; and were daunted by his iron heart. They got enough to eat, and their previous want made their then present scarcity seem like paradise begun. They were by themselves, but still they were away from their enemies.

Mexico was vanquished, California seized, much territory annexed to the United States, and the Mormons were now desirous to be recognized by the federal Government. Accordingly the people elected a Convention who drew up the Constitution of the State of Deseret, appointed delegates, sent them to Washington, and prayed admission into the Union. Brigham of course was Governor; the other offices were filled by the leading men of the Church. Congress in 1850 sheared some of the self-named and extensive proportions of "Deseret," and granted them a Territorial Government under the name of Utah. Fillmore, by the advice and intercession of Colonel Kane, who had embraced Mormonism in Iowa, appointed Brigham as the Governor of Utah, for the first term of four years.

Since that time, large bodies of emigrants have flocked in. The California excitement drove thousands through, who left much money and property. Brigham's policy of keeping the people to work constantly, began to show its fruits. Cities, towns, public buildings, roads, etc., were going up. A Temple block was dedicated, inclosed, and the Tabernacle erected. Meanwhile his influence began to increase; thousands came from England, prepared to believe him any thing he pretended, and every thing he said. They brought the skill of English mechanics added to the Mormon energy. Comfort and prosperity dawned upon the people; and Brigham had a moment's respite. The year 1852 came, and the Secretary and Judges appointed by

President Pierce to Utah, came with it. Mr. Brocchus and others made some slighting allusions to the Saints, and their conduct. Brigham was aroused. The man who had crushed Sidney Rigdon, in the very teeth of the Church, at a time pregnant with ruin for the whole system, would not be cowed by one man, especially when there were thousands to support him in what he might do, and they were a thousand miles "from anywhere." Brocchus was bruised, bent, broken; and the officers fled. Others were appointed; they yielded to Young, and remained.

In 1854 another cloud darkened the temporal horizon of the Church. The crops failed. Famine stared the people in the face. Hundreds were suffering want and anxiety. The people murmured, and many left. Brigham recalled his old tact and energy. "The Saints were unfaithful, therefore they were cursed;" or, rather, the Saints were cursed, therefore they were unfaithful. Brigham's famine sermons startled every body; they succeeded where every thing else would have failed. He stifled out complaint by cursing the murmurers. The people bowed to the yoke, and only worked harder than ever. There was more suffering, and more prayer. Brigham had frequently declared that "no other man should be Governor of the Territory." Colonel Steptoe came in the same year, with his appointment, generally suspected. Brigham courted the Colonel; got up parties for the officers; flattered, befooled, and used them as tools. Colonel Steptoe threw up his appointment; got up the following memorial to President Pierce; induced his officers and civil friends to sign it, and forwarded it to Washington, praying for the reappointment of Brigham Young to the office of Governor.

TO HIS EXCELLENCY FRANKLIN PIERCE,

PRESIDENT OF THE UNITED STATES.

Your petitioners would respectfully represent: that

Whereas Governor Brigham Young possesses the entire confidence of the people of this Territory, without distinction of party or sect; and from personal acquaintance, and social intercourse, we find him to be a firm supporter of the Constitution and Laws of the United States, and a tried pillar of Republican Institutions; and having repeatedly listened to his remarks, in private as well as in public assemblies, do know he is the warm friend and able supporter of Constitutional Liberty, the rumors published in the States to the contrary notwithstanding; and having canvassed to our satisfaction his doings as Governor, and Superintendent of Indian Affairs, and also the disposition of the appropriation for public buildings for the Territory,

We do most cordially and cheerfully represent, that the same has been expended to the best interest of the nation; and

Whereas his reappointment would better subserve the Territorial interest than the appointment of any other man, and would meet with the gratitude of the entire inhabitants of the Territory, and his removal would cause the deepest feelings of sorrow and regret; and it being our unqualified opinion, based upon the personal acquaintance which we have formed with Governor Young, and from our observation of the results of his influence and administration in this Territory, that he possesses in an eminent degree every qualification necessary for the discharge of his official duties, and unquestioned integrity and ability; that he is decidedly the most suitable person that can be selected for that office.

We therefore take great pleasure in recommending him to your favorable consideration, and do earnestly request his re-appointment as Governor, and Superintendent of Indian Affairs for this Territory.

Great Salt Lake City, Utah Territory, December 30, 1854.

J. T. Kinney, Chief Justice U. S. Supreme Court, Utah.

E. J. Steptoe, Lieutenant-colonel U. S. Army.

John F. Reynolde, Brevet Major 3d Artillery U. S. Army

Rufus Ingalls, Captain U. S. Army.

Sylvester Mowry, Lieutenant U. S. Army.

Lathett L. Livingston, Lieutenant 3d U. S. Artillery.

John G. Chandler, Lieutenant 3d U. S. Artillery.

Robert O. Tyler, Lieutenant 3d Artillery.

Benjamin Allston, Brevet 2d Lieutenant 1st Dragoons U. S. Army.

Charles A. Perry, Sutler U. S. Army.

William G. Rankin, Quartermaster's Clerk.

Horace R. Wirtz, Medical Staff U. S. Army.

Leo. Shaver, Assistant Justice of Supreme Court of U. S., Territory of Utah.

William I. Appleby, Clerk of Supreme and First District Courts U. S., Territory of Utah.

Curtis E. Bolton (Book-keeper of Mr. Perry).

A. W. Babbitt, Secretary of Utah Territory.

Joseph Hollman, U. S. District Attorney for Utah; and many Mormon signatures.

The Colonel left, believing Brigham to be an ill-used and belied man; and feeling that certainly, notwithstanding his fame in military and diplomatic circles, he was not the man to cope with this famous prophet and would-be reformer.

Other judges and officers were appointed; not one of them but sunk themselves, or was fiercely curbed by Brigham. One officer disgraced himself with an Indian squaw. Another was a notorious opium-eater, with which he killed himself. Another was accused of having gambling in his cellar. Another for taking a public prostitute, seating her on the bench with him, and being accessory to an attempted assassination. Another was a notorious drunkard. All fell, or all had to fall. It is a popular mistake that Brigham used physical force in any of these cases; he is too wise a man. Physical force is the sole property of brutes, and they are brutes who make it their sole property. But although he never struck, he has over and over again threatened and intimidated them. He has instigated annoyances of a thousand different kinds; frustrated their plans, and baffled their designs; forced them to act under a mental and moral duress; but he never yet attempted personal violence. They have all felt the pressure of his heavy hand, but none bear the marks of his fangs. Had they resisted him, however, I make no doubt but that some appointed individual would have sought a quarrel with the contumacious Judge, and have murdered him. Let another man give the Mormons the same reasons to be disliked or feared as Governor Boggs of Missouri, and Joseph Smith's successor will find another O. P. Rockwell to attempt to assassinate him. That Brigham Young has been accessory to several murders, I am compelled to believe; that he would not hesitate at such, if he thought it advisable and proper, I have not the slightest doubt; yet, I think his heart would condemn such an act, if not imperiously demanded by his policy.

To his policy he would sacrifice himself; to it he would willingly sacrifice his country; to it he will assuredly sacrifice the whole Mormon people, by arraying them against federal authority and power; and the immolation of a Judge or a Governor, would need but a small stretch of his conscience. While this is true as to his unscrupulousness, it is not true of his past conduct. The means he has employed to so completely rule the United States officials hitherto sent has been this—they have put themselves under his heel, and he has mercilessly trod them down, and compelled them to leave.

Brigham Young has one design, and only one. However wild in theory and impossible in execution, he entertains it seriously; and that is, to make the Mormon Church by-and-by control the whole of this continent. For this he really hopes, and to this end are all his efforts directed. By the native force and vigor of a strong mind he has already taken this system of the grossest absurdity and re-created it; molded it anew and changed its spirit; taken from beneath it the monstrous stilts of a miserable superstition, and consolidated it into a compact scheme of the sternest fanaticism; guided its energies and swelled its numbers; increased its wealth and established its power, and all with the same ability that characterized his triumph over Rigdon, or his direction of the emigration to Salt Lake. His success in the past only inspires in him confidence in his future, and relying on contemptuous disregard or fluctuating imbecility on the part of the Government, he is prepared to consummate his folly and his ruin.

I have seen and heard him very often; privately conversed with him; watched him in his family and in his public administrations; carefully endeavored to criticise his movements, and discover his secret of power, and I conscientiously assert, that the world has much mistaken the ability and danger of the man.

This is independent of his system; *that* is a piece of gross fraud, but it is a proof the stronger that he must be something of a man, to make so much out of so poor and ridiculous a foundation. In a few years he will follow others to the grave; Mormonism will lose his clear head and his iron fist. Under the vacillating weakness of Kimball, or the impetuous thoughtlessness of the old apostate, Hyde; the abstract ponderings of O. Pratt, or the good-natured want of energy of George A. Smith; the self-confident and self-exhibiting egotism of Taylor, or the wild theories of the others, Mormonism will decline. It must live its day, and die. Brigham is its sun, this is its day-time. Delusions have arisen in all ages; like meteors, the more rapid their progress, the more heat and light they have evolved—but the more speedy has been their extinction. It has been thus with other systems of imposture, and will be so with this.

Brigham Young is far superior to Smith in every thing that constitutes a great leader. Smith was not a man of genius; his *forte* was *tact.* He only embraced opportunities that presented themselves. He *used* circumstances but did not *create* them. The compiling genius of Mormonism was Sidney Rigdon. Smith had boisterous impetuosity, but no foresight. Polygamy was not the result of his policy, but of his passions. Sidney gave point, direction, and apparent consistency to the Mormon system of theology. He invented its forms and many of its arguments. He and Parley Pratt were its leading orators and polemics. Had it not been for the accession of these two men, Smith would have been lost, and his schemes frustrated and abandoned. That Brigham was superior not only to Smith, but also to Rigdon, is evident. To carry on Mormonism demands increasing talent and skill. Its position and progress becomes constantly beset with fresh and greater difficulties. The next President must be as superior to Brigham as he was to Smith, or Mormonism will retrograde. Such an one does not live in the Mormon Church.

Thus far with Brigham's past history. It may be interesting to ask what is his appearance and style. In person he is rather large and portly, has an imposing carriage and very impressive manner. To pass him in the street, he is one of those men we should naturally turn round to look after. In private conversation, he is pointed, but affable, very courteous to strangers, knows he is the object of much curiosity, takes it as a matter of course, and, so long as the curiosity is not impertinent, is very friendly. He talks freely, in an off-hand style, on any subject, does not get much time to read, and, therefore, often blunders grossly; he is much more of an observer than reader, thoroughly knows men, a point in which Smith was very weak, although he boasted "the Lord tells me who to trust." *Men* not books, *deeds* not words, *houses* not theories, the *earth* and not the heavens, *now* and not hereafter, is Brigham's view of matters. Hence his religion is all practical; and, consequently, hence his practical success.

Brigham in a council and Brigham in the pulpit are not the same. Under the force of his prophetic afflatus, he talks, till, on reviewing his remarks, he has to say, "Well, well, words are only wind." This is a remark he once made. In council he is calm, deliberate, and very politic; neither hastily decided, nor easily moved when decided. His shrewdness is often, however, baffled by a set of sycophants that he has around him. He has unjustly browbeaten and crushed several of his warm believers through the instigations of men "whom I thought I could believe." So complete is his ascendancy that they, however, have only bowed their heads and tried to do better. The same petty jealousies, secret maneuverings, pandering flattery, and entire self-abnegation, characterize his, as any other great man's satellites. One difference exists, and that is this, however bickering among themselves, they would all die for Brigham Young. One of the severest tests of greatness is the power to completely center in oneself a thousand interests and the deep affections of a thousand hearts. All really great men have done this. Philosophy has had its disciples, adventurers their followers, generals their soldiers, kings their subjects, impostors their fanatics. Mohammed, Smith, Brigham have all been thus. No man ever lived who had more deeply devoted friends than Brigham Young. The magnetism that attracts and infatuates, that makes men feel its weight and yet love its presence, abounds in him. Even his enemies have to acknowledge a great charm in the influence he throws around him. The clerks in his office and his very *wives* feel the same veneration for the Prophet, as the most respectful new-comer. It is thus also in his public orations; he soon winds a thrall round his hearers. Bad jokes, low ribaldry, meaningless nonsense, and pompous swagger that would disgust when coming from any one else, amuse and interest from him. I have seen him bring an audience to their feet and draw out thundering responses more than once. Sermons that appear a mere farcical rhodomontade have been powerful when they were spoken by him. His manner is pleasing and unaffected, his matter perfectly impromptu and unstudied. He does not *preach* but merely *talks*. His voice is strong and sonorous, and he is an excellent bass singer. His gestures are easy and seldom violent. He *feels* his sermons; the people see he feels them, and, *therefore*, they make themselves felt. He makes constant and unmistakable allusions to individuals; imitating their personal appearance and peculiarities, and repeating their expressions. Brigham is a good mimic, and very readily excites laughter. Much that tells, therefore, very gallingly to Salt Lake audiences, who understand the allusions and recognize the parties, seems ridiculous when read. Even on reading, after denuding his sermons of the ridiculous and obscure, there is an evident vein of strong, practical sense. They are, however, much garbled in printing, and are still more coarse and profane, when spoken. Brigham has no education. He never writes his letters, merely dictates them. This was also the custom of J. Smith. Smith's letters to A. Bennett, Clay, and Calhoun, and his address as candidate for the Presidency, which was thought to so clearly evince the man, were written by Phelps, the Mormon devil, W. Clayton, and others. In like manner, the epistles, addresses, and messages that simple Saints have believed were the divine effusions of "Brigham's graphic pen" (!) were written by General D. W. Wells, Albert Carrington, and others. His autograph, which is quite characteristic, dashed energetically up and down and curling off with a little flourish, is almost as far as Brigham's chirography extends.

Much interest is naturally felt as to his family. As a husband he is *kind* not *fond*. As a father he is necessarily negligent, indeed he makes a mockery of Solomon's injunction, "Bring up a child in the way he should go, and he will never depart from it;" quotes Solomon himself as a proof to the contrary, and says, "According to my experience it is, bring up a child and away they go." Brigham is a tolerably well-preserved man, considering his travels and hardships, and the constant mental and physical demands on his system. He sleeps by himself, in a sacredly private chamber behind his office. He, as some old philosophers, teaches the doctrine that cohabitation is entirely for the purpose of procreation, and that all cohabitation should, therefore, cease with pregnancy; nor be resumed until after weaning the infant! This rule he endeavors to keep, although the birth of children proves him to have violated his own law, certainly in one woman's exception. There is also another practice he has adopted which eminently proves the degrading nature of this Mormon institution. As cohabitation is merely for the purpose of procreation, therefore after his wives get past child-bearing, they are entirely discarded. They live in his house and eat at his table, but all attention from him, as a husband, ceases. Brigham believes that Solomon's injunction, "Waste not thy strength on women," might be peculiarly applied in these instances. These women, thus neglected, usually become "Mothers in Israel;" pretend to great piety, and endeavor to win the smile of approval as devotees, that is denied to them as wives. But Mormon piety is very peculiar in its nature; it is not the spiritual purity and holiness that might be imagined, but assumes quite a practical and Mormon cast: to convert young girls who dislike polygamy into advocates of the practice; to convince young wives who stand alone in their husband's affections, that it is their duty to persuade their husbands to take other wives; to visit the sick, and by anointing, and praying, and "laying on of hands," to endeavor to heal them miraculously; to teach newly-married wives their duties, which many of them do most indecently and even obscenely; to be present at child-births, and give motherly advice upon the most sacredly private affairs; to attend their weekly "council of health," and tell their own and friends' experiences; and disgustingly discuss the laws of procreation and *human nature* in general. Incited by feelings which are neither dead nor dormant, witnessing around them unblushing signs of sensuality, remembering the reasons that have induced the neglect they can not but feel, hearing but little conversation not connected with marriage, or birth, or their kindred concomitants, the vast majority of them are as above stated; and who can be surprised that such results should inevitably follow?

Brigham has not only these discarded wives, and those with whom he lives, but also the widows of Smith; besides many spiritual wives (temporarily married to other husbands) and likewise many women to whom he has been "sealed" as agent or proxy for some dead brother. Counting all these he has a very large number. Out of this number, there are only, I believe, about twenty-five with whom he lives. This, I think, includes the whole, but of this it is impossible to speak decisively. I can only say, that I am not acquainted with any more. It may be naturally asked, Where does he keep them? How do they live? What do they do? When does he visit them? etc., etc.

Brigham has some of his wives in his Lion House; others in his Mansion, and others in little houses, in different parts of the city. He intends to see them all once a week, and, if possible, once a day. This, however, owing sometimes to his ill health, sometimes to the press of business, and sometimes from bad weather, he is not able to do. His wives, if they want to see him, then, have to go to him. For thirty or forty women to be in a sick room, and all wanting to do something for their suffering lord and master, is no trifle for weak or disordered nerves. If he be sick, he has to name his attendant, and the rest go sadly away and weep, till their jealousy and anguish is over. Poor women! there is many and often a wet eye, a pained bosom, a dreary heart-ache, and deep sighs; but they murmur, "It is the will of the Lord," and try to stifle down the voice of nature that is pleading within them, against the monstrous cruelty. He may be in pain, and their kind hearts and soft hands may uselessly wish to attend or comfort him; he may die, and the whole of his family could not stand around his bed, to hear his last words or watch his last breath. They are the companions of his passions, and not of his life; panderers to his lusts, instead of being the partners of his affections; obliged to be satisfied with a passing nod, a casual smile, or an accidental confidence: crushing out every hope of happiness, every dream of girlhood, every wish and every necessity of their deep woman hearts; searing themselves into a premature age, and age bringing with it inevitable neglect, and yet, most of them appearing content to be thus degraded, for the sake of their religion; preserving themselves pure for their impure husbands, till the observer is almost compelled to think, that they must have ceased to be women altogether in heart, in soul, and in mind.

Brigham Young, imitating the sultan in his hareem, has imitated him also in having a favorite. This, of course, is vigorously denied by the men of Utah; the women, however, whose perceptions are far more acute, especially when sharpened by jealousy, know the men are trying to deceive them. It is contrary to human nature for men, however brutal or however refined, to have several wives without feeling a warmer love for some one of them than for the others. Brigham Young, I presume, would deny the charge directly, were any of his wives to dare to make it: but with so many eyes to watch his glances; to observe on whose face it lingers the longest; or seems most tender while regarding; or whom he gets to wait on him most, when sick; or whose company he prefers, when traveling; or who seems best acquainted with his views on private matters; or who exercises most influence over domestic arrangements; or who obtains the most attention if unwell; or who is always best provided with assistance; or at whose accouchments Brigham, in spite of himself, exhibits most anxiety; with so many eyes to remark, and so many hearts to treasure up such observations, it is impossible not to know.

Brigham has a favorite. She is a very good-looking person, of about thirty years of age. She is tall; her eyes are a very soft blue, large and full; her hair light brown; complexion very fair, and general expression very intelligent and prepossessing. I believe she is Brigham's third wife, and, I understand, he married her at Council Bluffs, Iowa. She has had six children, most of them, however, are dead. In her case, Brigham violated his own law. For a little while, he indulged his vanity so far as to wear his hair curled; much laughter and remark was occasioned by persons often noticing his head fixed up in papers and hair-pins, of an evening. This lady was the industrious hair-dresser. She is very devout in her religion and passionately devoted to her husband, that is, to her "undivided moiety" of a husband!

Mrs. Emeline Free Young, however, is not alone, either in her worth or her affection. Brigham is very much beloved by all his wives, notwithstanding his bitter attacks on some, and cruel neglect of others, of them. They all certainly believe in his authority, and are content to share his future glory, although that is so widely diffused, that it can come only in *homeopathic doses to any one of them.*

There are still very many who would like to be married to Brigham, notwithstanding the size of his family. Many great men, orators, tragedians, poets, or warriors have excited similar feelings in many bosoms. At Salt Lake the women not only feel, but express such wishes. Nature has implanted the feeling of sympathy and the sentiment of admiration; false education has taught many to mistake that sympathy for love, and that admiration for devotion: the Mormons have broken down the barriers of modesty, and the women, thus in error are permitted to indulge it, and gratify the new passion by a new marriage, if single; or by a divorce and then a marriage if previously united.

Great numbers have pestered Brigham so much to marry them, that he has been forced to declare, "My family is large enough, and I do not want to take any more."

I spent a few days at the house of an old gentleman from Pennsylvania, during the spring of 1856. He was a thorough German; honest, honorable, very hard working, and completely infatuated with Mormonism. He had a daughter, about twenty-two years of age, good-looking, intelligent, and very much courted by several wealthy and hard-working single young men, but had refused them all. She was moping, and doing her best to make herself miserable, and I learned that Melina had been spending a few weeks with Mrs. Emeline Free Young, had thus been thrown into the society of Brigham, had become so impressed and enamored of him as to love him. She told me that she had asked Brigham to have her, she promised him to labor for and support herself, told him of her love, and only wanted to call herself his wife. When I asked her, very gravely, what Mrs. Emeline said to all this, she told me,

"Why, brother Hyde, she was only desirous to add to her husband's glory!"

I demanded what reply Brigham made to this earnest and devoted appeal?

"Why, he told me that his family was large enough and he did not wish to extend it," replied the half weeping and foolish girl.

"Then as he refused you, Melina," said I, "why do you not marry some of these young fellows, who are constantly pestering you to go to parties and sleigh-rides?"

Her answer struck me forcibly. "Brother Hyde, it is a principle of Mormonism that, if we resolve, and keep on resolving, and keep on living up to our resolution, that we can accomplish what we want. Is n't that true?"

"Yes, to a certain extent, it is true, but what do you make of it?" I demanded.

"Just this; I am determined to be one of brother Brigham's wives; God showed him to me in a dream, and I know he will have me, if I only resolve and keep sticking to my resolution, and living for it and nothing else, and that is why I keep refusing all these fellows. I won't ride with them, nor dance with them, nor walk with them; I'll keep myself to myself, and I know I shall get my wish."

Her perseverance is commendable, whatever be said of its object; and so Miss Melina is "still sticking to her resolution."

Brigham has some seventeen or eighteen of his wives in his "Lion House." Each wife has a separate sleeping apartment, except in case of discarded ones who sleep by twos. The rooms are scrupulously clean and neat; sufficiently, but not well furnished. They are the sitting-rooms during the day-time for their occupants. When well, all in that and the adjoining house are expected to eat at the general table. It is a curious spectacle is Brigham's dining-hall. Wives, children, workmen, visitors, a crowd of hungry dinner-seekers. It needs no small amount of cooking, nor any slight quantity of edibles. Brigham keeps no servants; his wives, unless sick, wait on themselves. In that case, they must wait on each other. Cooking, cleaning, dairy-work, washing, mending, tending children, has to be distributed among them according to the taste or skill of each; or else, by the absolute and final dictum of the Prophet! Before the general table system was adopted, each wife was supplied in rotation, and by weight and quantity, with vegetables, fruits, etc. Like old feudal barons, Brigham is obliged to keep a steward and purveyor for his numerous dependants.

It must not be imagined that these wives lead an idle life. Brigham is a working man. Sternly practical in his views of policy, keeping the whole of the people constantly and diligently at work, he makes his household a pattern for the Saints. "There must be no idlers in Zion, no drones in the hive," is Brigham's hobby-cry, and consequently the whole of his family work. His sons among the stock, herding, branding, driving. His wives at household affairs, looms, spinning-wheels, knitting-needles, and quilting-frames. They boast very extensively of how many stockings, quilts, yards of flannel, linsey, and carpet they have made. "If a woman can not support herself, and partly provide for her family, she is only half a woman," say Mormon domestic economists. They try, therefore, to make their wives models of perfection;

they have to work hard. "To dress well is costly, and that is extravagant; and extravagance is a sin," say they; and, consequently, they conclude, "to dress well is a sin." Proud of a delaine, pleased with a muslin or content with a calico, they limit their wants to the wishes of their "lords," and are satisfied if none of the rest *have any better*. Roundheads could not be less costly in their dress; Puritans not more punctilious in the trifles of life. I have often thought, indeed, that Brigham tries to imitate the old Puritanic style in every thing, except his polygamy. Stern old fellows who would pray while they drew their swords; who would kill an antagonist for the love of God; who, in the fanatic hope of securing a heavenly kingdom, would tear down earthly governments, and sincerely rebel in the belief of doing their duty; to whom blood was but an incense to the Almighty, and whose foes were the especial enemies of the Eternal; these certainly present Mormon sentiments. Brigham's wives, although poorly clothed and hard worked, are still very infatuated with their system, very devout in their religion, very devoted to their husband. They content themselves with his kindness, as they can not obtain his love. Not being allowed to be happy, they try to be calm; and endeavor to think that this calmness is happiness. Because their hearts may not feel, therefore they freeze their hearts. As their religion is all their solace, they try to make it their only object. If it does not elevate their mind, it deadens their susceptibilities, and not being permitted to be *women*, they try to convince themselves that it is God's will for them to be *slaves*.

As before remarked, Brigham sleeps alone. He not only

practices, but publicly advocates this habit, and that, too, without any delicacy of thought or modesty of expression. The reasons he urges are very singular and ridiculous. "*Audit solum ad vocem libidonis.*"

Brigham has many small children living, and one of his wives is school-mistress to the whole. His two large houses are comfortably furnished, and he has a piano and melodeon, on which his daughters have learned to play. His family is necessarily very expensive, but he is a very excellent business man; and although he does not receive a cent from the Church in remuneration for his services, his position as President secured to him all the chances of selection in the commencement, and every opportunity of improvement since. To this must be added his past salary as Governor and Superintendent of Indian Affairs. He is a very extensive farmer, having the best locations; owns several saw and grist-mills, much stock and other property. No one's farms are better cultivated; no stock, finer breed; no mills make better flour than those of Brigham Young. His practical genius shows admirably in the improvement of his own property. Of course his position secures also many valuable presents. From a barrel of brandy down to an umbrella, Brigham receives courteously, and remembers the donors with increased kindness. Any new variety of fruit, or stock, is always sent up to "Brother Brigham, with Brother So-and-So's respects." I saw one man make him a present of ten fine milch cows. That man will some day get an exclusive grant to some nice pasture from the Legislature of Utah, or some rich claim to a wood kanyon; or an important privilege in a valuable ferry.

Although, of course, the Mormons indignantly disclaim such bribery; still it is thus at Salt Lake; and as says Sam Slick, "human natur is human natur, wherever the critter's found."

Brigham is a great lover of fruit, and a warm patron of the Pomological and Horticultural Societies of Utah; although some rigid Saints are inclined to view Mormon co-operation with outside Pomological or Agricultural Societies, as evincing a hankering after "the flesh-pots of Egypt."

Brigham's time is much occupied. He rises early, calls the whole of his family together. They sing a hymn, and he prays fervently, and they separate for the day's duties. He eats at the long table, and as his gustativeness is small, his fare is very simple; often consisting only of a bowl of milk covered with cream, and dry toast or bread. To make his rounds, "see the women folks," is his next duty. To these he is cordial and kind, but no more. He is not Brigham the lover or the husband, but Brigham the Prophet and President. They feel for him more reverence than love, watch his face and treasure his words; and torture every one of them into embodying the "key" to some great mystery. Then to his office, to meet his visitors and counsel with them. He is the director of every thing. From the slightest matter to the most important, the Saints all consult with Brother Brigham. Many absurd things have occurred in consequence of this. Men of every trade seek his advice, and view it as a revelation from God for them to follow. None can divorce but him, and to him all such cases come for investigation and action. No other can give permission to a man to take any wives subsequent to the first, and therefore all such parties apply to him. An old lady once went to seriously inquire "the word of the Lord" as to whether red or yellow flannel was best to wear next the person, and he as gravely advised her to "wear yellow by all means." C. V. Spencer was married to two ladies on the same day, and they disputing as to *priority*, he appealed to Brigham to determine the important question. Brigham's reply was characteristic. No speculation is entered on, no enterprise begun without seeking counsel from Brigham. He encourages and commands this: "If you do not know what to do in order to do right," said he, "come to me at any time, and I will give you the word of the Lord on the subject."—*Deseret News, June* 25th, 1856. He is fully obeyed in this. Although it occupies much time and involves much labor, it is very admirable policy. It acquaints him with every secret of their thoughts; associates him with every action of their lives; makes them feel him their truest friend, and renders him positively necessary to their prosperity. For them to uphold, cherish and love him is inevitable; and whatever may be said of his policy as a leader, or his conduct as a husband, all must acknowledge that Brigham is as true to his friends as he is unscrupulous to his enemies.

He often enmeshes the affairs of the people, so that none but himself can disentangle them. A French soldier once, seeing a shell about to explode, threw himself on to Napoleon the Great, and sprang with him into a depressed earthwork. "Look here," cried he, "you must not die. You have brought us into this scrape, and no one but you can bring us out. So it is with Brigham. Brigham, knowing the business of all, can blend interests, and plan more successfully than any one else ; hence, also, if any grow contumacious, he can very easily ruin them, without being seen. A Mr. Howard was a Mormon merchant, but grew dissatisfied in 1845, and determined to leave Salt Lake. No sooner was his intention known at head-quarters, than the line was drawn, and he found himself irrevocably entangled. His goods were seized and sold at auction, when they were bought in by the "*Church*" at a mere nominal amount; his store was sold also and likewise bought by the Church at their own price ; no one daring to bid against this unseen, but all-powerful inviduality ; and Mr. Howard found himself a ruined man. His wife was, however, a firm and fervent Mormon ; she pleaded and implored him to remain ; consented even to *procure for him another wife.* Several Mormons used their influence with him ; the "Church" threatened its anathema ; it alluded to his endowment covenants, and their penalties ; old infatuation was re-awakened, and Mr. Howard bent his head to "the will of the Lord ;" was re-baptized, blessed, and returned to his old allegiance ; helplessly sunk and hopelessly involved in the destiny of Mormonism. This case is but a sample of many similar. Mormonism has adopted *Romanism* as its model of government, and uses *Jesuitism* as its means of accomplishing its ends, and controlling its victims. Loyola might have learned something from Brigham Young. So universally is this unseen power felt, although very seldom traced, that it has become a very common saying among the faithful Mormons at Salt Lake, "When I obey counsel, every thing prospers with me ; when I neglect it, I prosper in nothing." This united action under the able direction of one powerful business mind, is the main cause of the rapid prosperity of the Mormons; but is at the same time a strong evidence of Brigham's administrative tact and ability. On several occasions, however, he has made great blunders, and had to retract. One very prominent error was the attempted settlement of Carson and Wash-ho Valleys. Being surrounded, however, with active, enterprising and ambitious men, whom he must constantly keep employed, it would be astonishing were he not frequently to fail. Not long will elapse before this Cromwell shall fall, and under the lax administration of Brigham's "Richard," or some more cautious than profound General Monk, this meteor shall fade, and

"The king shall hae his ain again."

Brigham Young is not a temperate man. He loudly urges young men to quit the use of tobacco and liquor, as well as tea and coffee. He made a solemn covenant before the whole Church in 1851 that he would cease using tobacco. Excited by his words, and stimulated by his example, all the men joined in the obligation, and much was thrown away. Brigham persisted for several weeks; grew languid and nervous; he accidentally met Ira S. Miles, who was just cutting his tobacco; the temptation overcame the Spartan heroism of this would-be Lycurgus, and he asked for a piece. It was given; Brigham chewed it with great gusto. "It is very good, brother Ira," said he. "That is a question between you and the Lord, brother Brigham," retorted Ira; "Joseph says that God denounces it as bad!" Since that time the people have followed the Prophet; the children imitate the men, and tobacco is the best article of merchandise at Salt Lake. Lewis has received many a hundred dollars from many a Mormon Gentile hater.

Not only with regard to tobacco, but also as to *liquor*, Brigham is decidedly intemperate. His two sons, Joseph A., and Brigham, jun., have long since been notorious for their indulgence; and I have seen Brigham intoxicated at the same time that he was seated in his office, pretending to give the "word of the Lord" to those who should consult with him! This was on the evening of Monday, April 7th, 1856. Mr. Alva L. Smith was in company with me, and he also noticed it, and remarked it to me, after we left the office. It had been conference-day. Brigham had spoken but very little; but had been observed to have been "*full of the spirit*" when he did speak.

The whole secret of Brigham's influence lies in his *real sincerity*. Brigham may be a great man, greatly deceived, but he is not a hypocrite. Smith was an impostor: that can be clearly established. Brigham Young embraced Mormonism in sincerity, conscientiously believed, faithfully practiced, and enthusiastically taught it. As devoted to Smith as Kimball is now to himself, he reverenced him as a Prophet, and loved him as a man. For the sake of his religion, he has over and over again left his family, confronted the world, endured hunger, came back poor, made wealth, and gave it to the Church. He holds himself prepared to lead his people in sacrifice and want, as in plenty and ease. No holiday friend, nor summer Prophet, he has shared their trials, as well as their prosperity. He never pretends to more than "the inward monitions of the Spirit;" and, not as Smith, to direct revelations and physical manifestations. No man prays more fervently, nor more frequently, than Brigham Young. No man can more win the hearts, or impress the minds of his hearers than Brigham, while in prayer. Few men can persist in believing him a hypocrite, after hearing him thus pray, either in his family, or in private meetings, or in public. I am convinced that if he be an impostor, he has commenced by imposing on himself. It is not impossible, as any reader of history knows, for men to be as grossly deceived as Brigham, and yet be honest in their intentions. The Florentine Savanarola is a strong pertinent illustration. Were it not for this real, constant, evident sincerity, he would expose himself before the entire people, and fall. He is a good specimen of a man in positive earnest; and what such a man can do. He is in earnest; if he makes nothing else felt, all feel this. Enthusiasm is the secret of the great success of Mormon proselytism; it is the universal characteristic of the people when proselyted; it is the hidden and strong cord that leads them to Utah, and the iron chain that keeps them there; and it is, too, the real reason of Brigham's triumph. This earnest, obstinate, egotistical enthusiasm has been nursed by wily men as deceived, but more ambitious; it has been fed by false miracles, justified by false logic, fanned by persecution, and cemented by blood.

Brigham, however deceived, is still a bad man, and a dangerous man; and as much more dangerous, being sincere in thinking he is doing God's work, as a madman is than an impostor; one being accessible to reason and inducement; and the other knowing no reason but impotence, and no inducement but constraint.

CHAPTER VII.

BRIGHAM THE PROPHET.

Intention of Mormonism—Smith's prediction—Their prayers—Christ coming in 1890—Where he shall descend—Brigham's position—Brigham on himself—Drawing "the sword of the Almighty"—Shedding blood—Brigham on prospects of Utah—Fanaticism—His army—His intention, if arrested—His method of government—Stealing—Bribery—On debt paying—Frightening apostates—Mormon missions and missionaries—Brigham's policy—His successor—Joseph Smith, jr.—Heber C. Kimball—O. Hyde—Parley Pratt—Joseph A. Young—Revelations—Adam the God of this world and Father of Jesus Christ.

We have viewed Brigham Young as a *man;* impartially certainly, and we believe correctly. However *interesting* such an inquiry may be, it is more *important* that he be accurately understood as a *Prophet.* Great abilities ever command respect, but the world have a right to demand the good use of great talents. The more skill evinced in crime only so far enhances the criminality.

That Brigham Young is a great man, there can be no question; that he is a great criminal we shall prove.

The real object of the Mormon Church is the establishment of an independent kingdom of which Brigham shall be king. This they believe is a temporal kingdom to be soon set up, and to be begun at Utah, in fulfillment of ancient and modern prophecies. It was Smith's intention in Missouri and Nauvoo. It was Brigham's object in leaving Nauvoo, and it is his design now at Salt Lake.

Joseph Smith, on May 6, 1843, said:

"If the government can not protect citizens in their lives and property, it is an old granny anyhow, and I prophesy in the name of the Lord God of Israel, that unless the United States redress the wrongs committed upon the Saints in the State of Missouri, and punish the crimes committed by her officers, that in a few years the government will be utterly overthrown and wasted, and there will not be so much as a potsherd left, for their wickedness in permitting the murder of men, women, and children, and the wholesale plunder and extermination of thousands of her citizens to go unpunished." —*Joseph Smith's Autobiography.*

This speaks for itself, especially when it is remembered that it is Brigham's favorite dogma, "The duty of the Saints is to fulfill the predictions of the Prophets."

Not only do they try themselves to accomplish this design, but even in their prayers, make it the chief end and object of their existence. President J. M. Grant, on the 24th July, 1856, the ninth anniversary of the entry of the pioneers into Salt Lake Valley, thus addressed the Almighty in a public meeting:

"May we accomplish the great work thou didst commence, through thy servant Joseph. May we have power over the wicked nations, *that Zion may be the seat of government for the universe*, the law of God be extended, and the scepter of righteousness swayed over this wide world."—*Deseret News, July*, 1856.

The Mormons never intend to spiritualize such expressions in their prayers. They use plain words to utter plain thoughts. "Never pray for any blessing that you are not willing to *help* to obtain;" is the constantly reiterated doctrine of this same man. With these men there are no figurative prophecies about Zion. Christ's kingdom is a literal kingdom: God's Zion is a particular location; Zion's triumph will be a temporal and physical victory. Utah, to these men, is this Zion; her enemies, the American people; her triumph, America's downfall; her reign, the subjugation of this continent. These are strange dogmas, but they are earnestly believed by these men; who as firmly think that it is the duty of the Saints to literally prepare a kingdom for Christ to come to. Nor do they imagine either that it will be very long before he does thus come. Said J. Smith, on April 6th, 1843:

"I prophesy in the name of the Lord God, that the commencement of the difficulties which will cause much bloodshed, previous to the coming of the Son of Man, will be in South Carolina (it probably may arise through the slave question); this a voice declared to me, while I was praying earnestly on the subject, December 25th, 1832.

"I was once praying very earnestly to know the time of the coming of the Son of Man, when I heard a voice repeat the following: 'Joseph, my son, if thou *livest until thou art eighty-five years old*, thou shalt see the face of the Son of Man, therefore, let this suffice, and trouble me no more in this matter.' "—*J. Smith's Autobiography.*

As Smith was born in 1805, this would make the date 1890. He often endeavored to make the "prophetic numbers" refer to this 1890, A.D. This is also as firmly believed by the Church, as the Book of Mormon. It is one of the most prominent promises made by the Elders to those whom they bless, that they "shall live to behold the winding-up scene." Smith promised this to Brigham; he likewise publicly prophesied in April, 1843:

"There are those of the rising generation who shall not taste death till Christ comes."—*Ibid.*

Not only have they determined *when* he shall come, but also *where* he shall come to. Said Brigham, on September 28th, 1856:

"Again, how does it contrast with Joseph's being sent forth with his brethren to search out a location in Jackson county, where the New Jerusalem will be built, where our Father and our God planted the first garden on this earth, *and where the New Jerusalem will come to when it comes down from heaven?*"—*Deseret News, October* 8th, 1856.

Those who have entered into the Celestial Kingdom, say the Mormons, must be ordained *kings* and priests: Brigham is thus ordained. He is the king to the people. The autocrats of antiquity, or the early sultans of Turkey, were not more absolute than is Brigham Young.

Said Kimball, September 21st, 1856:

"I have often said that the word of our Leader and Prophet is the word of God to this people. We can not see God, we can not hold converse with him, but he has given us a man that we can talk to, and *thereby know his will, just as well as if God himself were present with us.* I am no more afraid to risk my salvation in the hands of this man, than *I am to trust myself in the hands of the Almighty.* He will lead me right if I do as he says *in every* particular and circumstance."—*Deseret News, October* 1, 1856.

Brigham cites Kimball as the model Saint. Nor is this confined to him. Grant speaks equally plainly.

"There is a spirit of murmuring among the people, and the fault is laid upon Brother Brigham. For this reason the heavens are closed against you, for he holds the keys of life and salvation upon the earth; and you may strive as much as you please, but not one of you will ever go through the strait gate into the kingdom of God, *except those that go through by that man and his brethren,* for they will be the persons whose inspection you must pass."—*Deseret News, Dec.,* 1856.

The means to be adopted with reference to the unbelieving and those who will not hear, are equally pointed out. Said J. M. Grant, a prophet, seer, and revelator, on Sept. 21, 1856,

"We have been trying long enough with this people, and I go in for letting the sword of the Almighty be unsheathed, *not only in word but in deed.*"—*Deseret News, Oct.* 1, 1856.

What this really means may be determined by a subsequent paragraph.

"Brethren and sisters, we want you to repent and forsake your sins. And you who have *committed sins that can not be forgiven through baptism, let your blood be shed and let the smoke ascend,* that the incense thereof may come up before God as an atonement for your sins, *and that the sinners in Zion may be afraid.*"—*Ibid.*

And while this doctrine is publicly taught and *privately practiced*, they dare to assert they commit no murders!

Brigham is very candid about the position of the Mormons at Utah. Said he in Sept., 1856,

"I say as the Lord lives, we are bound to become a sovereign State in the Union, or *an independent nation by ourselves*. I am still, and still will be Governor of this Territory, to the constant chagrin of my enemies; and twenty-six years shall not pass away before the Elders of this Church will be as much thought of as kings on their thrones."—*Deseret News, Sept.* 1, 1856.

However ridiculous such an object may appear, it is still the real design of these foolishly infatuated people.

As before remarked, Brigham was ordained a *king* in their Temple; and the people in their hearts reverence him as such. As to the means they adopt to begin their kingdom, they have private courts of their own, in which they try their own criminals. A United States appointed judge makes his charge to a Grand Jury, and they are dismissed to their room The foreman has been previously instructed by the Church, and he directs the judgments and controls the consciences of his fellow jurymen. Bills of indictment are found or cast out as he directs; and *he* directs as advised by the "Church."

Should a Mormon be tried by a United States Court for a capital offense, and the evidence completely convict him, if he will throw himself entirely on Mormon law, to be administered by Mormon authorities, unmindful of the evidence, of their oath, or of the judge's charge, the jury will acquit the prisoner; even though *that same night*, as the Mormon jury of a Mormon court, they would pronounce him guilty without rehearsing the evidence. Carlos Murray was the nephew of Heber C. Kimball; he was accused of murder, and a bill of indictment was found against him. He was tried by the court in which Judge Drummond sat. The evidence was positive, and all thought he would be convicted. He confessed to H. C. Kimball that he was guilty of the crime, but demanded to be "*tried and punished by Mormon law,*" and implored to "*be saved from hanging by a Gentile court.*" The penalty of both judicatories was death; only, in the one case he would be "hung by the Gentiles;" and in the other, he would be "shot by his brethren." Kimball interfered, the jury were instructed, and they *acquitted* Murray. He was carried off by the sheriff's officers, all Mormons, from Fillmore to Salt Lake City, when Judge Drummond caused the whole party to be arrested, and brought before him as abetting the escape of a prisoner. Paralyzed under the duress of his position, with Brigham's hand upon him, and the excited populace ready to commit any outrage, Judge Drummond was forced to compound matters, and the result was that Carlos Murray got completely off. But the Mormon penalty was still over him; and Mormonism *never forgives*, although it often *delays* the blow. He was allowed to live as long as he labored to "build up the kingdom;" but that as soon as he forgot his duty or his obligation, the penalty was to be exacted of him. He was commanded to move his family into Salt Lake City, and permitted to go completely at large. The chains of superstition were around his soul, and they were far stronger than any chains about his limbs. He went to

Mary's river, a distance of 400 miles, got his family, and, with the intention of coming and living near the "authorities," and using his doomed life for the support of Mormonism, turned toward Salt Lake. The Indians, however, revenged their brother, whom he had killed, and murdered him. He would have been killed by the Mormons, just as soon as the superstitious terrors had subsided sufficiently to permit him to become disobedient and negligent.

There are several men who are now living in Utah in this condition. Their lives are forfeited by Mormon law, but spared for a little time by Mormon policy. They are certain to be killed, and they know it. They are only allowed to live while they add weight and influence to Mormonism; and, although abundant opportunities are given them for escape, they prefer to remain. So strongly are they infatuated with their religion, that they think their salvation depends on their continued obedience, and their "blood being shed by the servants of God." Adultery is punished by death; and it is taught, unless the adulterer's blood be shed, he can have no remission for this sin. Believing this firmly, there are men who have confessed this crime to Brigham, and asked him to have them killed. Their superstitious fears make life a burden to them; and they would commit suicide, were that not also a crime.

James Monroe had criminal connection with the wife of one Howard Egan at Salt Lake City, during his absence. Egan returned home, became satisfied of the circumstance, and deliberately shot Monroe. Brigham publicly applauded his action; George A. Smith, one of the Apostles, defended him in a United States Court, and he was cheerfully and immediately acquitted by a Mormon jury. The strict Mormon law, however, demanded that Egan should also murder his wife, as an adulteress; his heart and hand failed, and he spared her. He divorced her from him; but although he murdered his dishonorer, he could not overcome his own affection for his guilty and abandoned wife. He visited, talked with, wept over, and, *sic homo est*, he pardoned her. He forgot his resentment and his divorce, and, according to Mormon doctrine, committed adultery with his own wife. He was an adulterer, and the adulterer must die. He told Brigham, and offered his life. Brigham's reply was peculiar:

"Howard, go to the friends of James Monroe, tell them you have murdered him, and if they take your life, it is well. If they do not, go anywhere where there is fighting; join any party, and try and fall in battle; and, if you can not die there, go your way, and trust in the mercy of God and of your brethren.

Whether he took the advice or not I do not know. He is now in California, and were Brigham to call on him to-day to return and be killed, I fully believe he would immediately comply.

Another instance: Curtis E. Bolton, married a mother and daughter, and lived with both of them. During his absence as a Mormon missionary, it is said his step-daughter wife was prodigal of favors to some passing emigrants. On his return he divorced her; but, as she had no other home, she stopped with her mother, and called Mr. Bolton *father*, instead of *husband*. He loved her still with more than a father's affection, and they sinned, and she became *enceinte.* He was an adulterer; and by Mormon law, his life was forfeit. He tried to conceal his crime by adding to it. He compelled her to take some virulent drug, to endeavor to procure abortion. Destroying the life within her, she nearly lost her own. The residents of the twelfth ward, where Bolton lived, learned the incident. He was tried by an ecclesiastical court, condemned, and cut off from the Church. His life is forfeited, and will be taken by-and-by; but he still remains at Salt Lake City, a slave to his own superstition, and, although so circumstanced, was appointed in 1856 to go as a *working missionary* to Green river, among the Indian tribes.

Such men are necessarily reckless of all consequences. All their safety consists in their obedience. They might easily fly, but stronger bonds than links of steel, a closer prison than stone walls, retain them willing captives. The African flies not from his fetish-man; the children of the Orient never fled from their genii; the Roman can not escape the anathema of his priest; the Tartar cowers before the grand lama; and the equally devoted Mormon shudders and groans, but he still remains. It is not unnatural, it is only human nature degraded.

Such is a fair specimen of Mormon fanaticism. That these deluded men are sincere, madly, absurdly sincere, there can be no doubt; and there are thousands such in Utah. These men will fight, lie, rob, murder for Mormonism if commanded, and really believe that they are doing God good service. By means of such influence over the minds of large bodies of such men, Brigham hopes to execute his designs. Mormonism is attracting many sensible and educated men to its ranks. Mr. Bolton, above named, is an educated man, speaks several languages, has been editor of a French Mormon magazine, and firmly believes that he can establish the truth of his faith and the propriety of his devotion from the holy Scriptures; and he can construct an ingenious argument, too.

Nor does Brigham give much opportunity to a jury to decide according to their sense of justice, or their view of the evidence produced. A T. S. Williams was sued by a Mr. Leonard on an action of debt. As it was an important case, a jury was empaneled, consisting of several of the Apostles and some of the Bishops of Salt Lake City. They heard and decided the case. As, however, their verdict did not suit the prejudged opinion of Brigham, on the Sabbath following he gave that jury a most outrageous haranguing for being "old grannies," and for "selling their verdict;" he cursed Williams' lawyer, and sent him on a mission to the East Indies out of spite. Such treatment from "the Prophet" has rendered Mormon juries extremely solicitous to know *his* opinion before giving their verdict, and then to prove their confidence in his judgment by delivering a verdict accordingly. Hence in this way Brigham's will is pre-eminent in even Gentile courts of law; and thus is all justice frustrated at Utah. To be on good terms with Brigham, is to secure his favor; and to dare to oppose, is to be crushed under himself and friends. I could cite a dozen instances that I have seen of such favoritism. As to expecting that a Gentile can obtain jutsice against a Mormon, it is ridiculous; a jury would feel they were sacrificing their friends to their enemies in deciding against their brother.

Besides these means of self government, Brigham has adopted another method of destroying the influence and nullifying the appointments of the judges sent by the President of the United States. He has organized Probate and Magistrate courts throughout the Territory, and installed in them his most devoted creatures. An appeal can be made from the decisions of these to the Supreme Court, but any application for appeal is *almost always refused*. To speak contemptuously of such courts is to become a marked man; and ruin and danger are the inevitable consequences of such unfortunate significance.

Brigham not only has a nucleus around which to gather fanatic disciples; but he has also one about which to collect an army. In 1840, Smith organized the "Nauvoo Legion" and enrolled all the male Saints from sixteen to fifty years of age. Since then their numbers have been continually increasing, as all are compelled to enlist. This force, that still bears its old name, the Nauvoo Legion, is regularly drilled by competent officers, many of whom served in Mexico, with the Mormon Battalion, under General W. Scott. They are well armed and perfectly fearless. They completely re-organized in May, 1857. They have frequent parades, and likewise occupation, in forays against the turbulent Indians. The same fanaticism that characterizes their worship, or their labor, also signalizes their military evolutions. They do it with an object, and *work* at it. To them it is no holiday pastime; they do not play at soldiers. As devoted to Brigham and as convinced of his authority, they will as blindly and cheerfully obey, as the soldiers of Mohammed. The silk standard of

Mormonism would be as firmly and furiously sustained as was the silver crescent.

These men expect to fight, and are preparing for it. They even constantly pray for the time to come speedily when "the Lord shall arise as a man of war," when they can accomplish the saying of Isaiah, that they so love to quote, "The nation and people that will not serve thee shall perish," Isaiah lx. 12; or Smith's prediction, "And the wicked shall say, Let us not go up to battle against Zion, for the inhabitants of Zion are terrible and we can not stand;" "when one shall chase a thousand and two put ten thousand to flight."—*Doc. Cov.*, p. 136.

I presume that about eight thousand such soldiers might be mustered in Utah. The number is contemptible as a military *force*, but fearful as religious fanatics; ridiculous in comparison with their object; terrible in consideration of their delusion, and the ruin that would have to be consummated to subdue them.

I have heard both Brigham and Kimball gloat over the anticipation that "the time of warfare would speedily come." Said Kimball, "I will do as I did at Nauvoo; when they demanded our arms I loaded my old gun half way up to the muzzle, and prayed to God that the mean cuss who fired it off, might be blown into atoms." Said Brigham, "I carry two loaded revolvers on me constantly, and the man who touches me, to arrest me, dies. In the name of God I have spoken it." There is not the slightest question as to his keeping his oath, should such an event occur. Brigham bitterly reproaches the suffering of the Saints on the whole American people; but forgets *that it is Smith and himself who have occasioned it.* The criminals are not the *enforcers* of the law, but its *transgressors.*

Some very distressing cases of extortion have occurred, with the connivance and by the direction of the Prophet. In 1854, a Mrs. Du Fresne left the island of Jersey, Channel Islands, to come to the city of the Saints. She had some money more than she needed to defray her expenses, and intending to do the Church a kindness, offered to lend $2,500 to the President, S. W. Richards, at Liverpool, for six months, and required no interest. It was accepted gladly, and an order was drawn on Brigham for the amount, payable at sight. The old lady came to Utah, expecting to obtain her money as a fund to rely on, in case of desiring to invest it. She presented the order, it was dishonored. She demanded an explanation, and she was told she must either take a poor city lot and a hovel for the amount, or that she would have nothing. She expostulated, and was laughed at; reasoned with them, and was dictated to; got angry, and was turned out of the office. Without a remedy and without a hope she left Salt Lake City almost penniless. They made $2,500 by this saint-like transaction.

This nefarious system is in common vogue among the "authorities in Zion." Some gentlemen in England were induced by John Taylor to embark nearly $100,000 in the purchase of machinery to manufacture sugar from beet-roots, and cloth, at Salt Lake City. Great promises of profit were made by Mr. Taylor, both as a man and in his capacity as an Apostle of the Church. The machinery, sheep, and beet-seed were procured and forwarded, and with them went these credulous Saints. At St. Louis, one of the gentlemen became undeceived as to Mr. Taylor's real character and designs; and left the Church and returned to his business in Liverpool. The others went on to Salt Lake. Brigham took possession of the machinery; M. Delamere, one of the partners, robbed and ruined, had to work as a blacksmith's assistant to procure a livelihood; Mr. Coward, another of these victims, went into the kanyons and chopped down fire-wood till he became sick; Mr. Russel, another of these dupes, died, and the Church *administered on his estate.* This was bad, but a worse tinge was added to it. One of these gentlemen, although he had left a wife and family behind him in England, was induced to take another wife at Salt Lake City. She was an intelligent, educated English lady, but as deeply infatuated with Mormonism as the rest. With increased experience, her fanaticism has died out, and his has also much faded away; but they are now irrevocably disgraced in their own eyes and irretrievably bound to this atrocious delusion.

Nor is Brigham Young very chary about perjury, any more than extortion and murder. In 1852 beef was scarce in the Tithing-office; and the church herd was small, and very poor. Brigham Young, through General Wells, ordered a young man named Thomas Clayton, to fetch up a fat ox belonging to Messrs. Holladay and Warner, merchants then passing through Salt Lake City. It was driven in, killed, and paid to the workmen on the Temple! Messrs. Holladay missed the ox, traced it to the Church slaughter-yard, and prosecuted Brigham. The slaughterman was brought to the witness-box, and he stoutly denied the fact. This young man was now the important witness. He might fail, and Brigham went to him, and told him, " Get out of the affair, and get us out of the affair without lying if you can; but if you have to lie, Tom, *don't break down!*" He got them out of the affair by perjury; acquitting himself, however, by a *mental reservation.* He himself told me this incident, and rather boasted of it, as a proof how " *Brigham could come it over the Gentiles!*"

Brigham Young is not immaculate, either, on the score of corruption. Mr. Washburn Loomis, from Niagara county, N. Y., says, " he was sentenced to wear the ball and chain two years, and was pardoned by Brigham Young on his paying him $200 cash in hand. Young reported that he had given him a free pardon, and it was generally supposed he had; but, in fact, he had sold him it for $200. He required Mr. Loomis to keep it a profound secret."

This individual is, I believe, still in California. Like Horace Skimpole, however, Brigham might not consider this a *bribe*, but "simply a *gift*, my dear young friend."

That he does not entertain the strongest notions of honor is very evident from his own statements. A. Cyrus Wheelock had robbed an old gentleman from Lancashire, England, of a large amount of money, by borrowing without any intention of returning it. On arriving at Salt Lake, Mr. Lee requested payment, and was coolly told by Wheelock, " I used it for the poor Saints; I shan't pay it, and now what are you going to do about it?" Mr. Lee appealed to Brigham, who thus publicly sanctified repudiation:

"If an Elder has borrowed from you, and you find he is going to *apostatize, then you may tighten the screws upon him;* but if he is willing to preach the Gospel without purse or scrip, it is *none of your business what he does with the money he has borrowed from you.* And if the Lord wants it to use, let it go, and it is none of your business what he does with it. And if you murmur against that Elder, it will prove your damnation. The money was not yours, but the Lord Almighty put it into your hands to see what you would do with it."

Out of his own mouth Brigham condemns himself; and yet so strongly rooted is the delusion in that old man's mind, that he still remains in Utah, and bows his head to this extortion and robbery.

"'Tis true, 'tis strange; and stranger still, 'tis true!"

Still there are some who do leave the Church, and they cause Brigham a great deal of trouble. His predictions concerning apostates are very terrible and ridiculous. Says he:

"The moment a person decides to leave this people, he is cut off from every object that is durable for time and eternity, and I have told you the reason why. Every possession and object of affection will be taken from those who forsake the truth, and their identity and existence will eventually cease."

Annihilation, the heaven of Buddhism, is to be the final hell of Mormonism. Threats of violence, and the preaching of such dogmas, deter many from leaving, who otherwise would quit gladly. In some instances, however, this severity is directed on the other side. In 1852, Albert Smith, then living at Salt Lake City, differed from Brigham on some points of doctrine, and began to teach his heresy; thinking that a people who declaimed so loudly against modern intolerance, would be tolerant with regard to himself. He taught his opinions in his own house; the Mormons threatened to tear it down over his head. He called a meeting on the public square; the marshal dispersed his audience. He announced another meeting; but was driven from the ground, and Brigham, from the stand in the Tabernacle, uttered these apostolic words: "It is nasty stinking little apostates like these, who have brought our enemies upon us; and I tell Albert Smith that he had better clear right out, and that right straight, too, or *I will cut his damned throat, and send him to hell across lots!!*" Albert Smith sold his property for a trifle, and fled for his life. Since then, no one has had the hardihood and simplicity to publicly oppose Mormonism.

This tyrannical supervision is adopted in all their proceedings. Brigham and his coadjutors arrange all the political nominations in their ecclesiastical council meetings. The Mormon people know, that elected or not, these men will have the seats; and, therefore, very few vote, regarding the whole matter as a mere farce, intended only to maintain legal form, and preserve appearances. In 1845, among other nominations for representative for Salt Lake county, was one A. P. Rockwood. He was very much disliked; and a few men got up an opposition ticket, substituting the name of Stephen H. Hales in the stead of this A. P. Rockwood. It was the first and last opposition ticket in Utah Territory. A small body of voters were brought, and Hales obtained the majority, as very few had voted previously or since. Although he had the majority of votes, and was therefore legally elected, Brigham was insulted; such dangerous contumacy must be punished, or it might prove dangerous. Stephen Hales was accordingly sent for, by Brigham, who administered to him a severe reprimand, for *daring* to allow his name to be used as an opponent of "the Church nomination;" and by duress, he terrified and compelled Hales to resign the election, while Rockwood had the seat, and what to him was more important, and his real object, the *per diem.*

This tyranny of the hierarchy is also carried into private enterprises. Mr. William Nixon was a Mormon merchant, very liberal to the Church, and to the people. He had, in 1845, among other merchandise, some cooking-stoves for sale. I was standing in his store one day, when H. C. Kimball entered, and began to bargain for one of these stoves.

K. How much do you ask for one of these, Brother Nixon?

N. So much, sir (naming the price).

K. You ask too much, Brother William. They are only worth so much. You're growing too rich, sir; you're making money out of the poor Saints; you're taking advantage of your brethren.

N. (deprecatingly). No, Brother Kimball, you are wrong; they cost me more than that; their first cost was thus (making the calculation).

K. Don't tell me, sir; I know as well as you do. You're losing your love for truth; you're losing the Spirit, you're robbing the poor!

N. But, sir—

K. (angrily) I know, I tell you I know you, by the Spirit within me. We'll have to send you on a mission, to learn you to open the bowels of compassion for this people. You're getting proud and lifted up.

N. You wrong me, Brother Kimball; *take the stove at your own price;* but you really are mistaken.

K. (relentingly). Well, it is necessary to trim you down a little, I see; the Lord bless you, Brother Nixon!

Mr. Nixon added many more articles not included in the purchase, and consequently received a *double blessing* from this modern Apostle. Mr. Nixon got the blessing, and Mr. Kimball got the stove. This ought to have sufficed, but in the fall of the same year Mr. Nixon received an appointment as missionary to the Indians. Although it was made by one Prophet, another Prophet overruled, and Brigham cancelled it. In the spring of 1856 Mr. Nixon was sent to Carson Valley. He was a faithful Mormon, and he obeyed implicitly. He sold off his stock at a ruinous sacrifice; rented his store for a mere nominal amount; left his dwelling-house vacant, and several thousands of dollars due to him from many parties; took his family and went to Carson. His enormous loss of money, time, and business, will perhaps teach him never to *dispute with H. C. Kimball again.*

The greatest engine of Mormon power, without any question, is the *missions.* There are men in Utah whose oratorial ability and general information are far superior to Brigham's. The most infatuated can not help observing the difference. To keep them at home, would create schisms innumerable;

and in order to preserve his influence, he has to send them out to preach. O. Pratt is never at Salt Lake without weakening Brigham's hold on some mind, and therefore he is allowed to be there but very little. It is not their best men, by any means, whom the Mormons send on missions. A man who is wavering in his faith, and trembling on the verge of apostacy, is sent out to be *confirmed.* Too timid, or too undecided to renounce Mormonism entirely, he is compelled to advocate it. This is very admirable and far-seeing policy. Often a man is sent on a mission to punish him. A lot of "gamblers, thieving lawyers, loafers, and drunkards," were sent, in the spring of 1856, to Australia as missionaries. Some of these Brigham *cursed* most frightfully, and the whole of them he denounced. Said he, "You have been raising hell here long enough, now go and raise little hells of your own in Australia." He told them plainly, that he "sent them to get rid of them, and that he never wished to see them again." Some are sent because they are too indolent to work; some because they allow themselves to talk too freely about the authorities; some because they are in the habit of getting publicly intoxicated; some because they are in the way of some ambitious man in power; some because they are troublesome about some debt; some because their creditors dun them; some to England, because they were very poor, and Brigham wanted to help them out of the liberal purses of the European Saints. I can fill in names by dozens to every one of the above examples. The great idea of Mormonism is, that "the iniquity of the preacher makes no difference as to the purity of the principle; that the vices of the administrator can not affect the acceptability of the ordinance, *if he only possess the priesthood.*" Brigham Young lays down this principle very distinctly when speaking of Smith. Said he,

"The docrine he teaches is all I know about the matter; bring any thing against that if you can. As to any thing else, I do not care if he acts like a devil; he has brought forth a doctrine that will save us, if we will abide by it. He may get drunk every day of his life, sleep with his neighbor's wife every night, run horses and gamble, I do not care any thing about that, for I never embrace any man in my faith. But the doctrine he has produced will save you and me, and the whole world; and if you can find fault with that, find it."—*Deseret News, December*, 1856.

It is often quite useless, therefore, to attempt to convince a Mormon of his error from the iniquity of his ministers. They will admit the premises, but deny the conclusion. They forget that causes can only rightly be judged of by the effects they produce, and the efficacy of the principles by practices; for "the tree must be known by its fruits. Do men gather figs of thorns, or grapes from thistles?"

The question is often asked, "In the event of Brigham's death, on whom will the presidency fall?" Opinion is divided on this subject. All the old Mormons who knew Smith cling to his memory, and believe that Joseph Smith, jun., now at Nauvoo, will assume the position. At present he denounces the practice of polygamy, and brands Brigham as a usurper. He is much averse to conversing on the subject; but his grandmother informed me that he firmly believes in the authority and mission of his father. The character he bears at

Nauvoo is a very high one for intelligence and probity. Kimball says of him and his brothers:

"At present the Prophet Joseph's boys lay apparently in a state of slumber, every thing seems to be perfectly calm with them, but by-and-by God will wake them up, and they will roar like the thunders of Mount Sinai."

Still, the number of old Mormons is very limited; *the flame of Mormonism dies out very soon.* Brigham remarked this sadly. Said he, August 17th, 1856:

"How many of those before me were personally acquainted with Joseph, our Prophet? I can see now and then one; you can pick up one here and another there; but the most of the people now inhabiting this Territory never beheld the face of our Prophet; even quite a portion of this congregation never beheld his face. But few of this congregation have been assembled together more than a very few years, to receive and be benefited by the teachings from the fountain head, directly from the living oracles."

This is the case with this delusion everywhere. Twenty-one thousand persons had emigrated from Europe, from 1840 to 1855, to join the forces of this sect; at least one half of that number have apostatized. Were it not for the impetuous zeal of its missionaries, it would have long been extinct.

Many believe that when Brigham dies, Kimball may succeed him in the presidency. He is now the second man of this Mormon hierarchy. His history is that of Mormonism. He was born the 14th of June, 1801, and was baptized into Smith's Church in 1832. He met Smith in the September of the same year; accompanied him and Brigham Young to

Heber C. Kimball

Missouri in 1834; was ordained an Apostle in 1835, and was with Brigham in most of his important labors. He is a coarse, sensual man; calls himself "Brigham's echo;" is called by Young, "the model Saint." His sycophantic reverence for the "the President" is extremely ridiculous. Brigham always wears his hat in meetings. "I will uncover to God alone," says he. Said Kimball, June 29, 1856, before 3000 persons:

"I never feel as though I wanted to wear my hat when Brigham is present. I consider that the *master should wear his hat*, or hang it on the peg that God made for it, which is his head, of course."

Kimball is the most disgusting speaker of the Mormon community; and yet, much respected, and no little feared. His resentments are revenges! His face exhibits the man. Although only thirteen days younger than Brigham, he is very much more robust. He is a large, powerful man, with the most complete want of, and contempt for education. He sometimes boasts he has more wives than Brigham; I only know of *eighteen*, of whom, though not very *fond*, he is *very jealous*. By the law of the Church, Kimball should succeed Brigham; but, by the precedent of Brigham himself, O. Hyde, the President of the Twelve Apostles, should fill the chair. Kimball lacks the confidence of many persons. Orson Hyde's cupidity is too well known; his apostacy in 1838 too well remembered, and his impetuosity too much dreaded, for him ever to obtain the suffrages of the people. The man who, next to Brigham, possessed their love, was Parley Pratt, and he is dead—killed in his sins; the measure he has so often threatened on the seducer of any of his wives, a wronged and maddened husband has inflicted on him, and he has gone adulterous and bloody into the presence of God. May he find mercy!

Brigham Young has a son, Joseph A. Young. He was in 1851, '52, and '53, one of the most rowdy young men in Utah, celebrated for getting publicly intoxicated, riding horses to death, furious driving, etc. From the whisky-shop and their pot-companions, he and W. H. Kimball, Kimball's son, were sent to England, *to preach Mormonism.* The Saints, instead of being astonished thereat, said coolly, "Well, that will sober them down!" Joseph A. Young returned to Utah in 1856, and was immediately elected member of the Territorial Legislature for Salt Lake county. What is his mental caliber is not of course known thoroughly. His past does not speak very favorably for his future. If Brigham lives a few years longer, which he has every appearance of doing, and can prepare the way, Joseph A. Young will be the President of the Church. The Smiths feel the authority *has gone out of the family.* Brigham will endeavor to keep it in *his.* The Smiths were, the Youngs are now, the leading men of Mormonism; Brigham, President of the Church; Joseph, the President of the Seventies; John was President of the High Priesthood, and is now a Patriarch; Joseph A., a member of the Legislature, and certain to fill the next important vacancy, if he be at all decorous in his conduct, so as not too violently to shock the prejudices of the people.

Brigham has only once pretended to write a revelation, as

coming directly from God; and that was when the Church was leaving Winter Quarters for Salt Lake Valley. He then communicated the "order of traveling organization." He asserts that Washington was inspired by God to fight the British, and the Constitution Convention were inspired to frame the Constitution; and that he is only similarly inspired to lead the people. Yet Kimball always proposes to the vote of the Conference, "that we sustain Brigham Young as the *Prophet*, *Seer*, and *Revelator* of the Church." The people have often murmnred, indeed, that Brigham does not give "new revelations;" nor teach "new principles," as Smith did. As to the latter, Brigham tried his skill at invention in 1852, and discovered that *Adam was a polygamist*, and *that he was the God of this world; and the Lord and father of Jesus Christ!* This stupendous blasphemy he publicly taught, saying, "He is our God, and to him must we come, for we shall never have another." (Journal of Discourses, vol. i.) Kimball, of course, seized on this discovery with avidity, and pronounced it the height of inspiration. Said he, September 28, 1856:

"I have learned by experience that there is but one God that pertains to this people, and he is the God that pertains to this earth, the first man. That first man sent his Son to redeem the world, to redeem his brethren; his life was taken, his blood shed, that our sins might be remitted. That Son called twelve men and ordained them to be Apostles, and when he departed the keys of the kingdom were deposited with three of these twelve, viz.: Peter, James, and John. Peter held the keys pertaining to that Presidency, and he was the head."—*Deseret News*, *October* 8, 1856.

This new mystery was promulgated in England, and much written about it in the "Millennial Star," of 1853. A great many disbelieved it, O. Pratt among the number; many doubted it, as it contradicts all Smith's writings and teachings, and therefore Brigham commanded the Elders to "lay it aside, and not to teach it till the Saints were *more fully prepared!*"

Now, however, Brigham has laid down the order of things definitely. On May 28, 1856, he said that they were "the Apostles of Joseph Smith." Joseph is the God of this generation, Jesus is his God; Michael, or Adam, is Jesus' God and Father; Jehovah is the God of Adam, and Jehovah is inferior to Eloheim, who is in turn, subject to the grand council of assembled gods of infinity. All of these are polygamists, and they all rule over their own descendants, which are constantly increasing in number and dominion.

This barbarous and blasphemous polytheism comports strangely with God's declaration, Isaiah xlv. 5, 6, "I am the Lord and there is none else, there is no God beside me. That they may know from the rising of the sun and from the west, that there is none beside me. I am the Lord, and there is none else." But this blasphemous degradation of God fully accomplishes the words of Paul, Romans, i. 22, 23, "Professing themselves to be wise, they became fools; and changed the glory of the incorruptible God into an image, made like to corruptible man."

CHAPTER VIII.

CHRONOLOGICAL HISTORY OF MORMONISM.

1805. December 23. Joseph Smith, jun., born at Sharon, Windsor county, Vermont.

1815. April. His father and family remove to Palmyra, Wayne county, New York.

1820. March. Many revivals of religion in western New York, and Smith's mind becomes disturbed. Under the preaching of Rev. Mr. Lane he becomes partial to the Methodists.

April. Smith pretends to receive his first vision while praying in the woods. He asserts that God the Father and Jesus Christ came to him from the heavens; and, like Mohammed's Gabriel, told him that his sins were forgiven; that he was the chosen of God to reinstate his kingdom and re-introduce the gospel, that none of the denominations were right, etc.

1823. September 21. Smith proved forgetful of his pretended revelation and swore, swindled, lied, and got drunk as formerly; but says that an angel came to him while he was in bed, and told him of the existence and preservation of the history of the ancient inhabitants of

1823. America, engraved on plates of gold, and directs him where to find them.

September 22. Goes as directed and discovers them in a stone box, in a hill side between Manchester and Palmyra, western New York. He attempts to take them, but is prevented. The devil and angels contend about him; devil is whipped and retreats: he receives many instructions from the angel and begins *preparing himself for his future.*

1827. January 18. Smith married to Miss Emma Hale, afterward "Lady elect of the Church."

September 22. Receives the "plates" from the hands of the angel.

1828. July. Translation is suspended, in consequence of Martin Harris stealing one hundred and eighteen pages of MS., which have never been replaced.

1829. April 17. Translation recommenced, Oliver Cowdery acting as clerk.

May 5. Smith pretends that John the Baptist came and ordained Cowdery and himself "priests;" and commanded them "to baptize and afterward re-ordain each other."

1830. Smith was ordained Apostle by Peter, James, and John.

April 6. The Mormon Church organized at Manchester, New York, and consisted of J. Smith, sen., Hiram and Samuel Smith, O. Cowdery, Joseph Knight, and J. Smith, jun. Martin Harris, one of the witnesses, not being one among them!

1830. June. First conference at Fayette, New York.

August. Parley P. Pratt and Sidney Rigdon converted to Mormonism.

December. Smith is visited by Rigdon.

1831. January. The Church commanded to move to Kirtland, Ohio, where Rigdon had a body of persons converted to Mormonism as a nucleus.

May. The Elders sent out by twos to preach.

June 7. The first endowment given; Elders much disappointed in their expectations. Many ordained and sent out to preach. New branches growing up rapidly.

June 17. Smith and party start for Missouri to search for a location for "Zion."

August 3. Zion determined to be in Independence, Jackson county, Mo. Smith dedicates the "Temple block;" names the place "The New Jerusalem," and returns to Kirtland.

August 27. "The Kirtland Safety Society Bank," store, mill, and other mercantile operations commenced by Smith.

1832. February 16. Smith and Sidney Rigdon pretend to see in a vision the whole destiny of man, and his different degrees of glory and punishment.

March 22. Smith mobbed, tarred, and feathered for dishonorable dealing.

April 2. Smith visits Jackson county, Mo., where matters are in disorder; the Saints by their boasts and threats enraging the old citizens, and the "Church" quarreling among themselves about the *communism* that Smith had attempted to establish.

1833. March 8. The first presidency organized by the appointment of Sidney Rigdon and Frederic G. Williams as Smith's counselors.

July 23. The foundation of Kirtland Temple laid by Smith. The mob at Independence, Jackson county, Mo., rise against the Mormons, and extort a promise of half to leave by January, and all by April, 1834.

October 30. The mob destroys ten Mormon houses. Two of the mobbers are killed by the Saints. This was the first blood shed, and the Mormons shed it.

November. The Mormons fly from Jackson, and are kindly received in Clay county, Mo.

1834. February 20. Smith goes with companies from Kirtland to Missouri, to the relief of the Saints; organizes a small army, and begins to dream of physical conquest and temporal sovereignty.

May 4. Mormon Church first called "The Church of Jesus Christ of Latter-Day Saints" by Sidney Rigdon at a convention at Kirtland.

July 9. Smith returns to Kirtland, where his presence began to be needed.

1835. February 14. The first quorum of the Twelve Apostles ordained at Kirtland; and among them Brigham Young and Heber C. Kimball.

Classes of instruction and school of Prophets commenced. Sidney Rigdon delivers six lectures on Faith, generally attributed to J. Smith, being unaccredited to their author, and bound in the book of Smith's Revelations (Doctrines and Covenants).

1836. March 27. The Kirtland Temple, finished at a cost of $40,000, is dedicated; at which Smith pretends to see Moses, Elias, and Elijah, who give him different "keys" of priesthood, which guarantied to their possessors unlimited power in spiritual and temporal things.

June 29. The Mormons are requested by the citizens to move from Clay county, Mo., to Carrol, Davis, and Caldwell counties, they having become impudent, encroaching, and threatening. They wisely decide to move, and leave with friendly arrangements.

1837. June 1. O. Hyde and Kimball appointed to go to England as missionaries.

November. Smith's Kirtland Safety Society Bank broke, store seized, goods sold, and himself insolvent.

1838. January 12. Smith and Rigdon run away in the night from their creditors in Ohio, who were threatening their arrest for fraud.

March. They arrive in Missouri, and begin to scatter the Saints, in order to obtain political ascendancy in other counties of the State of Missouri. The citizens commence to murmur at being under Mormon rule.

About this time Smith pretended to obtain a revelation from God authorizing him to practice polygamy, and began to practice it accordingly.

July 4. Sidney Rigdon, in an anniversary oration, familiarly called by the Mormons "Sidney's Salt Sermon," threatens the Mormon enemies and apostates with physical violence.

1838. July 4. The Danite Band, or United Brothers of Gideon, organized, and placed under the command of David Patten, an Apostle, who assumed the alias of Captain Fearnot.

Martin Harris, Oliver Cowdery, and David Whitmer, the three witnesses to the Book of Mormon, are charged with lying, theft, counterfeit-coining, and defamation of Smith's character, and are cut off from the Church.

Orson Hyde, Thomas B. Marsh, W. W. Phelps, and many others apostatize from the faith, and give evidence against Smith, accusing him of being accessory to several murders and many thefts, and of designing to rule that part of the State of Missouri, and eventually the whole Republic.

August and September. Several *emeutes* occur between the mobbers and Mormons. The latter steal sixty or eighty stand of arms at Richmond, and fire on the militia, mistaking them for the mob, at Crooked river, where several are shot, when the militia return the fire, and David Patten is killed.

September 30. The militia, to avenge the death of their comrades, brutally attack the Mormon women and children at Hawn's Mill, shooting them down and burning the houses, and committing other barbarous atrocities on the women.

November. The Saints are kindly received at Quincey Illinois.

Smith arrested and about to be shot by the excited

military, but is handed over to the civil authorities, and is subsequently released.

1839. March 25. Brigham Young and others relay the foundations of the Temple at Independence, Jackson county, Mo.

May 9. Smith goes to Commerce, Ill., by invitation of Dr. Isaac Galland, of whom he obtains *gratis* a large tract of land, to induce him to settle there with the people. He accordingly receives a revelation, calls the Saints about him, and *sells* them the town lots he had received for nothing.

September. Brigham Young, H. C. Kimball and others leave for England as missionaries; O. Hyde, although previously appointed by "revelation," not accompanying them.

October. Smith and others go to Washington, to try and obtain redress from Congress for their injuries in Missouri.

5. The town of Commerce chosen a "Stake of Zion" by Smith.

1840. April 21. Commerce changes its name to Nauvoo.

October 3. Mormons begin preparing to build the Temple, and petition the State Legislature of Illinois for the incorporation of Nauvoo.

1841. February 4. Nauvoo incorporation act, passed in the preceding winter, begins to be in force. Nauvoo Legion organized. J. Smith, Lieutenant-General.

April 6. The foundation stones of Nauvoo Temple laid by Smith, with grand military parade.

1842. May 6. Governor L. W. Boggs of Missouri shot at by Orrin Porter Rockwell (now at Salt Lake City), with the connivance and under the instructions of Joseph Smith.

1843. J. Smith, mayor of Nauvoo, vice J. C. Bennet cut off for imitating Smith in his spiritual-wife doctrine.

July 12. Smith pretends to have a second revelation on polygamy, in order to conciliate his first wife, who was angry with his "ladies."

1844. February 7. J. Smith, as candidate for the Presidency of U. S., issues his address.

May 6. Smith and party destroy the material of "The Expositor:" suit issued against him in consequence.

June 24. The arms are demanded from the citizens of Nauvoo by the Governor of Illinois.

June 27. Joseph Smith, Jr., and his brother Hiram are shot in jail at Carthage, Illinois, by a gang of Missourians.

August 15. The Twelve Apostles, with Brigham Young at their head, assume the presidency of the Church; and address, as such, an epistle to the "Saints in all the world."

October 7. Brigham Young's authority is fully recognized by the majority of the Mormon people. Rigdon and all the contumacious members cut off, cursed, "and delivered to the devil to be buffeted in the flesh for a thousand years!" by Brigham.

1845. January. Nauvoo charter is repealed by the State Legislature

1845. February. Brigham Young and the Mormon authorities begin to seriously contemplate a general move to the west.

John Taylor, an Apostle, proposes Vancouver's Island, British America. Lyman Wight, also, then an Apostle, proposes Texas. Others suggest California, then but little known. Much dissension as to locality. Some valley in the Rocky Mountains finally selected.

May. The cap-stone of the Mormon Temple laid: and endowments soon after begin.

1846. January. Baptizing for the dead administered in the river Mississippi.

20. Pioneers leave Nauvoo to find some resting-place on the borders of Iowa. They select Council Bluffs.

February. Mormon companies cross the ice-covered river *en route* for Council Bluffs.

July. Brigham Young sells a company of his brethren as a Mexican battalion, for $20,000.

September. Nauvoo, in which many of the Mormons were remaining, was besieged by the mob.

1847. April 14. The pioneers leave their Winter Quarters, Council Bluffs, Iowa, for the Rocky Mountains, and by following the trail of Colonel Fremont, arrive at Salt Lake.

July 23 Orson Pratt and a few arrive at the Valley.

24. Brigham and main body of pioneers enter. This day, instead of the 23d, is always celebrated, as a compliment to Brigham, a species of sycophancy very customary from the Mormon people to the Mormon Prophet.

1847. December 24. Brigham Young nominated "President of the Church of Jesus Christ of Latter-day Saints in all the World," at a special conference. He appoints Heber C. Kimball and Willard Richards as his coadjutors. N. B.—He was not the appointment of God but the choice of the people, even by his own statement.

1848. April 6. His appointment confirmed at the General Conference at Kanesville, Iowa.

May. The Saints start for Salt Lake City, where they arrive in the fall.

September. Some of the Mormons who had sailed from New York for San Francisco, expecting the Church to locate in California or Vancouver's Island, as first intended, came in to Salt Lake Valley from the west.

1849. March 5. Convention held at Salt Lake City; Constitution of State of Deseret drafted by them, and Legislature elected under its provisions.

July 2. They send delegates to Washington to present Constitution, and petition for admission into the Union as a "sovereign and independent State."

August. Captain Stansbury, T. E., arrived to make survey of the Valleys and of the Salt Lake.

September 9. Bill organizing Utah Territory, signed by President Fillmore.

1850. February. Brigham takes oath of office as Governor of Utah Territory and Superintendent of Indian Affairs.

April 5. Assembly met, and State of Deseret was merged into Territory of Utah.

1850. June 5. "Deseret News" commenced under editorial charge of Dr. Willard Richards, "a prophet, seer, and revelator."

September. Judges Brocchus Day, Brandebury, and Mr. Secretary Harris arrive at Salt Lake.

22. Mr. Brocchus insults the people. Brigham threatens violence, and the judges leave Utah.

1851. The Salt Lake Tabernacle built.

1853. February 14. Temple excavations commenced.

April 6. Corner stones of Temple laid.

1854. August. Colonel Steptoe and soldiers arrive at Utah.

1855. May. Colonel Steptoe, having resigned the governorship of Utah, left with troops for California.

August. Judge Drummond, General Burr, Surveyor-General, and other U. S. officials arrive at Salt Lake.

1856. May. Judge Drummond left.

1857. April. General Burr and the other U. S. officials leave Utah and return to the States.

CHAPTER IX.

ANALYSIS OF THE INTERNAL EVIDENCES OF THE BOOK OF MORMON.

Introduction—The nature and purport of the book—Contents—Contradiction as to plates—As to Urim and Thummim—Hebrew language—Jewish materials for writing—Laban's plates—Jewish genealogies—The copies of the law—History of the Jews—Various Prophets of Bible and Book of Mormon—Prediction—Contradiction in Book of Mormon—Lehi's compass or Liahona—Natural history of America—Importations of stock—Elephants in America—Astronomical anticipations of the Book of Mormon—Contradictions between reputed authors of Book of Mormon—Solomon's Temple in America—Gifts of the Spirit before Christ—Jared's barges, what they were and what they brought—Precision of Book of Mormon Prophets—Plagiarisms from the Scriptures—Use of various terms not then known—Inconsistency—Prophetic apologies—Conclusion.

Mormonism claims as its founder, Joseph Smith. The pretensions of the system depend on the founder. If Smith be an impostor, Mormonism must fall. To commence an analysis of the system, we must begin with the pretensions of the Prophet. It is not enough for some to believe him to be a liar. To say that one has a right to believe him false, is to say others have the right to believe him true. Belief is the effect produced by evidence on the mind. Grounds of belief must, therefore, be searched for in the evidence. It is important to determine how much evidence ought to convince us. To believe without much proof is a sign of a weak mind. To be obstinately skeptical is a sign of ridiculous vanity. It is just as much to be avoided to say, "I am the standard for every thing," as to say "Every thing is my standard." The higher the pretensions, however, the stronger should be the evidence and the stricter the analysis. An amount of evidence that would justify belief in a trivial matter, would be wholly inadequate when offered to substantiate matters of vital moment.

The Book of Mormon claims our belief as being a revelation from God, inspired in its matter and translation. Is it true or is it false? This inquiry is important. O. Pratt, the ablest Mormon polemic writer, says, "The nature of the message in the Book of Mormon is such that, if true, none can be saved and reject it; and if false, none can be saved who receive it." Pretensions involving such important interests demand the very best of evidence. Happily for the world, it is not a question of events and persons between whom and us centuries have rolled their mists of prevarications, contradictions, and falsehoods. Young men remember its rise. Living witnesses are conversant with the whole of its history.

Professing to be a revelation from God, its evidences must be worthy of God; because God can do nothing unworthy himself. God, in the first place, would not send a book that would not commend itself and endure critical examination. God, in the second place, would not send it in a manner that would not sustain the most rigid scrutiny. God, in the third place, would not send it through a person whose character would not bear the most searching inquiry.

The nature of the book, the circumstances attending its production, and the character of its producer are the subjects proposed for discussion in the three ensuing chapters.

The Internal Evidences of Book of Mormon

I. What is the book?

1. It purports to contain a history of America from shortly after the destruction of the Tower of Babel, to the fifth century after Christ. It asserts that this continent was peopled by three different families.

First. The family of Jared who emigrated from the Tower of Babel, and whose descendants were entirely destroyed more than 600 years B.C.

Second. The family of Lehi, a Manassehite, who emigrated, about 600, B.C., from Jerusalem; the righteous part of whose descendants were destroyed 400, A.D., and the wicked part of whose descendants are now the American Indians.

Third. The "people of Zarahemla," Jews, who emigrated from Jerusalem about eleven years after Lehi, and the descendants of whom were destroyed by the wars or mingled among those of Lehi.

The history of the wanderings and wars of these several families was engraved by their Prophets on different plates; sometimes of gold, sometimes of brass, and sometimes of "ore" (as stated in the B. M.) These plates were religiously preserved until they all fell into the hands of Mormon, one of the descendants of Lehi, who made an abridgment of the whole, A.D. 384; when he buried the originals, together with certain other curiosities, in a hill; handed the *abridgment* to his son, Moroni, to which Moroni added an "abridgment of the history of the people of Jared," and finally boxed them up and buried them in a hill in New York State, A.D. 400. It is asserted that they lay in this box till the 22d of September, 1827, when they were given by an angel to Joseph Smith, who "translated them by the gift and power of God." A portion of this translation constitutes the Book of Mormon.

2. In this book there are mentioned certain other plates and curiosities, and most of which, if the book be correct, must still be in the hill "Cumorah," between Palmyra and Manchester, N. Y. A list of these curiosities is subjoined, to aid us in further remarks; the pages of the Book of Mormon (3d European ed.) on which they are described, are also stated:

1. Plates of Laban, B. M., pp. 9, 11, 144, 145.
2. Brass genealogical plates of Lehi, B. M., p. 11.
3. Brass plates of Lehi, afterward abridged by Nephi, B. M., pp. 3, 44, 62.
4. Brass plates of Nephi, containing "more history part," B. M., pp. 16, 138.
5. Brass plates of Nephi, containing "more ministry part," B. M., pp. 16, 144.
6. Ore plates of Nephi, containing "mine own prophecies," B. M., p. 44.
7. Plates of Zarahemla, containing "genealogy," B. M., p. 140.
8. Plates of Mormon, containing abridgment of Nephi's "more ministry part," B. M., p. 141.
9. Plates containing record from "Jacob to King Benjamin," B. M., p. 141.
10. Plates containing record of Zeniff, B. M., p. 161.

11. Plates (golden) of Ether, B. M., pp. 161, 189, 312, 516.
12. Plates of Alma's "account of his afflictions," B. M., p. 196.
13. Plates, Jared "brought across great deep," B. M., p. 530.
14. Copies of "Scirptures," out of which sons of Mosiah "studied 14 years," B. M., pp. 255, 271.
15. Many records "kept by people who went northward," B. M., pp. 394, 395.
16. Twelve epistles from different prophets at various times, (B. M., *in loci*).
17. The round ball, or "Compass of Lehi," B M., pp. 33, 145, 314.
18. The sword of Laban, B. M., pp. 8, 143, 145.
19. The engraved stone of Coriantumr, B. M., p. 140.
20. The sixteen stones that "God touched with his finger," B. M., p. 520.
21. The two-stone interpreters of Mosiah, B. M., pp. 162, 204.
22. The two-stone interpreters of Jared's brother, B. M., pp. 522, 523.
23. A white stone, "Gazelem," B. M., p. 212.
24. A brass breast-plate, found with Ether's plates (No. 11), B. M., p. 161.

Besides these, there were the plates containing Mormon's abridgment of the whole history (B. M., pp. 142, 443, 444, 507), and Moroni's "few plates," B. M., p. 507, the professed translation of which constitutes the present Book of Mormon. These plates, Smith says, were bound into a volume by three rings passing through the back edge.

3. There is one oversighted contradiction that stares us in the face, about the plates themselves. On p. 507 we are told that Mormon buries all these curiosities, "except these few plates" (his abridgment of the history) which he gives to his son Moroni. On p. 509, we are told Moroni fills up his father's plates, and says, "I have no more room on the plates, and ore I have none, for I am alone." The plates of his father, the book with rings, are all full. He has no more plates nor ore to make any of; and yet, the matter of *forty-seven closely-printed pages of pretended translation follows directly after.* Where does Smith pretend to have got the originals of the forty-seven pages of printed translation? He only professed to find *one set of ring-bound plates*, Mormon's abridgment. They were not in that, for Moroni "filled them up;" he did not make any more plates, "for he had no ore, and was alone." Then where were the originals of this subsequent matter?

4. Another and a graver difficulty presents itself next. Mormon, it is said, buries all the curiosities, giving Moroni *only* "these few plates." Moroni fills "these few plates," and then buries them up. Joseph Smith says he found, with these plates, the two-stone interpreters of Jared's brother (No. 22 in list), the breast-plate (No. 24), and the sword of Laban (No. 18). How could these few plates, which Moroni pretends to have buried, be with these other curiosities, *which Moroni did not have?* They were buried apart, and yet they were found together!

5. Lehi professes to live at Jerusalem in the beginning of the reign of Zedekiah. The scenes, characters, and habits

must belong to this age. They must not belong to a period 500 years antecedent or posterior to this time. When any thing is definitely known of this period, for the Book of Mormon to directly contradict it, must be a proof of imposture. Nephi states, Book of Mormon, page 1, "I make a record in the *language of my father*, which consists of the learning of the Jews *and the language of the Egyptians*." The almost foolish reverence felt by the Jews for their Hebrew language is well known. They used to believe that it was given by God to Adam in the garden, and spoken by man before the languages were confounded. It was in Hebrew that God had talked with Abraham and spoke on Mount Sinai. The imagery of Job, the tenderness of David, the expressiveness of Solomon, the sublimity of Isaiah, were all in Hebrew. They thought that while it was an especial gift, it was almost an especial sign to them. It was the only language in which they could name God. In the days of Hezekiah the pure Hebrew of Moses to David began to decline. Till 784 B. C. was the "golden age" of Hebrew literature. After this time it became corrupted with its cognate dialects. These were Aramœan, Syriac, Chaldee, Phœnician, Samaritan, but not Egyptian. The Egyptians were hated by the Jews. Briton slaves felt not a fiercer hatred to the Latin tongue of their masters than the descendants of the Jewish bondsmen to the language of their Egyptian taskmasters. For a Jew to adopt so thoroughly the "language of the Egyptians," that a Jewish prophet should call the Egyptian the "*language of his father*," is contradictory to every thing that is known of the time and people. On page 2 we are told Lehi lived in "Jerusalem all his days." He was constantly talking to the Jews, his fellow-citizens of the holy city; mingling with them in their festivities, markets, synagogue, and houses; had learned to talk among them; had never left Jerusalem; continually read the prophecies, which were in *Hebrew*, and yet we are told that his language was *the Egyptian*. Nephi pretends that God gave revelations to Lehi, and although the Eternal had never used any thing but *Hebrew*, and was communicating to a *Hebrew*, yet we are informed that God talked in the "language of his father," which was the "language of the Egyptians." Is not this requiring the world to believe too much, and, therefore, a strong presumptive evidence of ignorant imposture?

6. The plates. We must remember that it is a *Hebrew* youth, who "has lived at Jerusalem all his days," until he leaves for "the wilderness." He had no other privileges than those enjoyed by others of his circumstances and time. He did as others did. His ideas could extend but very little further than others. The writing materials then in use, and it was then only very few who could use them, would be those such a youth would be familiar with. Now the Jews did not use plates of brass at that time. Their writing materials were

1. Tablets smeared with wax.
2. Linen rubbed with a kind of gum.
3. Tanned leather and vellum.
4. Parchment (invented by Attalus of Pergamos).
5. Papyrus. (M. Stuart, O. Test. Can.)

All the writings of the Jews long anterior and subsequent to Zedekiah were in *rolls*. (Isa., xxxiv. 4; Jer., xxxvi. 25;

Ezek., iii. 9, 10; Ps. xl. 7; Zech., v. 1, etc., etc.) These rolls were chiefly parchment and papyrus. The use of papyrus was as ancient as Hermes, 1500 B. C. Ancient monuments, in Mr. Abbott's collection, whose date are at least 1600 B. C., bear representations of the inkstand and stylus. On this papyrus, were not only the ancient writings of Egypt, but the early copies of the Pentateuch. The use of this material superseded the stones filled with lead (Job), Hesiod's leaden tables, Solon's wooden planks, the wax tablets, so clumsy and easily erased. This material rolled up could be bound with flax and sealed. Isa., xxix. 11; Dan., xii. 4; Rev., v. 1. (*Vide* Kitto, Watson, Calmet.) The Jews used this material. The Egyptians, whose language Nephi gives his father, used this material. Had Lehi or Nephi really lived then, they would have used this material. Contradiction and inconsistency are stamped on any other assertion. This is another strong proof of imposture.

7. From pages 7 to 11, Book of Mormon, there is an account of Nephi's return to Jerusalem to steal from his kinsman, Laban, some plates of brass, on which were engraven certain matters. He murdered him, cheated his servant, broke into his house, carried them off, took the servant prisoner, and returned to his father in the wilderness, *thanking God* for enabling him to accomplish so many notable things, so worthy of a prophet and so honorable to the Deity!

What were the contents of these plates? On p. 10, "Then he (Lehi) beheld that they did contain the five books of Moses, * * * and also a record of the Jews from the beginning even down to the commencement of the reign of Zedekiah, king of Judah, and also the prophecies of the holy prophets, even down to the commencement of the reign of Zedekiah; and also many prophecies which have been spoken by the mouth of Jeremiah; * * * also a genealogy of his fathers, and of Laban, who was also a descendant of Joseph." To an uneducated youth like Joseph Smith, all this would not appear extravagant; but let us see in what position he has placed himself.

First. The genealogies were kept by public registrars, and were written in Hebrew on rolls of papyrus and parchment, not on plates, nor in the Egyptian language. They were very extensive, embracing all members of the family, and were sacredly preserved.—(*Kitto.*) This mass of names, embracing from Joseph, son of Jacob, down to Lehi, even though they had been, as pretended, engraved on *brass plates*, would have formed an immense volume and a great weight.

Second. They contained not only the genealogies, but the Pentateuch. A few years before this reputed time, in the reign of Josiah, king of Judah, "the book of the law" was lost. Not one copy was to be found. The few copies, and they were few, that had existed, had doubtless been destroyed by Manasseh. The nation was in the dark, directed only by tradition. Eighteen years of Josiah's reign had thus passed away. He had broken the idols, dispersed the idolaters, repaired the Temple, reinstated the high-priest; and Hilkiah went in to the holy of holies before the Lord. He "found the book of the law" hidden in the house of the Lord. He sent it to Josiah, and Saphan, the scribe, read it before the king; "who, when he had heard it, rent his clothes." (2

Chron., xxxiv. 19.) The only remaining copy was found; and so great had been the ignorance of its contents, that all Judea stood rebuked and cursed. Here, according to the Bible, a few years before, had all Judea lost the law, and Josiah, the good, who had been eighteen years on his throne, was so ignorant of it; and now Smith impudently makes God say that Laban's father had a copy of this very same law engraved on *brass plates*, and although side and side with their genealogy, and, therefore, all Jerusalem constantly seeing it, *yet entirely ignorant of it!* Is not this impudent imposture?

Third. These copies of the Scriptures, which Smith, soon after this period, makes very common indeed in America (Book of Mormon, pp. 249, 255, 271), were scarce at any time among the Jews. Jehoshaphat sent the Levites and priests, the depositaries of the Word, (not Joseph's but Aaron's descendants) with the "law of the Lord" to the people, and they had to carry it with them; it was not where they went (2 Chron., xvii. 7, 9). So scrupulous were the Jews in making copies of the Scriptures, that they would not only copy the letter, but imitate its faults and even size. This involved much labor, and the copies were therefore very few. To have told one of those old Levites, so punctilious and even superstitious, that some one had copied their law in the language of the Egyptians (idolaters and enemies) in the first place, and had it durably engraved on brass, when they were handling so delicately those papyrus rolls, he would have called it an infamous imposture. Every wise man will imitate the skepticism of that Levite.

Fourth. These plates contained, also, a "record of the Jews from the beginning till the reign of Zedekiah." By whom written and compiled? The four books of Kings and Chronicles were not compiled till Ezra, many years after Zedekiah. Who compiled these?

Fifth. These brass plates contained "all the prophecies *of all* the prophets from the beginning down to Zedekiah," together "with some of the prophecies of Jeremiah." Let us glance at the list. It embraces the whole Assyrian period: Joel, Hosea, Isaiah, Micah, Nahum, Jonah. All these lived in the golden age of Hebrew literature, and all anterior to Zedekiah; although Smith does not seem to have been aware of this, and only quotes or names Isaiah in his book. These, however, *are only a part* of the prophets who had written. Besides these, there is the Book of the Wars of the Lord, Num., xxi. 14; Jasher, Jos., x. 13; Statutes of Kingdom of Israel, 1 Sam., x. 25; Acts of Solomon, 1 Kings, xi. 41; Nathan and Gad, 1 Chron., xxix. 29; Ahijah and Iddo, 2 Chron., ix. 29; Shemaiah, Jehu, Sayings of the Seers, Isaiah's History of Uzziel, Life of Hezekiah, Life of Jehoshaphat, Lamentation over Josiah. Besides all these, which must have been on those wonderful plates, if the Book of Mormon be true, there are prophets mentioned and quoted in the book, about whom our Scriptures and Hebrew history are silent: Zenoch, Zenos and Ezias, Book of Mormon, pp. 411, 429, 455; besides all these there was "Jacob's Prophecy about Joseph's Coat," Book of Mormon, p. 336; Joseph's prophecies, "than which not many greater," Book of Mormon, p. 62. All this vast mass of matter, it is pretended, was on these singular brass plates: the Pentateuch, history, prophecies, and of course the Psalms, for was not David a prophet? Add to all this the genealogies of their families ever since Abraham! One man could never have carried it all. A narrative so full of absurdities and positive contradictions of all fact, can not come from God, and must therefore be an imposture.

8. Lehi prophesies, on p. 11, "These plates shall go forth to all nations—never grow dim, nor perish." "These plates" are not, as the Mormons often try to apply the passage, the plates on which the Book of Mormon was engraved, *but the plates of Laban.* The Mormons claim literal interpretations of Scripture. It was the *plates* that should never grow dim, the *plates* that should never perish, the *plates* to go forth to all nations. Where are they? It is pretended, Book of Mormon, p. 507, that Mormon hid them up, and there they are still. If Laban's plates were to be the ones to go to all nations, why dig up Mormon's plates? If they both are to go, why not send both? It is evident that in commencing the Book of Mormon, Smith was not quite settled as to the exact plot of the affair, and after Cowdery had once written it, it could not be erased.

9. Nephi's ball or compass, Book of Mormon, p. 33, can not endure the application of any rule of criticism. "He beheld on the ground a ball of curious workmanship, and it was of fine brass; and within the ball were two spindles, and *the* one pointed the way we should go in the wilderness." How they could look into a *brass ball*, how they were to know which one spindle was *the* one, and what was the use of the other, are questions that need some answer, before believing that God inspired so vague and meaningless a sentence. On

p. 35, these spindles, *inside* this *brass ball*, did not work independently of its possessors, but " according to the faith and diligence and heed we did give unto them." It was only one spindle, before, that pointed. " And there was also written on *them* (not the ball, but on these *fine spindles*) a new writing, plain to be read, which did give us understanding concerning the ways of the Lord, and it was written and changed from time to time." Nephi builds a ship by himself in a few weeks (it took Noah and all his men 120 years to build his ark), launches it, takes this " compass" on board, and sails. His brethren, however, rebel against, and bind him. The miracle of his compass, the still greater miracle of building a ship, when he " *had even to melt the ore he found in the rocks in order to make tools*," every tree to cut down, and every plank to hew out, and yet he completes, launches, and fits it for sea—*all by himself, and in a short time*, do not convince them. When they bind him, the " compass did cease to work," p. 42. His frightened brethren " are driven backward three days ;" then " they loosed me, and I took the compass, and it did work whither I desired it." Here is a jumbled mass of vague inconsistencies. If the compass " ceased *to work*," how could Nephi tell they were driven backward or forward, or sideward ? As they had lost their way, how did Nephi know in which direction to " *desire* it to work ?" One thing is painfully noticeable, Smith is very cautious not to give the slightest clew as to where they sailed from, how long they were reaching that point, in which direction it lay from Jerusalem. All the rivers and valleys he makes Lehi name with *new names*. The little that is written about it only serves to mislead the reader. It is not the plain honest narrative of an honest man; it certainly is not the luminous narrative of a God-inspired man. Telemachus' Mentor, building a ship on the island of Calypso, is rational, compared with this statement of Nephi's ship-building. His voyage across the island-dotted sea to America is a mystery of navigation. This vagueness, inconsistency, evident effort at being antique, is impossible in an honest narrator of facts, ridiculous in a prophet; but perfectly natural in an ignorant impostor.

10. "We found upon the land of promise (Central America) that there were beasts in the forest of every kind; the cow, and the ox, and the ass, and the horse," Book of Mormon, p. 44. This is a palpable falsehood, and eminently displays the impostor's *hoof*. "When horses were first brought to Mexico, by Hernando Cortez, they were objects of the greatest astonishment to the aborigines, who thought they lived on flesh as well as their riders, and brought flesh to feed them with. They thought that they devoured men in battle, and that their neighing was a demand for prey" (Herera, Dec. ii., lib. vi.) "They invented a new weapon, with which to catch and fight them" (Ib., Dec. v., lib. viii., quoted Robertson's History of America). This occurs in a country and among a people, *where the Book of Mormon makes horses quite common*. The first horse the Utah Indians ever possessed, they tied up till it died of starvation; they thought it need not eat. South American horses have all sprung from those introduced by the Spaniards. Cuba obtained her horses from Spain; Mexico got hers from Cuba. West American horses sprang from the Canadian, imported by the French.

Eastern America from the importations of British stock (Youatt on the Horse, *in loci*). It may be objected the stock could not have increased so rapidly since that time, 1500; but the wild horses of the Ukraine and Tartary have all descended from a few that escaped from their masters at the siege of Azoph, 1657. "The first horses brought to America were imported by Columbus on his second voyage, 1493. The first horses landed in United States territory, were brought to Florida by Cabeça de Vaça, who imported forty-two head, 1527. De Soto, in 1539, imported a still larger number, etc., etc. (Report of Superintend. of Census, U. S. A., 1852.) And yet Smith makes horses abundant in America, 600 B. C., which, Book of Mormon, p. 517, he makes imported in "air-tight, whale-like barges" from the plains of Shinar, after the destruction of the Tower of Babel! They found "cows and oxen." Cows and other domestic animals were all imported. Columbus, in 1493, brought a bull and several cows. In 1553, the Portuguese took cattle to Nova Scotia and Newfoundland. In 1611, Sir Thomas Gates imported 100 cows and some bulls. In 1624, E. Winslow brought 3 heifers and 1 bull, etc., etc. (Superintendent's Report, Census, 1852.) "They also found the ass." "Washington was the first man who imported the ass into America" (Ency. Americana, Art. Ass.) Since his time, the raising of mules has become quite a business in this country. To say that these animals were here, that they lived till the fifth Christian century, and then became so extinct as to leave no trace, and be remembered by no tradition, is requiring a miracle to sustain imposture. Smith has evidently overreached his knowledge of fact. This contradiction of well-known truths can not have been made by a prophet, and is, therefore, positive proof of imposture.

11. But Smith not only makes all these animals flourish "in large flocks," just subsequent to the destruction of Babel, but on page 533, he says, "The people had silks, and all manner of cattle and sheep and swine, and also *elephants* and *cureloms and cumons.*" What these cureloms and cumons mean it is impossible to decide. The present elephant is not a native of America, and never since the creation of man has it been an inhabitant of this continent. Prior to his advent on the earth, when the climate of North America was very different from what it has since been, gigantic species of elephants and mastodons lived, died, and left their bones in the post pleiocene formation of this country, as well as in northern Europe; but here, Smith pretends that so recently as shortly before Christ, the people had them and used them, when their forms are seen upon no ruin, carved on no temple, represented by no idol. Sheep; "neither North nor South America can boast any aboriginal, primiitive, domestic sheep; those which have received the name of 'natives' having been brought at early periods by the colonists." (American Shepherd, New York Agricultural Society, 1854.) Swine are certainly not aboriginal to America. The earliest swine were imported by De Soto, in 1539, who brought 13 sows. The Portuguese took swine to Newfoundland, 1553. In 1609 the English im-

ported 600 swine and many sheep and fowls. So plentifully had the imported swine increased that, in 1627, the Indians fed on the hogs that roamed the woods, half wild. The Spaniards took swine to their settlements in southern America, where they also increased very rapidly. Does not such jumbling up of inconsistencies and contradictions not only demand the strongest possible evidence to substantiate, but become a positive proof of forgery and imposture?

12. "All things denote that there is a God, yea even the earth and all things thereon; yea and its motion; yea and also all the planets which move in their regular form." Book of Mormon, p. 293. Here is the gist of Paley's design argument anticipated. Not only the Egyptians but also the Greeks and all the world accepted Ptolemy's theory of the solar system. The earth was to them the stationary center, around which *all* the stars revolved. What the Jews knew of astronomy they had acquired from the nations around them. God revealed spiritual and not physical truths! He certainly did not reveal to them a treatise on astronomy. Their acceptance of the Ptolemaic theory is evidenced in all the astronomical allusions of Job, David, and Solomon. Believing all the stars to move, the word *planet* was neither needed nor used. Copernicus, when he discovered that some stars moved, while others were stationary, divided the heavenly bodies into planets (from Gr. *planeo*, I wander), the moving bodies, and the fixed stars. The Manassehite Alma, however, is far wiser than all the rest of the prophets. He overturns all the astronomical theories, and just as *an illiterate itinerant might, to-day*, use a weak version of Paley's

argument. It is a question of probabilities. Is it the most probable that this Alma could have used such language, anticipated the discoveries of 2000 years' later date, excel all the other prophets, quote the circumstances as *a well-known fact* on which to base an argument, when every thing we know proves it not to have been known at all; or is it the most probable to believe it the ignorant forgery of an illiterate impostor? This, however, is a small thing. On page 421 there is an attempted refutation of the modern infidel argument about Joshua and the sun. Smith pretends that this argument was used by people *who believed the same theory of astronomy* as the ancients and therefore could *not feel its pertinence and therefore could not have used it.* "The earth goeth back and it appeareth unto man that the sun standeth still, yea, and behold this is so, for *sure*, it is the earth that moveth and not the sun." Here are all the prophets transcended; Ptolemy refuted; Copernicus and all his discoveries anticipated 2000 years before he was born. The only pity is, that this was not published, however, *until* 200 *years after he was dead!*

13. One great peculiarity of the Book of Mormon is the number of direct contradictions among its inspired men. We will quote a few examples. On page 3, it says Lehi left Jerusalem because "God directed him in a dream;" but on page 411, we are gravely told Lehi was "*driven out by the people.*" On page 109, Nephi tells his brethren, "We are descendants of the *Jews;*" and on page 113, he says, "the *Jews* from whence I come;" yet on page 235, Amalek testifies that "Nephi and his brethren were of the *tribe of Ma-*

nasseh." On page 517, we are assured that "the Lord led Jared and his brother out to America;" but on page 406, the reader is divinely instructed that it was "*the Devil.*" All the world have considered America was a continent; all the writers in the Book of Mormon call it a continent; but the Lord is made to tell Jacob "it is an isle of the sea." (Book of Mormon, page 78.) "At the death of Christ," it is predicted that "darkness shall cover the *face of the whole earth for three days.*" (Book of Mormon, page 428.) The New Testament says three hours; and the Roman records do not even notice that casualty. It is certain that darkness did not cover the earth for three days. Smith not only regulates the motions of the planets, but on pages 426 and 434 he makes a "new star." Not a brilliant conjunction of stars, but a *bona fide* new planet, for he makes it move too. Where is it now?

14. The Nephites build on America (Book of Mormon, page 65) "a temple like unto Solomon's;" and this poor family had come to this land destitute a few years before. They "offer burnt offerings therein," page 145. They "ordain *high priests*," page 208; and priests, page 225. If the Bible be true, there could be but one temple; but one holy of holies; but one high priest. The location for that temple was to be Jerusalem, the city of God. No high priest could be chosen out of the tribe of Levi and of the seed of Aaron. "The stranger that approaches thereto shall surely be put to death." Yet here it is asserted that Jews or Manassehites dared to break God's most holy law, administer God's most holy ceremonies, usurp the authority of God's most holy priesthood,

and that the Lord blessed and sanctioned this violation of his word. They were not Levites; they were strangers; they did go into the holy of holies, and yet Jehovah falsified his own threat and favored the transgressors!

15. In the holy Scriptures, we are informed that the Saviour had to die in order that his disciples might obtain the gift of the Holy Ghost. "If I go not away, the Comforter can not come." "He, when he is come, shall bring all things to your remembrance, and show you things to come." John xiv. Smith makes the Nephites far more favored. On page 234, the reader is divinely informed, that "there had been made known unto them that which has been, which is, and which is to come; having *been visited by the Spirit of God*, having conversed with angels and spoken to by the voice of the Lord, and having the spirit of prophecy and the spirit of revelation, and also many gifts; the gift of speaking with tongues, and the gift of preaching, and the *gift of the Holy Ghost*, and the gift of translation;" and all this, Smith pretends, occurred more than *three hundred years before Jesus Christ came.* If we believe the New Testament is true, we must reject the Book of Mormon as an imposture.

16. Come we to a still more startling proof of imposture. From page 517 to 526 of the Book of Mormon is contained an account of how Jared, his brother, their families and friends were miraculously conducted to this continent from the plains of Shinar. They are commanded to gather "their herds and flocks, two of each kind, male and female," also "all kinds of animals after their kind, male and female," also "fowls of the air," likewise "swarms of bees;" beside these,

they "did prepare a vessel, in which they did carry with them the fish of the waters," as well as "seeds of the earth of every kind." With this mass of material they cross the ocean, on which they are tossed about for "*three hundred and forty and four days.*" (Book of Mormon, page 526.) How did they cross? Not only have they to take all these creatures, but they have to carry with them *food* for all of them for a *year.* Not only food, but *fresh water* for the same length of time, and some of the animals need so much. What means were adopted? They crossed in eight *barges,* which are thus described (page 519): "And they were *small* and they were *light* upon the water, even like unto the lightness of a fowl upon the water; and they were built after a manner that they were exceeding tight, even that they would hold water like unto a dish; and the bottom thereof was tight like unto a dish; and the sides thereof were tight like unto a dish; and the ends thereof were peaked; and the top thereof was tight like unto a dish; and the length thereof was the *length of a tree:* and the door thereof, when it was shut, was tight like unto a dish." "And Jared cried unto the Lord, we shall all perish, there is no light to steer by, and in them we can not breathe for there is no air." "And the Lord said, behold thou shalt make a hole in the top thereof and also in the bottom thereof; and when thou shalt suffer for air, thou shalt unstop the hole thereof and receive air. And if it be so that the water come in upon *thee, ye* shall stop the hole thereof that ye may not perish in the flood." But the light difficulty needed another remedy. "And Jared did molten out of a rock, sixteen small stones, and they were white and clear, even as transparent glass." (N. B. *Glass at the time of the deluge!*) These stones he brought before the Lord, and "behold the Lord stretched forth his hand, and touched them one by one with his finger." He then placed them, one in each end of his eight barges, "and they shone in the darkness." While they were "as a whale in the sea, swallowed up in the depths of the sea, and the mountain waves should dash upon them." Eight canoes are formed of as many trees, hollowed out inside, peaked at the ends, having a shut down door. And now, Smith pretends, that "two of each kind of animals," "fowls of the air," "swarms of bees," "a large vessel containing fish of the waters," "all manner of seeds of the earth," "twenty-two grown persons and their sons and daughters" (page 526), all the food they would need for a year, and all the fresh water they would require, with vessels in which to carry it; all this vast amount of matter is snugly stowed away in eight canoes, "*which were small and light* like unto a fowl, *and only the length of a tree!*" It would be folly to attempt to apply figures either as to their capacity to receive, and much less to sustain these things. To attempt to palm such a statement on to man as a revelation from God, is the act of an impostor.

17. God, in the predictions of the Bible, has left a species of ambiguity. Pretended prophets take especial care to leave nothing vague in their predictions, when their prophecies do not profess to come to light *till eighteen hundred years after the accomplishment of the event foretold.* This is peculiarly the case in the Book of Mormon, about the coming of the Saviour into the world. The most minute incident of his

life, from the first sign of his advent till his final ascension, as it is left us by the Evangelist, is definitely foretold. While, however, it predicts every thing of which we have any account, it is silent about those things of which we have no account! His mother should be a virgin, named Mary, who should conceive by the Holy Ghost, p. 227. The star in the east, p. 426. He should be born at Jerusalem, p. 227. *Not at Jerusalem but at Nazareth*, p. 20. His name should be Jesus Christ, pp. 76, 226. Lamb of God who taketh away the sins of the world, Redeemer, Maker of heaven and earth, coming to and rejected of his own, Only-begotten, full of grace and truth, High Priest, etc., pp. 17, 150, 235, 246, 223. His baptism by John and descent of Holy Ghost as a dove, p. 17, 110. Has twelve apostles, heals sick and casts out devils, pp. 29, 21. Is spitten on, smitten, scourged, p. 45. Crucified, p. 21. Three days in sepulchre and rises on third day, pp. 96, 150. Ascends into heaven, p. 180. His people in America calling themselves Christians one hundred years before he came, p. 335. John's Apocalypse, p. 29. Is not this "fitting prophecy to the event?" If it were true, it would be most extraordinary that the Lord should thus singularly favor these Israelites with so much clearer views of his scheme of salvation, and, therefore, so signally neglect the Jews, when the Jews were "his own," and he declares that he had "cast the Israelites out from his sight."

18. From page 2 to page 428, pretending to embrace a period from 600 B. C. to A. D., I have counted no less than 298 direct quotations from the New Testament; some of them, paragraphs of verses; some of them, sentences from verses.

Besides these, there are whole chapters of the Old and New Testament copied *verbatim*, and often not acknowledged. Below is the list:

Isaiah, chs. 48 and 49 are from pages 46 and 50, B. M. (3d European edition).

Isaiah, chs. 50 and 21 are from pages 68 and 71, B. M.

Isaiah, chs. 2 and 14 are from pages 79 and 94, B. M.

Isaiah, ch. 52 is from page 477, B. M.

Isaiah, ch. 54 is from pages 480 and 481, B. M.

Malachi, ch. 3 is from pages 482 and 483, B. M.

Matthew, chs. 5, 6, and 7 are from pages 457 and 464, B. M.

1 Corinthians, ch. 13 is from page 556, B. M.

"In the Hebrew manuscripts of the Old Testament there have been counted 800,000 different readings, as to consonants alone. (M. Stuart, Old Tes. Can., p. 192.) How comes it then, with such a margin for slight differences, that all the above quotations are copied in the *exact words of King James's translation?* The style of thought and expression in the original of the Book of Mormon and these interpolations, are entirely different. From the nervous, luminous English of the Bible, Smith wallows in the fogs of his own barbarous twaddle. The slightest investigation will show that Smith copied them *verbatim* from the English translation of the Scriptures; will show him to be an impostor.

19. I might urge the utterance of ideas and the use of words which these ancient writers, if genuine, could not have known, as an argument against the authenticity of the book. Such as "Bible," not employed to express the idea of the united Scriptures, till Chrysostom, in the fifth century. Or

"dissenters," a word of Latin origin, a language not then known, and the word not employed till Wickliff, and not generally till 1662, the great era of non-conformity. Or "church," which Smith puts into a Jew's mouth, 600 B. C. (B. M., p. 9), but which was not thus employed till after Christ's ascension. Or "martyr for Christ," or "cimeters." Another strong evidence of forgery may be found on page 513, "*For do we not read*, that God is the same yesterday, to-day, and forever, and that in him is neither variableness nor shadow of changing?" The first part of this sentence is to be found in Paul's epistle to the Hebrews, chapter xiii., ver. 8: "The same yesterday, to-day, and forever." The closing clause was written by James, i. 17: "Father of lights in whom there is no variableness nor shadow of turning." The Nephites do not pretend to have these epistles; how, then, could "*they read*" what they did not have? Smith made a terrible oversight here.

20. When the prophets of the Scriptures had predictions to utter or events to narrate, conscious of their authority, they spoke without circumlocution or excuse. Many men are forced to concede their dignity who question their veracity. With these compare Smith's *pseudo* Prophets of the Book of Mormon; "Many shall say we have a Bible, and there can not be any more Bible." (p. 107.) "Neither am I mighty in writing like unto speaking." (p. 113.) "Condemn me not because of my imperfections, neither my father, because of his imperfections, neither them who have written before him, but rather give thanks unto God that he hath made manifest unto you our imperfections, that ye may learn to be more

wise than we are." (Strange talk for an *inspired Prophet!*) "And if our plates had been sufficiently large we should have written in Hebrew, and if we could have written in Hebrew, behold ye would have no imperfection in our record." (515). Whatever imperfections we find, therefore, we must attribute to the records not having been written in Hebrew. They were not written in Hebrew, because their plates were not large enough. But they made their own plates; they had abundance of gold, as we are over and over informed. They might have made their plates, consequently, just as large as they pleased. It is impious to charge the omniscient God with such trifling puerilities.

The Book of Mormon consists of two parts. One is stolen, and the other original. Its copied part consists of plagiarisms, culled from the commonest books, collected without knowledge, and combined without skill. Its original part is a mass of contradictions, and miracles sublimed into absurdities. To attempt to palm the whole on human credulity, as a revelation from God, is folly and fraud.

The Well against which Jos. Smith was shot after his death.

CHAPTER X.

THE EXTERNAL EVIDENCES OF THE BOOK OF MORMON.

Mormon style of proof—Attacks on the Bible examined—Laws of evidence—Contradictions between statements—Urim and Thummim—Affidavits as to Smith's statements—Contradiction of probabilities—Weight of book—Smith's previous character—Affidavit of eleven citizens—Of fifty-one—Of different individuals—Smith's witnesses—Contradictions—O. Cowdery—Harris Whitmer—Of the eight witnesses—Analysis of testimony—False grounds of the Mormons—Examination of prophetic evidence—Summary.

A FEW of the many evidences of imposture, contained in the Book of Mormon, have been examined in the last chapter, and the result of which, must be the conclusion that the book does not commend itself, either to the judgment or the heart. The Mormons have two ways of defending their book. One is by a constant retreat to its external evidence, and the other by an acrimonious assault on the Bible. It is not that the nature of the book shall prove the authenticity of its pretensions; but that the pretensions of the book shall prove its authenticity. The idea is not to receive the Prophet for the sake of the book, but the book for the sake of the Prophet. The Mormons have ever shrunk from a full investigation of the internal evidences of their book; but have sought refuge under affidavits and testimony. This is wise policy too, from the fact that it is more easy to avoid personal attacks, and cripple personal investigation, than to protect a printed book. The book remains, awkwardly remains very often, to refute its advocates. No sympathies can be aroused, no feelings awakened by critical disquisition; whereas, all have so much of the hero in them, that a spice of romance, a dash of suffering, plead loudly in extenuation of grave faults and serious deficiencies.

To attack the Bible is not the way to establish their pretended revelation. Even though they could prove every word of the Bible to be false, it would not prove their book to be true. Not only would it not establish it, but would destroy it—bury it under the mass of ruins they had created It is not enough to show that the Book of Mormon is as *good* as the Bible; it must be better, or it is a forgery. It must be better first, in the subject-matter; because the writers of the Book of Mormon pretend to far greater light on the important themes of human salvation. They assert that God was so much more gracious to them, as to give them so much more knowledge about the coming, mission, and death of the Saviour, that they organized churches in his name; called themselves Christians; obtained the Spirit with all its gifts; died martyrs for his sake, and all hundreds of years before he came, while the Jewish prophets were only cheered by a dim ray and comforted by a hope that the Messiah would come. "They looked forward to his day, and were glad." Men so much more blessed, ought to so much more exceed their comparatively neglected brethren. Not only in matter, but it must excel the Bible in style. All that the translators of the Bible claim is strong patience and unwearied research. The Book of Mormon translator claims *inspiration* as his means of production. With the Bible it is only human sagacity, increased by labor and invigorated by study; with this other book, Smith says that "therein is the wisdom of God made manifest." As far then as the wisdom of God is superior to the sagacity of men, so far should the Book of Mormon surpass the Bible. Nor can the "Saints" shirk this corollary. The Bible was handed down in MSS. with considerable differences; singularly preserved, it is true, but not without some important alterations. The Book of Mormon is written by Prophets, engraved on metal plates, hidden by a Prophet, found by a Prophet, translated by revelation. It is God throughout on whom it is charged. If it do not exhibit God throughout, it is a forgery. To attempt to extenuate any failings on the plea of human fallibility, is to charge weakness on the Omnipotent. To show that there are errors in the Bible, is a proof of the fallibility of the translators. To show errors in the Book of Mormon, is either to prove Smith an impostor, or it is to find God at fault!

The book does not commend itself; does the manner of its production commend it? It would be well to determine what are the laws of evidence by which to judge. They may be comprised in the following formula:

I. Statements must agree with themselves.

II. Statements must agree with principles previously known.

III. Statements must agree with collateral facts.

IV. Corroboration without collusion among disinterested witnesses

V. Their joint evidence must preponderate over conflicting testimony.

First. Statements must agree with themselves.

Joseph Smith, born in 1805, sees an angel in 1820, who tells him his sins are forgiven. In 1823 he sees another angel who tells him of the existence of certain plates, their locality, and his destiny to obtain, translate, and publish them. Next morning, 22d September, 1823, Smith goes to the place, has a look into the stone box containing them, again sees the angel, endures a conflict with the powers of darkness, receives much instruction, and is finally commanded to cover up the box for four years. On the morning of 22d September, 1827, he goes to the box in the hill and obtains the plates with the "Urim and Thummim," and commences the translation. Now what does he see? The plates, about 7 by 8 inches large, and about six inches thick; besides these there were the "Urim and Thummim, two white stones set in the rim of a bow," and "a brass breastplate worn by the ancients" (*vide.* J. Smith's Autobiography). This is the first statement with regard to the matter. On page 189 of Smith's Revelations (Doctrines and Covenants) is another statement in which "the sword of Laban and the brass director of Nephi" were added to the list. Which is true? If he only saw the plates, interpreters, and breastplate, as he said he did in his early statements, how comes he to change it *two years afterward?* Whichever is true, or if they both be false, the first-law evidence would determine his rejection.

Another very serious discrepancy occurs as to this Urim

and Thummim. In the Book of Mormon there are two mentioned. One, p. 522, is possessed by Jared's brother, who seals them up with his plates, and hides them. These plates and interpreters, according to the Book of Mormon, have never been found. Ether, the last surviving descendant of Jared's company, engraves a succinct history of his forefathers on twenty-four golden plates and dies, p. 549. These plates of Ether are found by the people of Limbi, about 120 B. C., p. 161. With these plates was brought the breast-plate referred to, but with them neither the plates of Jared's brother, nor his interpreters. They have not been found. Besides these, there is another pair of interpreters, possessed by one Mosiah, who declares he received them, they "having been handed down from generation to generation," p. 204. All that Mosiah knew about Jared was by means of Ether's plates of gold which he interpreted by his two interpreters. The interpreters of Mosiah were handed down to Mormon. If the Book of Mormon be true, these must be the interpreters Smith obtained; but, in his Revelations, p. 189, two years after, he says, "they were those given to Jared's brother." Here is a palpable contradiction between Smith in the Book of Mormon and Smith in the Doctrines and Revelations, and by the first law of evidence, he should be rejected.

Not only has Smith contradicted himself in his own works, but still more extensively in the statements he has made to his companions and neighbors; many of these have testified to such contradictions.

Peter Ingersol, one of Smith's most intimate friends, makes affidavit, and says, "that Smith told me the whole affair was a hoax, that he had no such book, and did not believe that there was such a book in existence; but, said he, as I have got the damned fools fixed, I shall carry out the fun."

Willard Chase testifies that "Smith came to me, wanting me to make him a chest to put his Gold Bible in, and promised me a share in the book to do so. He told me he was commanded to keep it two years, without letting it come to the eye of any one but himself."

Isaac Hale, Smith's father-in-law, also affirms, "I asked Smith who was to be the first to see the book of plates? He said it was a young child."

Rev. N. C. Lewis testifies that "Smith told me he was commanded to exhibit the plates to all the world at a certain time, then about eighteen months distant, and promised that I should see the plates. When that time came, he said he had been deceived."

Henry Harris testifies that "Smith told me that he could not obtain the plates until he was married, and that no one was to see them but himself and wife."

Alva Hale testifies that Joseph "promised me that I should see the plates, and appointed a time; but when it came, appeared angry, and refused to keep his word."

Levi Lewis testifies that "Smith told me that God had deceived him, and that this was the reason he did not show them."

Sophia Lewis testifies that she "heard Smith say the book of plates could not be opened by another person than his first-born, which was to be a male; and that she was present at its birth, and that it was still-born, and much deformed."

The question is, are these deponents to be believed? Either they are perjurers, or Smith is an impostor. These, one Smith's father-in-law, are parties well known and respected where they lived. They are perfectly disinterested. Its success would cost them nothing. *Had they been disposed to assist in the imposture, they could have made a great deal.* Although testifying to additional circumstances, they all confirm each other's statements. Either they are *all* perjurers, or they *all* tell the truth. The above are but a selection from many. The Smiths never could, and did not, oppose to these affidavits any thing but a bare denial, *but moved out of that part of the country*, where they could obtain no converts. They must be believed; Smith did contradict himself, and should therefore be rejected.

II. Statements must be probable.

In 1823 Smith disinters the box, looks into it, covers it up, and leaves it for four years. When he first visited it, "the crowning top of the box was visible from the road, though not sufficiently so to attract the attention of the traveler unless previously directed to it." It was thus in 1823. After the snows and rains of four winters such a box would be quite bare, and would have been inspected and robbed. To say that God should act thus in preserving "his holy word" is ridiculous and improbable.

Smith avers, that after receiving these plates, etc., he was "waylaid by two ruffians, one armed with a club; still keeping the plates, etc. concealed, he beats them off, runs from them, and arrives at his father's house, a two miles' run, before them." (Smith's Autobiography.) *This* may appear a small feat till we remember what he had to carry. "The plates of gold measure 7×8 inches, and six inches thick, and are fastened through the back edge with three rings." A box of tin, 10×14, and 3 inches deep, weighs about 125 lbs. gross. The box may weigh 10 lbs., leaving the nett weight of tin 115 lbs. Now $10 \times 14 \times 3 : 115 :: 7 \times 8 \times 6 : 92$ lbs. Had these gold plates been tin, they would have weighed about 90 lbs. But the relative weight of tin and gold is as 19·25 to 7·58. So that $7{\cdot}58 : 19{\cdot}25 :: 92 : 220{\cdot}44$. Hence, this mass of gold plates, as they were not so compactly pressed as boxed tin, would have weighed nearly 200 lbs. Besides these plates, he had, according to his third story, a breast-plate of brass, Laban's sword, the crystal interpreters, the "brass ball with spindles" director of Lehi. Yet he packs this horse load, keeps these large and awkward shaped things *completely concealed*, and, at the same time, beats off and outruns two empty-handed men a distance of two miles. Statements must be probable, and, therefore, these ought to be rejected.

III. Statements must agree with collateral facts.

What is Smith's previous character? While the prophets and apostles were poor, many of them ignorant, and some of them very young, still their characters were irreproachable. Smith's youth, ignorance, and low position would be no valid argument against him; but what was his reputation? Only those who know him best can testify. Such disinterested testimony we subjoin:

Affidavit made by eleven residents of J. Smith's village.

"We, the undersigned, being personally acquainted with the family of Joseph Smith, sen., with whom the Gold Bible, so called, originated, state, that they are not only a lazy indolent set of men, but also intemperate, and their word not to be depended on, and that we are heartily glad to dispense with their society."

Signed by eleven male residents of Manchester, Ontario, N. Y., November 3, 1833.

On December 4, 1833, fifty-one other men of standing and reputation made affidavit to a similar effect. "We, the undersigned, have been acquainted with the Smith family for a number of years while they resided near this place, and have no hesitation in saying, that we consider them destitute of that moral character which ought to entitle them to the confidence of any community. They were particularly famous for 'visionary projects,' spent much of their time in digging for money which they pretended was hid in the earth. Joseph Smith, sen., and his son Joseph in particular, were considered entirely destitute of *moral character and addicted to vicious habits.*"

This was signed by fifty-one men of well-known reputation.

Williard Chase made affidavit before Judge Smith, that "I have regarded Joseph Smith, jun., from the time I became acquainted with him, as a man whose word could not be depended on. After the family became Mormons, their conduct was more disgraceful than before. Although they left this part of the country without paying their just debts, yet their creditors were glad to have them do so rather than to have them stay."

Parley Chase affirms, "I was acquainted with the family of Joseph Smith, sen., both before and since they became Mormons, and state that not one of the male members of the

Smith family are entitled to any credit whatever. They were lazy, intemperate, and worthless men; very much addicted to lying. In this they frequently boasted their skill. Digging for money was their principal employment. In regard to their Gold Bible speculation, they scarcely ever told two stories alike."

Joseph Capron testified that "the whole object of the Smith family appeared to be to live without work. While digging for money, they were constantly harassed by creditors who are still unpaid."

Henry Harris testifies that "the character of Joseph Smith, jun., for truth and veracity was such that I would not believe him under oath. I was once on jury before a justices' court, and the jury could not and did not believe his testimony to be true."

Levi Lewis testifies "he knows Smith to be a liar; that he saw him intoxicated at three different times while pretending to translate the Book of Mormon; that he has heard him say adultery was no crime."

Barton Stafford, on oath before Judge Baldwin, testified, "Joseph Smith, sen., was a noted drunkard, that most of his family followed his example, especially Joseph Smith, jun., the Prophet, who was much addicted to intemperance. That he got drunk in my father's field, and that when drunk would talk about his religion."

Here are positive statements made by men who knew Smith well; who had known him long; who had no motive to exaggerate. They are not bare assertions uttered without thought, and repeated without exactness, but deliberate, written affidavits. No attempt has been made to meet them, only to cry persecution and *run away*. To cry persecution is not to answer grave accusations. To run away is to tacitly admit, if not the direct charge, certainly their inability to refute it.

We are bound in all honesty to believe these solemn assertions of over seventy well-known and well-reputed men. To believe them is to reject Smith. To commence God's work of salvation on the earth, required his Son, Jesus Christ, and the new testament of his blood. God would not select such a work as the Book of Mormon to continue the object that needed his Son to commence. He would neither select such a work, nor choose such a man to introduce it, nor in such a manner.

IV. There must be corroboration without collusion among disinterested witnesses.

To judge the Book of Mormon by the precedent laid down in the Bible, it is extraordinary for a Prophet to need witnesses at all. But Smith's only crutch are his twelve witnesses. He has introduced them and they must be cross-examined. A jury who knew him best, believed him the least. If not to be believed by a jury *on another's case* he ought not to be believed by the world *on his own*. We have seen that he has so contradicted himself that we can not believe him for his own sake; now, can we believe him on the evidence of his friends? The Book of Mormon says, "There shall be three witnesses." These records were to be shown to no more than three. When Moses brought down from the mountain the tables of stone, on which God had written the law, and brake them in pieces before the people, the pieces lay there in the sight of all, a God-marked ruin, symbol of Israel's folly. These plates obtained in secrecy by a drunkard, a liar, and a cheat are to be secretly shown to three persons on whose testimony it is pretended, God will condemn the world. The Book of Mormon says he shall show them to three witnesses, Smith showed them to eleven! Not only the Book of Mormon, but Smith pretends to get a revelation in March, 1829 (Doc. and Cov. p. 172), and makes God to say, "I will give unto these three witnesses power that they may behold and view these things as they are, and to *none else will I give this power* to receive this same testimony among this generation." This is in March, 1829, yet in 1830 he pretends that eight others saw and handled the plates and bore not only the same but a still more explicit testimony. Out of his own mouth does Smith condemn himself and his witnesses.

On page 189, Doctrines and Covenants, Smith pretends that God has said, these three witnesses should see the plates, *and breast-plate, and sword of Laban, Urim, and also the miraculous directors of Lehi.* "You shall testify of *them*, that you have seen *them* with your eyes." Now, in their testimony, prefixed to the Book of Mormon, they assert nothing of the kind. They say that they did see the plates, *but not one of the other things* that God said they should testify about. If they had seen them they would have testified of them; if they had seen the plates they would have seen these *other things* also, according to their pretended God's word; they did not testify of them, therefore, they did not see them.

They did not see these curiosities; either then, they did not see the plates or Smith's god is a false and deceiving god. If they did not see the plates their testimony fails. If they did see the plates, and not these *other things* also, their god fails, and Mormonism falls in either case. It may be urged this promise was contingent on their *faith;* and that may have failed them. Paragraph 3 of the same revelation says, "Wherefore *you have received* the same power and *the same faith*, and the same gift like unto him" (Joseph Smith). They had the faith but yet did not see these things. Paragraph 2 of the same revelation says, "You shall testify you have seen them *even as my servant Joseph has seen them.*" If Smith had seen, they should see; if they saw, they should testify. They did not testify, therefore, they did not see them. They did not see these things, consequently *Joseph Smith never saw them either*, for they were "to see them even as Joseph saw them." This conclusion is inevitable. Smith's witnesses, therefore, only prove him an impostor!

THE TESTIMONY OF THREE WITNESSES.

"Be it known unto all nations, kindreds, tongues, and people unto whom this work shall come, that we, through the grace of God, the Father, and our Lord Jesus Christ, have seen the plates which contain this record, which is a record of the people of Nephi, and also of the Lamanites, their brethren, and also of the people of Jared, who came from the tower of which hath been spoken; and we also know that they have been translated by the gift and power of God, for his voice hath declared it unto us; wherefore we know of a surety that the work is true. And we also testify that we have seen the engravings which are upon the plates; and they have been shown unto us by the power of God, and not of man. And we declare with words of soberness, that an angel of God came down from heaven, and he brought and laid before our eyes, that we beheld and saw the plates, and the engravings thereon; and we know that it is by the grace of God the Father, and our Lord Jesus Christ, that we beheld and bear record that these things are true; and it is marvelous in our eyes, nevertheless the voice of the Lord commanded us that we should bear record of it; wherefore, to be obedient unto the commandments of God, we bear testimony of these things. And we know that if we are faithful in Christ, we shall rid our garments of the blood of all men, and be found spotless before the judgment-seat of Christ, and shall dwell with him eternally in the heavens. And the honor be to the Father, and to the Son, and to the Holy Ghost, which is one God. Amen.

"Oliver Cowdery,
"David Whitmer,
"Martin Harris."

Several sound objections can be urged against this testimony. 1. There is no date nor place. 2. This is not three separate affidavits, "corroborating without collusion," but *one* testimony, signed by three men. 3. Who wrote this statement—which of the three—was it the three conjointly—or *neither of them?* Compare these words with Smith's pretended revelation, Doctrines and Covenants, p. 173, and any one will see the author of the Revelation is the author of the testimony. This testimony is, therefore, drawn up by *Smith himself.* There is necessarily corroboration, but there certainly must have been collusion!

But who are these witnesses? As the salvation of the

world is made to depend on their testimony, it is important we know how much their evidence is worth. O. Cowdery was a school-master, became clerk for Smith to write his translation, in 1829, after Harris had become dissatisfied. He, too, soon grew to desire a stronger evidence of Smith's pretensions; so, in April, 1829, Smith gets a revelation to appease him, saying, "Did I not speak peace to your mind concerning the matter? *What greater witness can you have from a god?* (In passing, it is a singular coincidence that Mohammed used this same argument.) And, behold, I grant unto you a gift, if you desire it of me to translate, even as my servant Joseph;" but not *these plates;* oh! no, but (par. 12), "there are other records kept back; you shall assist in bringing to light those parts of the Scriptures." He begins to write again, but is again disturbed in mind, and another revelation is obtained for him. He tried to exercise "his gift," but *failed*, and Smith puts these words into the mouth of God:

"Be patient, my son, for it is wisdom in me, and it is not expedient that you should translate at this present time. Behold, the work which you are called to do, is to write for my servant Joseph; and, behold, it is because that you did not continue as you commenced, when you began to translate, that I have taken away this privilege from you. Do not murmur, my son, for it is wisdom in me that I have dealt with you after this manner. Behold, you have not understood; you have supposed that I would give it unto you, when you took no thought, save it was to ask me; but, behold, I say unto you, that you must study it out in your mind; then you must ask me if it be right, and if it is right,

I will cause that your bosom shall burn within you; therefore, you shall feel that it is right; but if it be not right, you shall have no such feelings, but you shall have a stupor of thought, that shall cause you to forget the thing which is wrong: therefore, you can not write that which is sacred, save it be given you from me. Now, if you had known this, you could have translated; nevertheless, it is not expedient that you should translate now. Behold, it was expedient when you commenced, but you feared, and the time is past."

Can any man read this wire-working, and charge it on the Being who says, "As far as the east is from the west, so are my ways from men's ways?" Oliver is foiled, and submits. A short time after the organization of the Church, Hiram Smith charges Oliver Cowdery, in print, with going to his house, while he, H. Smith, was in prison, "and ransacking and carrying off all the valuables; compelling my aged father, by threatening to bring a mob over him, to deed over to him about one hundred and sixty acres of land, to pay a note, he said I had given, for $160, which note was a forgery!" Sidney Rigdon, J. Smith's counselor, at Independence, Mo., in 1838, charged Cowdery and David Whitmer, both witnesses, with being "connected with a gang of counterfeiters, thieves, liars, blacklegs of the deepest dye, to deceive and defraud the Saints." Joseph Smith (Times and Seasons, vol. i., pp. 81, 83, 84) charges Cowdery and Whitmer with being "busy in stirring up strife and turmoil among the brethren in 1838 in Missouri;" and that "they were studiously engaged in circulating false and slanderous reports against the Saints," and he demands, "Are they not murderers at heart? Are not their consciences seared with a hot iron?" These vile men were consequently cut off from the Church, being too deeply implicated to deny their testimony, and too thoroughly defamed beforehand for such denial to have weight.

Martin Harris was a rich farmer. Before he became acquainted with Smith, he had been Quaker, Universalist, Restorationist, Baptist, Presbyterian. He was a violent, quarrelsome man, "known to frequently whip and kick his wife, and put her out of doors." (Richard Ford and G. W. Stoddard's affidavits.) Lucy Harris, his wife, affirms that "her shoulders and back were often black and blue in many places;" "once he beat me so severely that marks remained more than two weeks;" "once he struck me over the head several times with the butt-end of a whip three or four feet long." His first acquaintance with Smith was by Smith's "going to him and saying, 'I have a commandment from God to ask the first man I meet to give me $50 to help me to do the Lord's work in translating the Golden Bible.'" Martin believed, contributed, grew intimate, and became scribe. Not satisfied, however, he wished to see the plates; but Smith put him off, giving him a slip of paper, with some of the characters inscribed, and sent him to Professor Anthon of New York, who warned him of being hoaxed. Harris returned dissatisfied, and still wanted to see the plates; and Smith, to give him a quietus, obtained a revelation, March, 1829 (Doc. and Cov., p. 171), and says, par. 2, "Behold, if they will not believe my words, they would not believe you, even if it were possible for you to show them all these things I have committed unto you. Oh! this unbelieving generation, mine anger is kindled against them;" and in par. 5, Harris is commanded to say no more about it, "except he shall say I *have* seen them, and they have been shown me by the *power of God, and not of man.*" Observe, this is March, 1829. The revelation given immediately previous to their seeing the plates was in *June*, 1829; so that here is Smith's pretended God, wanting Harris to testify that *he had* already seen the plates, three months before he pretended to have seen them at all. God wanting Harris to lie!

Harris, however, is not satisfied even with all this spiritual machinery at work around him. He determines to steal 118 pages of translation he had made, hoping that Smith would reproduce it, and by comparing the two to examine how far verbatim were his revelations. Smith is too cunning. He obtains a revelation commanding him not to retranslate, but promising that a better and fuller account of the same matters should be found in the next book; and he then plays off Cowdery against Harris as scribe. The book is finished, the "testimony" is gotten up, his signature extorted the *last* when it ought to have been the *first*, and it goes to the world. But we may, perhaps, be astonished to find, that though Harris's testimony has convinced many thousands who have embraced Mormonism, it did not convince Harris himself, nor deter him from desiring to *commit murder and adultery*. In March, 1830, Smith has to severely rebuke him, and got a revelation commanding him to "repent, and keep the commandments which you have received by the hand of my servant Joseph, in my name; and it is by my almighty power that you received them." "Repent, lest I smite you and your sufferings be sore—how sore, you know not; how exquisite, you know not; yea, how hard to bear, you know not. For behold, I, God, have suffered these things—which suffering caused even God, the greatest of all, to tremble, because of pain and blood at every pore. I command thee not *to covet thy neighbor's wife, nor seek thy neighbor's life.* And again I command thee to impart freely of thy property to the printing of the Book of Mormon. Pay the debt *thou* hast contracted with the printer!" (Doc. and Cov., p. 194.)

In 1837 Smith prints this language about his coadjutor and witness: "There are negroes who have white skins as well as black ones. Granny Parish and others, *who acted as lackeys, such as Martin Harris!* But they are so far beneath my contempt, that to *notice any of them would be too great a sacrifice for a gentleman to make.*" (Elder's Journal, 1837.) This is rather hard, remembering that he had completely ruined Harris. We must, however, believe the prophet, and urge that to notice the testimony of Martin Harris is "*too great a sacrifice for a gentleman to make!*" And yet it is on the testimony of such a man, the Mormons believe and contend, that God will condemn mankind.

Notwithstanding the declaration of the Book of Mormon, or of Smith's pretended revelation of March, 1829, that God would give the testimony to "these three, and to none else," yet Smith felt that their testimony wanted bolstering up, and he has, therefore, added the testimony of eight others. Although by the revelation above, it is evident that the testimony could not have been given by God, and is, therefore, worthless; still it ought to be examined.

"*Testimony of the Eight Witnesses.*

"Be it known unto all nations, kindreds, tongues, and people unto whom this work shall come, that Joseph Smith, jun., the translator of this work, has shown unto us the plates of which hath been spoken, which have the appearance of gold; and as many of the leaves as the said Smith has translated, we did handle with our hands; and we also saw the engravings thereon, all of which has the appearance of ancient work, and of curious workmanship. And this we bear record with words of soberness, that the said Smith has shown unto us, for we have seen and hefted, and know of a surety that the said Smith has got the plates of which we have spoken. And we give our names unto the world, to witness unto the world that which we have seen; and we lie not, God bearing witness of it."

CHRISTIAN WHITMER.	HIRAM PAGE.
JACOB WHITMER.	JOSEPH SMITH, Sen.
PETER WHITMER, Jun.	HIRAM SMITH.
JOHN WHITMER.	SAMUEL H. SMITH.

Observe, there are three Smiths, four Whitmers, and Page, a relation of Cowdery's, who make the above statement. There is no need to investigate their characters. To acknowledge their testimony true, will add no weight to the Mormon cause. But their testimony destroys itself.

First. There is neither date nor place. Second. It is not an affidavit. Third. It is evident that Joseph wrote it himself. Fourth. It contradicts the testimony of the three. It needed an "angel from heaven" to show the plates to the three witnesses who were, it is said, chosen by God; Smith himself showed these things to these eight whom he himself chose. Fifth. The three, although *chosen* by God, saw only with the "eye of faith," saw, but touched not; these, *forbidden* by God, "handled and hefted them." They were so sacred that Smith divided his translating room with a blanket, he sitting on one side, his scribe on the other, to prevent Harris from seeing them; so professedly sacred, that it needed many revelations, the delay of three years, many warnings, menaces, and maledictions, the maintenance of profound secrecy, and the adoption of subterfuges and fanatical paraphernalia, before these three could get a glimpse of them; and now, it is pretended, they were freely handled and loosely *hefted* by these eight men, who had been forbidden by God. These statements differ; one is certainly false, and whichever it is, Smith is an impostor. Sixth. Smith says, that "when the plates were translated, they were given back to the angel." How then could he show them to these eight men? Seventh. Smith pretends to have found one book "bound by three rings passing through the back edge, and a part of them was sealed." These men "handle the leaves," not of the whole, sealed as well as translated, but of *the part* that "Smith had translated." Either he must have broken those sacred rings, or they must have handled the whole. It is to confirm this ringed book their testimony is advanced. But they did not see this ring-bound book, and therefore their testimony is worthless. Eighth. If Smith did show them some plates, which we are willing to believe he did, they could not tell whether they were "the leaves Joseph Smith had translated;" they could not tell that "they were the plates of which have been spoken;" they could not tell whether they were "*as many*" as translated. All *they* had was Smith's *bare word.*

All *we* have is Smith's *bare word* too. But we have already shown that that word, even on oath, would not be believed by a jury of his acquaintances. Unbelievable in trivial matters, how shall we credit him when universal salvation is at stake? Ninth. They were confessedly ignorant men. Their statement of "ancient work and curious workmanship," is the opinion of men who necessarily know nothing about it. For an astronomer to obtain the testimony of an infant school as to the correctness of the "nebular theory," or the undulation of light, and who should require the world to believe it on their testimony, would be just as wise as to require the world to believe the Book of Mormon on the testimony of these men. Who shall charge God with making the salvation of the world depend on the contradictory opinions of these men, as to something of which they are entirely and confessedly ignorant?

V. The testimony of the witnesses must preponderate over conflicting evidence.

The testimony produced against Smith has never been met. Recrimination or silence has been their manner of treating it. The cry of "persecution" has been raised, and they "ran away." Such evidence demands attention and refutation, or it demands belief. Orson Pratt, the ablest Mormon writer, says, "We must prove these men did not see what they pretend, before we can disprove the Book of Mormon." (Authenticity of Book of Mormon.) This is an error. The *onus probandi* rests with the affirmative. It is impossible to prove a negative. Truth is that which *is*. Falsehood is that which *is not*. We can prove truth, or that which *is*, but we can not prove that which *is not.* The affirmative produce their case, and the negative examine it. It is for them to prove that Smith's previous character was good; that his word is to be believed; that his statements were consistent; that they were probable; that they did agree with collateral facts; that there was no collusion; at the same time that there was full harmony among disinterested witnesses of unimpeachable character. Till they do this, the world is not responsible for unbelief. Till they do this, to believe Smith, is a sign of a hastily and easily satisfied mind. They have not done this, therefore men should not believe.

Still they are not without an argument. They rely greatly on their prophetic proof. They try to show that God was to reveal himself to Ephraim; quote the promises made to that tribe; refer to Ezekiel, xxxvii. 15, 28, inferring thence that the stick of Judah is a book, the Bible; that the stick of Ephraim is also a book, the Book of Mormon. To establish the identity of the Book of Mormon with this book or stick, is now the grand difficulty. They use Isaiah, xxix., and attempt to wrest it to mean the coming forth of the Book of Mormon from the ground; the inability of Professor Anthon to decipher the characters, etc., etc. This is their tower of strength,

> "Which if to totter, is their all to fall."

"And the Lord rejected all the seed of Israel, and afflicted them, and delivered them into the hands of the spoilers, until he had *cast them out of his sight.* Therefore the Lord was very angry with Israel, and removed them out of his sight: there was none left, but the tribe of Judah only" (2 Kings, xvii. 18, 20). God says he rejected them, and cast them out of his sight. Smith says he led them to America, and blessed them "above the house of Judah." Which is right? It is a question between God and Joseph Smith. To believe the one, is to reject the other.

Admitting that Ephraim was to be blest, as pretended, it does not help the Book of Mormon. There was not a single Ephraimite on the continent of America, according to their book itself. The Nephites were descendants of Manasseh (Book of Mormon, p. 235). The people of Zarahemla were *Jews*, and were of the "seed of Zedekiah" (Book of Mormon, p. 411). These not being Ephraimites, their record can not be the "stick or records of Ephraim." The Mormon prophetic argument falls to the ground, therefore, because Ephraim's promises do not refer to others. Again, Ezekiel says, "Write, for Joseph the stick of Ephrain and for all the house of Israel, *his companions*." Wherever Ephraim is, all the house of Israel are there also. Not an isolated family, as Smith pretends, separated by thousands of miles of sea and land, but with Israel, *his companions*. If the papyrus roll of the Bible be properly symbolized by a stick, a stick can not mean a book of gold plates. We find, then,

I. Statements must agree with themselves.

Smith has over and over again contradicted himself, and must, therefore, be rejected.

II. Statements must agree with known principles.

Smith has transcended all probability, and must, therefore, be rejected.

III. Statements must agree with collateral facts.

Smith's character, both previously and at the time, was notoriously bad, and, therefore, must be rejected.

IV. Disinterested and unimpeachable witnesses must, without collusion and preconcert, confirm each other's statement.

There was preconcert and collusion among Smith's witnesses; they were all deeply interested; they were men of such bad character that the Mormons themselves accused and criminated, and finally cut them off; and their testimony is contradictory. Therefore Smith must be rejected.

V. Their evidence must preponderate over all conflicting testimony.

So far from this, their testimony destroys itself, and, therefore, Smith must be rejected.

As Joseph Smith is the founder of Mormonism, and as, consequently, the truth of Mormonism depends entirely on the pretensions of Smith, so, therefore, all should reject Mormonism.

CHAPTER XI.

REAL ORIGIN OF THE BOOK OF MORMON.

Credibility of testimony—Money-digging in New York—Chase's peep-stone—Smith's mode of translating—Page's stone—Smith's plates—Wiley's plates—Cupidity of Smith's family — Smith's object—W. Harris's inducement—O. Cowdery's inducement—Origin of name—Origin of matter—Spalding's relations testify—Smith's means of obtaining MS. of Spalding—Incidents of Book of Mormon—Religious decisions—Religious style—Grammatical construction—The Bible.

The Book of Mormon is not what it pretends to be, a revelation from God; then, what is it? What is its real origin? Is Smith the author, or had he assistance? If he had accomplices, who were they, and what were the inducements held out to them? What was their object? Were they victims to his deceit or accessories to his fraud? These become not only interesting but important questions. To these questions a reply is attempted in this chapter.

It is very difficult to detect, in ordinary cases, evidences of fraud. Unless by the exposure by an accomplice, it is necessary to make a minute investigation of the circumstances of the case, remembering the third law of evidence, "Things must agree with collateral facts."

The apologists for the Book of Mormon boldly demand "What object could Joseph Smith and these witnesses have had if the transaction be a fraud?" There are three motives that induce deceit—the desire for wealth, reputation, and power. The whole of these actuated Smith; the first of these induced the witnesses. This will be clearly established.

It is important here, however, to determine what testimony is credible on this subject? The Mormons ever brand as "liar and perjurer" any who oppose and testify against them. They require us to believe Smith on testimony that no jury would receive. We require them to disbelieve Smith, on testimony any jury would credit; the testimony of disinterested witnesses well cognizant of the facts, corroborating each other's statements without collusion, which are also confirmed by circumstances known, and which would compel the assent of any unprejudiced examiner.

It was quite common in the western part of New York, about thirty years ago, for men to dig for treasure which they supposed had been hidden by Captain Kidd and others. Many plans were tried and much imposition practiced by means of divining-rods, dreams, and seeing-stones. It was not at all a new thing for Smith, therefore, to pretend to the power of seeing where gold was by the use of a "peep-stone," nor did it surprise the inhabitants of that locality.

Willard Chase, before Judge King, Wayne county, N. Y., swears that, in 1822, as Joseph Smith (then seventeen years old) and himself were digging a well, he found a curious white stone, about twenty feet from the surface. "Joseph Smith put it into his hat, asserting that by putting his face to the top of it, he could see in the stone." The next day Smith borrowed the stone, which Chase reluctlantly lent. Smith soon began to publish what wonderful things he could see in it. Chase ordered its return. In 1825, Smith borrowed it again, alleging he wanted it for an important purpose and promised its immediate return. In the fall of 1826, Chase sent for it, when Smith refused to restore it; Chase insisted on its restoration, Smith persisted in his refusal. In 1827, Chase swears, "Smith told me of having found his Golden Bible, and he said, 'If it had not been for that stone of yours (acknowledging it to be mine), I could not have obtained the book.' He then wished me to make him a chest to put his book into, but I refused." In 1830, Chase again demanded the stone of Hiram Smith, Joseph's brother, in the presence of Martin Harris. "Hiram replied that I could not have it, for *Joseph used it in translating the new bible.*" "I represented to him that the stone was mine and that I must have it; when Martin Harris flew into a rage, called me a liar, and took me by the collar. Hiram joined in the scuffle, shaking his fists at me and abusing me in the most scandalous manner." Chase could never afterward obtain that stone.

The testimony of Willard Chase is confirmed by Isaac Hale, Smith's father-in-law, who affirms "I first became acquainted with Joseph Smith in November, 1825. He was then in the employ of a set of men who were called 'money-diggers,' and his occupation was that of seeing, or pretending to see, by means of a stone placed in his hat and his hat placed over his face. In this way he pretended to discover minerals and hidden treasures. The manner in which he pretended to read and interpret his plates was the same as when he looked for 'money-diggers,' with the stone in his hat, and his hat over his face, while the book of plates was at

JOS SMITH, Jr.

the same time hidden away." Peculiar importance attaches itself to the testimony of Isaac Hale, from the fact of some of the "translation" being done at his house, till he became disgusted with their knavery and turned them all out of doors; and that Smith was still cheating in 1825; *two years* after pretending to have had his vision.

In this stone of W. Chase, was the real origin of Smith's Urim and Thummim. The ancient Urim and Thummim was in Aaron's breast-plate, "on his heart." Ex., xxviii. 30. Smith, however, fixed his into golden rims, and put them on his eyes. "Each was so large," says Martin Harris, "that a man could look, with both eyes, through one stone."

Nor was Smith's the only stone among his believers. In September, 1830, Smith had to get a revelation, commanding Cowdery to "take his brother, Hiram Page (one of the eight witnesses to the Book of Mormon) between him and thee alone, and tell him that those things which he hath written from *that stone* are not of me, and that Satan deceiveth him." (Doc. and Cov., p. 203.) While Page conceived he had an equal right to obtain revelations through his stone, Joseph could endure no rival to his pretensions. His only means of power was by keeping himself the sole revealer of God's will and word. To share with another the raft that was bearing him on, was to sink himself. It was a contest between Joseph Smith and Page. Page was the weakest, and he went down.

Here, then, is the origin of the Urim and Thummim idea; what suggested that of the golden plates? It is a fact that Smith did copy some characters on to a slip of paper, which he sent by Martin Harris to Professor Anthon. It is also a fact, that the description of the characters made by the Professor, does somewhat resemble the description of the glyphs of Otolum, made subsequently by Professor Rafinesque (Atlantic Journal, 1832, Professor Rafinesque). Of this similarity O. Pratt makes great capital as a proof of the Book of Mormon. I admit the resemblance. It is also a fact that eight men testified that Smith had shown them several plates curiously engraved; that they "did handle and heft them;" and that they knew Smith had them. Although, as before shown, these plates could not have been the pretended golden Bible, yet I think there can be no doubt that these men told the truth as to seeing and handling certain plates, and that Smith had them. Unless Smith had got something, he could never have originated the idea of the book; could not have copied the characters sent to Professor Anthon by Martin Harris; still more, those characters could not have happened to resemble engravings subsequently found; and as these eight do not pretend, as do the three, to have seen them with all the ridiculous concomitants of the eye of faith and coming of angels, it is reasonable to believe that Smith really possessed some plates. If their testimony be credible, it proves that he not only had them, but that he kept them, and not delivered them "up to the angel," as he elsewhere pretends. To possess the plates is one thing, to have received them from God is quite another. To admit that he had them does not admit the truth of the Book of Mormon.

"How did he get them?"

"On the 16th of April, 1843, a respectable merchant, by the name of Robert Wiley, commenced digging in a large mound near this place. He excavated to the depth of ten feet, and came to rock. On the 23d, he and quite a number of the citizens, with myself, repaired to the mound, and after making ample opening, we found plenty of rock, the most of which appeared as though it had been strongly burned; and after removing full two feet of said rock, we found plenty of charcoal and ashes; also human bones, that appeared as though they had been burned; and near the eciphalon a bundle was found, that consisted of SIX PLATES OF BRASS, of a bell-shape, each having a hole near the small end, and a ring through them all, and clasped with two clasps. The ring and clasps appeared to be iron, very much oxydated: the plates first appeared to be copper, and had the appearance of being covered with characters. It was agreed by the company that I should cleanse the plates. Accordingly, I took them to my house, washed them with soap and water, and a woolen cloth; but, finding them not yet cleansed, I treated them with dilute sulphuric acid, which made them perfectly clean, on which it appeared that they were completely covered with characters, that none, as yet, have been able to read. They were found, I judge, more than twelve feet below the surface of the top of the mound.

"I am, most respectfully, a citizen of Kinderhook,

"W. P. HARRIS, M. D."

The following certificate was forwarded for publication at the same time:

"We, citizens of Kinderhook, whose names are annexed, do certify and declare, that on the 23d of April, 1843, while excavating a large mound in this vicinity, Mr. R. Wiley took from said mound *six brass plates*, of a bell-shape, covered with ancient characters. Said plates were very much oxydated. The bands and rings on said plates moldered into dust on a slight pressure."

ROBERT WILEY,	J. R. SHARP,
GEORGE DECKENSON,	IRA S. CURTIS,
W. LONGNECKER,	FAYETTE GRUBB,
G. W. F. WARD,	W. P. HARRIS,

W. FUGATE.

The characters on these plates also resemble Professor Anthon's description: "The characters were arranged in columns like the Chinese mode of writing, and presented the most singular medley I ever saw. Greek, Hebrew, and all sorts of letters, more or less distorted, were intermingled, with sundry delineations of half moons, stars and other natural objects, and the whole ended in a rude representation of the Mexican Zodiac." (Professor Anthon's letter.) Professor Rafinesque describes the glyphs of Otolum, Mexico, as being "written from top to bottom like the Chinese." "The most common way of writing is in rows, and each group separated." (Atlantic Journal for 1832.) This similarity between the characters on Wiley's plates and Professor Rafinesque's description, does not prove that Wiley got his plates from an angel. However much the characters on Smith's plates may have resembled either of the above, it does not any the more prove that Smith got his plates from an angel either. Wiley found his plates while digging for water. It would be just as natural for Smith to have found his plates while digging for gold! To prove the resemblance only proves the possession, and not the means of obtaining possession. We have before shown that any impartial person must disclaim all idea of Smith getting his book as he pretends. Every careful reader must be compelled to admit that Smith did have some plates of some kind. Smith's antecedents and subsequents, show that he did not have genius sufficient to originate the whole conception, without some palpable suggestion. The having chanced to have found some plates in a mound, as Wiley found his, or as Chase discovered Smith's "peep-stone," would be just such an event as would suggest every particular statement Smith made about his plates, at the same time account for what is known; and, therefore, it is more than reasonable to conclude that Smith found his plates while digging gold. This entirely destroys all the shadow of argument so laboriously compiled by the Mormon apologists, which, even without this, although their strongest argument, only proves that he had some plates, but at the same time has no force of proof as to Smith's obtaining them from an angel.

It is certain that Smith began to feel his friends on the subject of this Golden Bible for some time before he pretended to possess it. Peter Ingersol testifies on oath that "J. Smith, sen., told me a book had been found in a hollow tree in Canada, giving an account of the settlement of this country before its discovery by Columbus." The views excited by Smith among his family were, that they should grow wealthy by this Gold Bible discovery. Abigail Harris, on the 28th November, 1833, testified:

"In the early part of the winter in 1828 I made a visit to Martin Harris, and was joined in company by Joseph Smith, sen., and his wife. The Gold Bible business, so called, was the topic of conversation, to which I paid particular attention, that I might learn the truth of the whole matter. They told me that the report that Joseph Smith, jr., had found the Golden Plates was true, and that he was in Harmony, Pa., translating them. The old lady said, also, that after the Book was translated, the Plates were to be publicly exhibited —admittance, twenty-five cents. She calculated it would bring in annually an enormous sum of money—that money would then be very plenty, and the Book would sell for a great price, as it was something entirely new; that they had been commanded to obtain all the money they could borrow for present necessity, and repay with gold. The remainder was to be kept in store for the benefit of their family and children. The old lady took me into another room, and after closing the door, she said, 'Have you four or five dollars in money that you can lend until our business is brought to a close? The Spirit says you shall receive four-fold!' I told her when I gave, I did not expect to receive it again, and as for money, I had none to lend. In the second month following, Martin Harris, and Lucy, his wife, were at my house. In conversation about the Mormonites, she observed that she wished her husband would quit them, as she believed it was all false and a delusion. To which I heard Mr. Harris reply, '*What if it is a lie; if you will let me alone, I will make money out of it!*' I was both an eye and ear witness of what has been above stated, which is now fresh in my memory, and I speak the truth and lie not, God being my witness."

This lady was a member of the Society of Friends, and was widely known, and universally esteemed.

Joseph Capron testifies that "Joseph Smith, jun., at length pretended to find his Plates. This scheme, he believed, would relieve his family from all pecuniary embarrassment. His father told me that when the book was published, they would be enabled, from the profits of the work, to carry into successful operation the money-digging business. He gave me no intimation at that time, that the book was to be of a religious character, or that it had any thing to do with revelation. He declared it to be a speculation, and said, 'When it is completed, my family will be placed *on a level above* the generality of mankind!'"

The Book of Mormon, p. 510, says, "No one shall have the Plates to get gain." Did Smith make nothing by his imposture? Mohammed was rich, and became poor; was respected, and became despised; was elevated to positions of authority and influence, and had to flee for his life; but Smith was miserably poor, universally despised and hopelessly degraded, and his imposture opened before him prospective wealth, influence, and power. In 1843 he owned mansions at Nauvoo; he had given revelations commanding the faithful to support him; and although he was proverbially the best wrestler in the county, he pretended that the Lord said, "My servant Joseph shall not have strength to work!" and, therefore, compelled the "Church" to sustain him. Smith had inveigled Harris into paying the printer, and the profits of the Book of Mormon came to him, who called himself on the title-page of the first edition, "Author and Proprietor." He was the Mayor of the city and General of the Legion. Who will say that this "money-digging youth, living by his wits," had made nothing by his imposture? Who can not but perceive abundance of motive for attempting it? Who can not but be convinced that it was imposture he attempted?

What inducements could this poor boy hold out to Martin Harris and the others to obtain his connivance? The testimony of Abigail Harris (his own sister!) can not be impeached nor misunderstood. Lucy Harris (his wife!) confirms this statement in every respect. In her affidavit she affirms:

"Whether the Mormon religion be true or false, I leave the world to judge; for its effects on Martin Harris have been to make him more cross, turbulent, and abusive to me. *His whole object was to make money out of it.* I will give a proof of this. One day at Peter Harris's (Abigail Harris's husband) house, I told him he had better leave the company of the Smiths, as their religion was false. To this he replied, '*If you would let me alone, I could make money out of it.*' It is in vain for the Mormons to deny these facts, as they are well known to most of his former neighbors."

Testimony so positive and direct must be received, especially coming from his sister and wife.

The inducement held out to Oliver Cowdery is evident from Smith's own revelation. (Doc. and Cov., p. 108.) "Seek not for treasures but for wisdom; and, behold, the mysteries of God shall be unfolded to you; and *then* you shall be made *rich*." This was in April, 1829, just after Cowdery began to write for Smith; and *even then* it is necessary to rebuke him for his too impetuous desires to be *rich*.

The real origin of the Urim and Thummim; of the form of the record, its material, and copying of some of the characters; Smith's object and inducements to his coadjutors is evident. Now, how account for the *matter?* "There are over five hundred different names, many incidents, and much doctrinal information. How could an ignorant boy compile such a work?" First. Its name. The only language in which the word is found is Greek. Μόρμω, Μόρμος, a bugbear. (*Vide* Donnegan's Lex.) Smith, however, finds for it the following singular etymology:

"Before I give a definition, however, to the word, let me say, that the Bible, in its widest sense, means *good;* for the Saviour says, according to the gospel of John, 'I am the Good Shepherd;' and it will not be beyond the common use of terms to say that GOOD is among the most important in use, and though known by various names in different languages, still the meaning is the same, and is ever in opposition to *bad*. We say from the Saxon, *good;* the Dane, *god;*

the Goth, *goda;* the German, *gut;* the Dutch, *goed;* the Latin, *bonus;* the Greek, *kalos;* the Hebrew, *tob;* and the Egyptian, *mon.* Hence, with the addition of *more*, or the contraction *mor*, we have the word MORMON, which means literally more good. Yours,

"JOSEPH SMITH.

"NAUVOO, *May* 19, 1841."

We remark on this: First. For "an ignorant man" it is a ridiculous affectation of pedantry. Second. As it is the "reformed Egyptian that no man knoweth," we have only Smith's word for it. Third. It is singular that the "reformed Egyptian that no man knoweth," should have the *Saxon* word "more" for a prefix, especially in the Anglicized contracted form of "mor." And Fourth. That though perfectly consonant with an ignorant impostor, the above would be perfectly absurd from an inspired prophet.

Second. Its matter.

John Spalding, brother to Solomon Spalding of Crawford, Penn., testifies that

"Solomon Spalding was born in Ashford, Conn., in 1761, and in early life contracted a taste for literary pursuits. After he left school, he entered Plainfield academy, where he made great proficiency in study, and excelled most of his class-mates. He soon after entered Dartmouth college, with the intention of qualifying himself for the ministry, where he obtained the degree of A. M., and was afterward regularly ordained. After preaching three or four years, he gave it up, removed to Cherry Valley, New York, and commenced the mercantile business, in company with his brother, Josiah. I made him a visit in about three years after, and found that he had failed, and was considerably involved in debt. He then told me he had been writing a book, which he intended to have printed, the avails of which he thought would enable him to pay all his debts. The book was entitled, the 'Manuscript Found,' of which he read to me many passages. It was a historical romance of the first settlers of America—endeavoring to show that the American Indians are the descendants of the Jews, or the lost tribes. It gave a detailed account of their journey from Jerusalem, by land and sea, till they arrived in America, under the command of NEPHI and LEHI. They afterward had quarrels and contentions, and separated into two distinct nations, one of which he denominated Nephites, and the other Lamanites. Cruel and bloody wars ensued, in which great multitudes were slain. They buried their dead in large heaps, which caused the mounds so common in this country. Their arts, sciences, and civilization were brought into view, in order to account for all the curious antiquities found in various parts of North and South America. I have recently read the Book of Mormon, and, to my great surprise, I found nearly the same historical matter, names, etc., as they were in my brother's writings. I well remember that he wrote in the old style, and commenced about every sentence with, 'And it came to pass,' or, 'Now, it came to pass,' the same as in the Book of Mormon, and, according to the best of my recollection and belief, it is the same as my brother Solomon wrote, with the exception of the religious matter. By what means it has fallen into the hands of Joseph Smith, jun., I am unable to determine.

"JOHN SPALDING."

Martha Spalding, the wife of John Spalding, says:

"I was personally acquainted with Solomon Spalding, about twenty years ago. I was at his house a short time before he left Conneaut; he was then writing a historical novel, founded upon the first settlers of America. He represented them as an enlightened and warlike people. He had for many years contended that the aborigines of America were the descendants of some of the lost tribes of Israel, and this idea he carried out in the book in question. The lapse of time which has intervened prevents my recollecting but few of the leading incidents of his writings; but the names of Nephi and Lehi are yet fresh in my memory, as being the principal heroes of his tale. They were officers of the company which first came off from Jerusalem. He gave a particular account of their journey by land and sea, till they arrived in America, after which disputes arose between the chiefs, which caused them to separate into different lands, one of which was called Lamanites, and the other Nephites. Between these were recounted tremendous battles, which frequently covered the ground with slain; and their being buried in large heaps was the cause of the numerous mounds in the country. Some of these people he represented as being very large. I have read the Book of Mormon, which has brought fresh to my recollection the writings of Solomon Spalding; and I have no manner of doubt that the historical part of it is the same that I read and heard read more than twenty years ago. The old obsolete style, and phrases of, 'And it came to pass,' etc., are the same. Signed,

"MARTHA SPALDING."

This Solomon Spalding appears to have been, like some other authors, exceedingly vain of his productions; and read his manuscripts so often to his friends that they still recollect its style and harsh names.

"CONNEAUT, Ashtabula Co., Ohio, Sept., 1833.

"I left the State of New York, late in the year 1810, and arrived at this place about the 1st of January following.

Soon after my arrival I formed a partnership with Solomon Spalding, for the purpose of rebuilding a forge which he had commenced a year or two before. He very frequently read to me from a manuscript which he was writing, which he en-entitled the 'Manuscript Found,' and which he represented as being found in this town. I spent many hours in hearing him read said writings, and became well acquainted with their contents. He wished me to assist him in getting his production printed, alleging that a book of that kind would meet with a rapid sale. I designed doing so, but the forge not meeting our anticipations, we failed in business, when I declined having any thing to do with the publication of the book. This book represented the American Indians as the descendants of the lost tribes—gave an account of their leaving Jerusalem, their contentions and wars, which were many and great. One time, when he was reading to me the tragic account of Laban, I pointed out to him what I considered an inconsistency, which he promised to correct; but by referring to the Book of Mormon, I find, to my surprise, that it stands there just as he read it to me then. Some months ago I borrowed the Golden Bible, put it into my pocket, carried it home, and thought no more of it. About a week after, my wife found the book in my coat pocket, as it hung up, and commenced reading it aloud as I lay upon the bed. She had not read twenty minutes till I was astonished to find the same passages in it that Spalding had read to me more than twenty years before, from his 'Manuscript Found.' Since that I have more fully examined the said Golden Bible, and have no hesitation in saying, that the historical part of it is principally, if not wholly, taken from the 'Manuscript Found.' I well recollect telling Mr. Spalding, that the so frequent use of the words, 'And it came to pass,' 'Now it came to pass,' rendered it ridiculous. Spalding left here in 1812, and I furnished him the means to carry him to Pittsburg, where he said he would get the book printed, and pay me. But I never heard any more from him or his writings, till I saw them in the Book of Mormon.

"HENRY LAKE."

These affirmations are abundantly confirmed by similar affidavits by John N. Miller, Aaron Wright, Oliver Smith, Nahum Howard, Artemas Cunningham, and many others, all well acquainted with Spalding, and most of them entirely unacquainted with Smith.

Whatever the cause, it is evident that the leading ideas of the two works are identical. If Smith tells *the truth*, it is still evident that Spalding imagined a novel containing the truths that it "needed God to reveal," *long before God revealed it;* so that, if Smith be believed, it makes a novelist *as wise as the angel.* It is absurd, however, to say this; such a resemblance without plagiarism would be a greater miracle than all the rest. Either Smith plagiarized Spalding's work or Spalding, Smith's. Spalding died before Smith wrote, therefore Smith must have plagiarized Spalding's novel.

But how did Smith obtain Spalding's book?

Spalding wrote this MS. during the years 1810, 11, 12, in Ohio. In 1812, he left Ohio for Pittsburg, where he resided two years, and went thence to Amity, Pa., and died in 1816. After his death Mrs. Spalding, widow, went to reside at Onondaga county, N. Y., remained there till 1818, when she removed to Hartwick, Oswego county, N. Y., where she resided till 1832. Mrs. Spalding, widow, says, that she believes the MS. was put into a trunk with some others, and that she had it at Hartwick, from 1820 to 1832.

In 1825 Smith, by his own statement, was employed by a man named Stowell, to dig for him. Stowell's residence was close to Hartwick, where this trunk was. After the publication and recognition of the Book of Mormon, this trunk was examined and only *one* manuscript was found. The other papers that had been in the trunk were gone. This MS., that was then found, was the commencement of a novel on the subject of the Indians, purporting to bring their forefathers from a colony of Latins. Spalding, after writing a few pages, had abandoned this idea as being too recent; and had commenced his *other* MS., which was then missing. This real MS. of Spalding's has never since been found. Where was it? Who had taken it? Mrs. Spalding declares that this trunk was full of Mr. S.'s papers, and among them, she believes, this now missing MS. The trunk is emptied of all but one paper. Shortly before she missed them, a book is published, which every one recongizes as a plagiarism from this identical MS. Smith, the author of this plagiarism, is proven to have been in the vicinity about the same time that he began to talk about having found "this book." What is the inevitable conclusion? It was there in the trunk; he was there to take it out of the trunk; he publishes a book, and every body recognizes the plagiarism; the trunk is searched, and it is not found. The case is clear. Smith stole the MS., altered and used it. But it had been altered; there were many things in it that Spalding would never have written. Smith was from 1825 to 1827 "obtaining instruction," as he calls it. He was a year less in altering and extending it, than Spalding was in writing it! The objection is urged that "Smith was too ignorant to adapt and alter this novel. Spalding described an idolatrous, Smith a religious people."

These adaptations and additions are the very strongest evidences of imposture. The religious incidents are copied from the Bible, and from the best-known events of history subsequent to the Christian era. Book of Mormon, p. 235, contains an imitation of Daniel reading the writing on the wall: pp. 23, 28, quote the Apocalypse, and talk of "the Church of Rome:" p. 24 tells of the American Revolution: pp. 179, 184, 249, 280 are borrowed from the history of Nero, Caligula, and Fox's Book of Martyrs; p. 201 has an imitation of Paul's miraculous conversion; with this difference, Paul was struck blind for three days, and Alma was struck dumb for three days; p. 207 teaches the modern doctrine *vox populi; vox Dei;* pp. 232, 251, contain a copy of Peter's miraculous escape from prison. Ananias lying to the Lord, imitated on p. 241. All the spiritual gifts enjoyed hundreds of years B. C., on p. 234. Repetition of Moses watering Jethro's flock, on p. 258. The fall-down Spirit of modern camp meetings anticipated, on pp. 263, 272. Preaching from pulpits, introduced on p. 296. A prophet of God introducing "*scalping*," on p. 330. Shadrach's deliverance from the furnace, repeated on p. 401. Elijah's rain and drought miracle plagiarized, on p. 417. Imitations of Daniel in lion's den, on pp. 489, 495. Raising of the dead, p. 449. "Candles" invented, on p. 451. Animal magnetic *shocks* anticipated, on p. 41.

The above quotations speak for themselves as to the sources

whence Smith derived his incidents. The Mormons not only contend for incidents, but "imporant decisions on points of religious controversy." He determines none of the *great questions* pending in the world at large, but only the minor difficulties that would have been likely to have reached a western village. He was "awakened at the age of thirteen" by Mr. Lane, an earnest Methodist minister. His proclivities are decidedly Methodist therefore, and consequently "free grace" abounds in the Book of Mormon. The Campbellites convince him of "adult baptism for remission of sin," hence this dogma is propounded and administered *in the name of Christ, four hundred years before he came.* Infant baptism he ferociously attacks. On p. 567 he says, "Behold, I say unto you, that he who supposeth little children need baptism, is in the *gall of bitterness and bonds of iniquity* (plagiarism), for he hath neither *faith, hope, nor charity* (plagiarism), wherefore, should he be cut off in the thought, he must go down to hell!" Universalism affects his sympathies, and he teaches "different amounts of punishment as well in duration as in degree." Roman apostolic succession pleases him, and he gets ordained. "Total depravity" is disputed, Smith decides in the negative, with a wire-drawn distinction between kinds of sin. Calvinism repels him, and he opposes it. Christ's atonement does not satisfy him, and he runs into Pelagianism, yet he makes Christ's blood "cleanse swords and cimeters" a hundred years before it was shed, B. M., p. 285.

This is a fair sample of Smith's controversial decisions. His theses do not commend him or his work.

Specimens of his religious style of expression prove their

nineteenth century origin. "The cold and silent grave, whence no traveler returns," on page 55. Shakspeare quoted 2,200 years before Hamlet was written! "Final state of our souls;" "arms of mercy extended;" "pour out their hearts in prayer;" "awakened to a sense of their condition;" "live without God in this world;" "from nature up to nature's God;" "oh! blessed Jesus, who saved me from an awful hell" (400 years before he came); "sing redeeming love and grace" (400 B. C.); "vital parts of body" (2,000 years before Hervey's discovery); "satisfy demands of justice and encircle them with the arms of mercy."

Examples of grammatical structure plead loudly for his claims to inspiration. "More history part," p. 16. "Shepherd hath called and *art* calling," p. 223. "Nevertheless *they* did not remain *an* entire peace," p. 400. "Stabbed by a garb of secrecy," p. 412. "They yieldeth." "They buried their *weapons of peace*," p. 278. "No afflictions save swallowed up in joy," p. 298. "I, the Lord, delighteth in the chastity of women," p. 118. "Harrow in my desires, the firm decrees of a just God," p. 288. These are in the *third European edition!* Hundreds of graver errors were expunged in the course of the six editions that preceded this.

Any candid reader must feel that such incidents so glaringly plagiarized from the Bible and school-books, such decisions on points of religious controversy, such cant phrases, and such a style of composition is unworthy of God; that, indeed, to associate the name of God with ideas so gross and ridiculous, is an outrage against his wisdom and glory; and, therefore, can not but conclude that Smith's pretensions are imposture.

There is no new truth to be learned from the Book of Mormon. Destroy the Bible, and two thirds of the world's literature is destroyed; for, however controverted and disobeyed, it has molded ages and toned all thought. Take away this book, and its loss would be unknown. Some deny the *authenticity* of the Bible; but no lover of gorgeous poetry, sublime description, profound reason, massive simplicity, and melting tenderness; no admirer of historical antiquity, legislative polity, unity of design yet variety of authors, has ever failed to applaud the Scriptures. Independently of its claims as a revelation, but viewed in the light of its merits as even a human work, it is an ornament to its nation, a monument of literature, a text-book for the world, and deserves its high title, "Bible," *the* book above all books. The heart sickens as we turn to the Book of Mormon. Not because it is not clothed with the veneration of centuries, but its indistinctness of narration, its universal plagiarism, its glaring solecisms and anachronisms, its direct contradictions, and its mouthing cant disgust while they bewilder the reader. To attribute to God a work that would disgrace a literary man, is to degrade God below that man's level.

CHAPTER XII.

THEORETICAL POLYGAMY.

Position—Anti-scriptural—Adam—Noah—Lamech—Abraham—Jacob—David—Book of Mormon denounces David—Christ—Paul—Christian dispensation—Anti-natural—Proportions of the sexes—Nature confirms Scriptures—Irrational—Woman's position the test of progress—Children's dependence on the mother—Wife—Races—Different laws of marriage—Single prophets—Lowest races most prolific—"Polygamy a preventive of prostitution" examined—Anti-Mormon—Revelation—Utah census.

PRACTICAL polygamy results in many evils wherever it exists. As we can only well judge causes by effects, we must conclude it to be practically erroneous. It then becomes an important query, Can a principle be practically false, and yet remain theoretically true? It is certain, say its apologists, that polygamy was practiced, and woman degraded, in the Hebrew nation; it is not evident that God blamed the practice or punished its adopters therefor. Were it so heinous an offense, it is probable that he would have expressed his disapprobation; and, as the Scriptures are silent, we must conclude he favored and intended it. This is all their real argument when stated in brief. It needs but the slightest smattering of logical acumen to discern the sophistry of the whole; as it is merely the *argumentum ex silentio*, which is the weakest of all proof.

As this dogma is made a strong-hold of faith, with these deluded people, a brief investigation of its evidences may perhaps be useful and interesting:

I affirm, I.—Polygamy is anti-scriptural.
II.—Polygamy is anti-natural.
III.—Polygamy is irrational.
IV.—Polygamy is anti-Mormon.

I. Polygamy is anti-scriptural.

1. In investigating this position, it is necessary to view the whole of the Scriptures, neither limiting ourselves to the ante-Abrahamic nor the ante-Christian periods. God's dealings are to be viewed as a whole. In the beginning Adam was created pure and holy, and God bestowed on him *one wife.* If polygamy had been the Lord's way of "*peopling the earth,*" then, of all other times, polygamy would have been instituted. Why was it not? Malachi, ii. 15, tells us the reason: "And did he not make *one?* Yet had he the residue of the Spirit. And wherefore one? *That he might seek a godly seed.* Therefore, take heed to your spirit, and let none deal treacherously with *the wife* of his youth." God had the residue of the Spirit; had it pleased omniscient wisdom to have created more, omnipotent power would have performed it. He did not do so, "because he sought a godly seed." The only inference that can be deduced from this passage, is, that as the seed of monogamy is godly, because of the monogamy, then the seed of polygamy must be ungodly. History, sacred and profane, will sustain this position. Polygamy produced men like Ishmael, whose first greeting was a curse, "His hand shall be against every man, and every man's

hand against him;" brothers, like Joseph's brothers, selling him to slavery, and dooming him to death; women, like Rebekah, cheating her husband on his death-bed; wives, like Leah and Rachel, contending disgustingly together about Jacob's bed; sons, like Reuben, committing incest with his father's concubine; or, like Amnon, defiling his sister Tamar; or, like Absolom, threatening his father's life; or, in later times, like the Chinese, the Turk, and the savage; or the neglected children of Mormon parentage. God sought a godly seed, and *monogamy* was the means he instituted.

2. When Adam and Eve were formed, and God rested from the work of creation, he gazed at the labor of his hands, and pronounced it "very good." The fiat of universal approbation went forth. Monogamy was then instituted and practiced, and that was "very good." To seek to amend that monogamy by polygamy, is for man to attempt to improve the God-approved institution of divine appointment. Until Jehovah just as explicitly declares *polygamy* to be "very good," we have no right to charge it on his wisdom or design. Two things essentially opposite can not be both true at the same time. Monogamy was "very good;" polygamy must, therefore, be "very bad."

3. When the Lord destroyed the inhabitants of the earth, because of their wickedness, he saved Noah and his three sons, and only *one wife* each. Peter says, "eight persons were saved in the ark." Any argument as to "more rapid increase of population," will certainly apply to Noah. Any argument as to polygamy "being a peculiar blessing," will apply to Noah too; for, while holy enough to be saved from

the flood, he was far more holy than many subsequent polygamists. But God destroyed the inhabitants of the earth, because they were ungodly and corrupt. He saved Noah and his family in order to repeople the world with upright and holy descendants. To obtain this end a second time, he a second time instituted monogamy. Had he selected a polygamist, he would have contradicted his prior sanction and institution of monogamy. To produce the same *result*, he adopted the same *cause*. "Therefore gave he *one*, *because he sought a godly seed*."

4. God sought a godly seed by means of monogamy. Was it a godly man who first infringed this law of purity? Gen. iv. 19, 23. Lamech had two wives, Adah and Zillah. But we learn from ver. 23, that Lamech was a murderer. The Mormons believe that the "mark" put on Cain by God was a black skin; that he and his descendants, the negroes, are peculiarly and especially cursed; that in fact they can not be saved in the "celestial kingdom." They also contend that a murderer can not be saved "in this life, nor in that which is to come." Lamech, this twice-cursed man; cursed in being a black descendant of Cain, doubly cursed, according to their own faith, in being a murderer, was the first example of polygamy. In adopting the principle, they have accepted a murderer as their model.

4. The Mormons make much capital of Abraham being a polygamist. One important fact must be observed here. There is a great difference between *example* and *precept*. To adopt any practice, because a certain good man did so, is often folly. Christ is a model in all things, because "in him

there was no sin." Before even prophets and patriarchs can be imitated as models, they must be proven infallible and immaculate. "All Scripture is written for our *instruction*," all Scripture however, is not written for our *example*. Abraham practiced polygamy; true, but Abraham drove out his wife and child to die in the wilderness. If the mere fact of Abraham's practicing polygamy be a warrant for me to commit it, then, *pari passu*, his wife and child desertion should be also imitated, for the same reason. The most rabid Mormon will not advocate child-desertion, even though Abraham practiced it; and ought not, therefore, to advocate polygamy, even though practiced by Abraham. To deduce from the apparent silence of God on this polygamy, an approval of it, is fallacious. God did not apparently condemn the driving out Hagar and Ishmael to die in the wilderness. Who will infer from that silence an approval of abandonment and murder? If the taking of Hagar be right, *per se*, then her desertion is right, *per se;* but if desertion be wrong, as it is; then polygamy is wrong, as it is.

It is well to remember, too, that all the blessings promised to Abraham were received by Isaac, the son of Sarah, his first and lawful wife. It should also be remembered that this Isaac was a monogamist, and that his blessings were none the less sure, and none the less glorious.

5. Jacob's polygamy is a "tower of strength" for the Mormons. Especial emphasis is laid on his sons being the heads of the house of Israel. View Jacob's polygamy first as a temporal matter, and let any pure mind read the sacred historian's simple and unsparing account of Jacob's household

as written in Gen. xxx., and they will not envy Jacob's polygamy. View it as a spiritual matter, and compare the blessings pronounced on the monogamist Joseph, and his two sons, Ephraim and Manasseh, and that on Jacob's own head. "Thy blessing is above the blessing of thy father's, even to the bounds of the everlasting hills," Gen. xlix. Jacob practiced polygamy, doubtless true; but Jacob cheated his father, defrauded his brother, and out-maneuvered his father-in-law. If Jacob's example may be urged as an argument in favor of one, it may in favor of all these practices. If the apparent silence of God be construed into *approval* of the one, then equal silence may be construed as an approval of all. Noah got intoxicated, therefore, I ought to drink. Jacob was a polygamist, therefore, I ought to take four wives. They are both equally forcible, and both equally fallacious!

6. David's practicing polygamy, while being a man after God's own heart, is another powerful Mormon argument in favor of polygamy. "Have I not given thee thy master's wives?" demands Nathan. David was Saul's son-in-law. For David to have cohabited with his father-in-law's wives, would have been *incest.* Yet David was certainly a polygamist. To say that "David was a man after God's own heart," *to be king over Israel,* does not involve divine acquiescence in all David's deeds. So far from this, David was severely rebuked and especially cursed, and the Mormons believe that he is still in hell. Viewing his polygamy in a temporal light, it entailed care and misery upon him; it surrounded his life with pain, and shortened his days. Viewed in a spiritual light, it led his heart from God to the gratification of the lusts of the

flesh; it brought upon him the full force of the word of Malachi. His "seed was ungodly" because he had more than "one." He had "dealt treacherously with the wife of his youth." He had not "taken heed." To contend that God approved polygamy because Jacob's sons were offsprings of a polygamist, is fallacious. We know that God disapproved of David's adultery with Bathsheba; and yet Solomon, whom he afterward blessed, was Bathsheba's son. As he pleased to bless the child of one marriage he condemned, he may also have condemned the marriages that produced other men whom he blessed. It is evident that "in the beginning it was not so," and either God must have changed or polygamy must be ungodly.

Mormons, however, above all, should never use this argument. Smith's Book of Mormon, page 118, says, "*Behold David and Solomon truly had many wives and concubines, which thing was abominable before me, saith the Lord.*" To say that God approved the practice, on their own faith, is to say that he approved of what to him was abominable. For them to insist on its practice because of David's example, is to destroy their own book. If this book be correct, it was *abominable* before God. If it was not abominable before God, their book is false. If their book be false, then Mormonism is a humbug; but if the book be correct, then David's polygamy was abominable, and to urge his example, is only to destroy the force of all the rest, by putting all the rest on the same level with his "abominations." Their book aside, however, it needed *God* to give the wives of Saul to David, even if we admit the illustration as of force; if, then,

David be any example, before I can practice polygamy, *God* must give me the wives: but God's command to all men is, "Take heed and do not treacherously against *the wife* of thy youth."

7. Whatever be the opinion left on the mind by the Old, the New Testament is explicit on this subject. "Whosoever putteth away his wife, except it be for fornication, and marrieth another, committeth adultery." (Matt. xix. 9.) Here are two actions concerned; 1, the repudiation; 2, the second marriage. In one of these two is involved adultery. It is not in the repudiation, be it just or unjust. It must, therefore, be in the second marriage. Though you put away your first wife altogether, cease to live with her entirely, unless she has committed fornication, *even then*, says the Saviour, you can not take a second wife without committing adultery. If marrying a second wife, the first being put away, is adultery, certainly marrying a second, the first being not put away, must be adultery also. Grant that the law of marriage and divorce under Moses permitted polygamy; Jesus, in changing the law of divorce, changed the law of marriage. The practice of the church is the best exponent of their doctrine, and it is certain that the early Christian church did not only not practice polygamy, but many of the apostles did not marry at all.

8. Paul, however, is still more definite on the subject. 1 Cor. vii., 2: "To avoid fornication, let every man have his own wife, and every woman her own husband." Each man is to "have his own wife" to and for himself. If *she* infringe that law it is adultery. So likewise, each woman is to "have her *own* husband," and to herself and for herself also. If *he*

infringe that law it is adultery. The fourth verse gives a reason: "For the wife hath no power over her own body, but the husband; and likewise also the husband hath no power over his own body, but the wife." In marriage he just as much becomes *hers* as she *his*. Her exclusive right, therefore, to a pure husband is just as stringent as his exclusive right to a pure wife. If it be not adultery for him to have many wives, it is no more adultery for her to have many husbands. She is bound, however, to keep herself solely for her husband, and he is equally bound to keep himself solely for his wife. "The bed undefiled is honorable," Heb. xiii. 4. The husband can defile the bed equally with the wife. "There is neither Jew nor Greek, bond nor free, *male nor female*, for ye are all one in Christ." That which is the law of Christ for the male, is, therefore, for the female also; equally as much as that which is the law for the Jew is the law for the Greek. Say that the law of Christ accords to the *man* unlimited choice, it must also to the *woman*, for "they are both one in Christ." God makes men and women *one*. Mormonism makes men kings and women slaves, therefore Mormonism is not of God.

9. Christ told the murmuring Jews that "Moses truly said so, for the hardness of your heart, *but in the beginning it was not so*." If, in the course of man's decadence, woman was degraded, it was the mission of Christ to save those who were lost; to restore them as they were "in the beginning." If, in the course of man's religious education, at the times of man's ignorance, God hath winked, he, in the revelation of a higher law, has elevated humanity to a higher position. As man draws his mental and moral natures more from the

woman than man, so to elevate mankind God must elevate their *mothers*. In the beginning men and women were equal and *one*, "*a* male and *a* female." Christ is the "restorer of all things as in the beginning," and, therefore, according to the Scriptures, monogamy must prevail. We can easily grant and only strengthen our position, that Jacob and David degraded women, for it is only an additional proof of the superiority of Jesus' gospel over Moses' law; in that he lifts up the fallen, and that in him ancient superstition and female slavery is a olished; for "there is neither male nor female, they are all one in Christ Jesus." They were one before the fall, God formed them "one pair," pronounced them "one flesh;" Christ makes them "one" again in the redemption.

II. Polygamy is anti-natural.

Nature in the proportion of male to female births distinctly manifests her will on the subject of marriage. There are more males than females born into the world. In the United States' census of 1850, the whole number of nativities in the United States were stated as 19,553,068 persons. Of these 10,026,377 were males, and only 9,526,691 females; leaving a surplus, in the United States alone, of nearly 500,000 on the male side. Had all these lived, attained the age of maturity, and intermarried, there would still have been nearly half a million of men without wives. By the British census of 1851, it is seen that the increase of the population of England during the then preceding fifty years, was 102 per cent. in the proportions of 105 males to 97-5 females; the increase of Scotland, for the same period, had been 78 per cent.; in the proportions of 84 males to 73 females. Instead, therefore, of a surplus of females, as the polygamy argument would require, there are, at least, 5 per cent. more males born. These, however, are but the births; the deaths may be unequal. After all the heavy demands of the fifty years ending 1851, on the male population of Great Britain, to supply men for the continental war, by sea and land; the East Indian war, and increase of soldiers after the cessation of the war; the war on the Cape of Good Hope; the many accidents on the ocean, and the draining emigration of an enormous plurality of males to the United States and Australasian colonies; still the population of Great Britain and Ireland was 13,537,052 males to 14,082,814 females, or an actual plurality of females of only three per cent. In Prussia, 1849, there were 8,162,805 males to 8,162,382 females, an actual plurality of males *living*. In the United States, and Australasian colonies, this is also the fact. As there are more males than females who emigrate, therefore, in all countries *to which* emigration comes, there is a plurality of males found; and in all countries *whence* they come, there are more females left. In the Sandwich Islands, in 1853, there were 37,079 males and only 33,940 females; a positive plurality of 3,139 males, or nearly 10 per cent.

While it is true that more males die from *accidental*, it is also true that more females die from *natural*, causes. This, also, helps to maintain the constant equilibrium of the sexes, and even leaves a small plurality of males. The works of nature are not, however, to be computed from one people or for one period. A census of the whole world, if taken, by centuries, would prove that the greater liability of males was more than compensated by the plurality of births ot nearly $5\frac{1}{2}$ per cent., or a surplus of 55,000 to every 1,000,000 of nativities. It must be so. Were the plurality of births female instead of male, with a constantly-increasing and excessive mortality of the males, and a constantly-increasing proportion of female births, the relative proportion of the sexes would become frightfully deranged in a few years. Any mathematician can add figures to this formula. Nature, in this respect, proves a very glorious truth; that the God of revelation who created man and woman "one pair," is the God who in nature preserves man and woman in pairs too! and, therefore, polygamy is anti-natural, because, for any one man to take more than his one woman, *is a robbery inflicted on the rest of mankind!*

III. Polygamy is irrational.

Reason is the faculty that adapts means to ends, and is founded on experience. What are the objects of marriage and how are they best subserved? Paley and others have ably shown, that one object of marriage is not only the *procreation*, but also the *elevation* of children. Now the history of the world's progress is traceable by that of women. The nation that degraded women was itself degraded. Those nations who most respected her mission and position, were the most celebrated and powerful. Those nations were always monogamist. The priests of Egypt, the conservators of human knowledge, were monogamists. The Grecians, who have given to every science a name and to many sciences a birth-place and master, were monogamists. Rome, whose very name recalls visions of universal dominion, intellectual pre-eminence, and physical strength, was monogamist. Roman matrons, mothers, wives, virgins, would have despised polygamy; they helped to make Rome the thing it was! Woman is the inciter of the artist and the model for the art. Had it not been for being the chosen recipients of God's word, the polygamist Jews might have lived unnoticed and died unknown.

2. The position of children depend on their mothers. Children assimilate more to their mother's than their father's nature. Universal philosophy, confirmed by universal experience, testifies that to make slaves of women they will bear but slaves. The child's earliest and hence strongest education depends on the mother. "If ever I was any thing, or am any thing, or ever shall be any thing, I must attribute it to my mother," said J. Q. Adams. "My mother," said Napoleon, "first inspired me with the wish to be great." Memory loves to linger round the names of such women as Washington's mother; those of Cromwell, Edwards, Wesley, Kossuth, Lamartine and others—mothers and men polygamic countries could never have produced.

3. Woman's influence as a wife is by no means inferior to that of a mother. The caliber of a man's mind is determinable by the female society he prefers; because the man's mind is toned by the female society that he keeps. Those who entertain a low opinion of woman's mission, generally act so as to keep them degraded. Some of the greatest men have had the best wives. She helps to form the character that he exhibits to the world. She is often the real artizan, but whose name is not on the production. Degrade the wife, and consequently you degrade the husband, the possessor of the wife.

The true glory that a woman adds to a man is not, can not be the mere sensual extension of gratification, nor the material benefit of numerous posterity, but mental and moral. Gems are valueless and unknown if they be not polished. To say that three fifths of the world are polygamists, is to say, therefore, that three fifths of the world are degraded. Polygamy compares with monogamy as Greece with Persia, Assyria with Rome; or, in our own day, as England compares with Turkey; North America with India; France with China. The Anglo-Saxon race who are giving language, laws, literature, commerce, and religion to all the earth; who are filling the world with their steam-engines and printing-presses; directing by their stronger energy, and instructing with their superior wisdom, are the monogamic descendants of monogamic ancestors. Degrade the position of Anglo-Saxon women to that of Circassian slaves, and you degrade Anglo-Saxon men to the level of the Turks, those slaves' masters; for universal experience asserts, that to degrade the woman, is to share her fall.

4. No rational argument can be drawn from the marriage laws of any one people for the peremptory regulation of any other. The laws of marriage have been as various as circumstances of nations. Among the Jews marriage was obligatory. An unmarried youth of eighteen was disgraced. Girls might marry at twelve years and one day; boys at thirteen and one day. The Medes compelled the citizens of one province to take each seven women; while in another, they compelled each woman to take five husbands. In Pegu a woman can be purchased for a certain time; while among the Chinese,

the wealthy buy their wives, and the poor beg theirs from foundling-hospitals. The good-looking girls were sold among the Assyrians, to furnish dowers for those whose good looks could not win a husband. Some modern reformers advocate the breaking down of all restraints, and let passion roam wild, unchecked by any thing but satiety, and undirected but by caprice. The objects of marriage, however, which are "private happiness, production, best eduction, and establishment of most healthy offspring; peace of society, administration of government, and encouragement of industry," are best subserved by monogamy. Political science repeats the command of revelation, "Let every man have his own wife, and every woman her own husband!"

5. The Mormons contend that a man's glory will depend on his kingdom, and that kingdom on his family. Hence, it is argued, no family, no kingdom. Many of the greatest prophets were not married men. There is no right to suppose that Enoch or Elijah were married, and whose glory surpasses that of these men? Samuel was not married, and what prophet greater than he? John the Baptist was not married, and yet "a greater prophet was never born of woman," said Jesus. John the beloved, Peter, and others of the apostles, preferred "to be eunuchs for the kingdom of God's sake;" and Paul himself advises the Church, "He that giveth in marriage doth well, but he that giveth not in marriage doth better;" and, himself a bachelor, set an example of celibacy to the Church.

6. Such a principle as the above, would be unworthy of God; because it would favor the gross and animal, to the

prejudice of those who, by their predominant intellectuality, are far better fitted to govern families. It is a well-known fact that the lower we descend in the scale of animated nature, the more prolific do the races become. Swine are more prolific than horses. This is not only a fixed principle that seems to obtain in the animal, but may also be traced in the human economy. Those races not most famous for mental energy, are often most famous for their numerous families. The men of great genius who have, by the powers of their intellect and mental resources, enlightened and advanced the world, have been remarkable for the smallness of their families. In many cases they have left no children after them, either to disgrace their names or increase their renown. Washington, no son! Jefferson, Madison, Monroe, no sons! Shakspeare, Milton, Byron, no sons! The direct families of Coleridge, Walter Scott, Earl Chatham, and Napoleon, and scores of others, are extinct. It almost seems as though their mental consumed their physical nature; and like the blossom of the giant aloe, could only bloom once in a hundred years.

7. It is however urged that polygamy prevents prostitution. This is a powerful argument in the conviction of women's minds and hearts in its favor; besides giving scope for fervent declamation to their Elders. The fact is gladly admitted that there are no prostitutes and bawd-houses at Utah. The enunciated penalty on discovered adultery is *death!* It is far more the *dread of this penalty*, therefore, than the practice of polygamy, that prevents prostitutions. Even were it otherwise, the remedy is worse than the disease. Appalling though the number of prostitutes may be, they are still comparatively

few when the whole number of virtuous women is remembered. Happy homes by far exceed the number of degraded unfortunates. To save these degraded *few*, *all* womanhood must be degraded according to this strange view. To prevent comparatively *few* from ruin, *all* must be sacrificed. The evil is partial, while the remedy is universal; or to use a forcible but common phrase, "the plaster is bigger than the sore!" Besides this, universal polygamy presupposes *a plurality of females*, when the real fact evinces a *plurality of males*. Polygamy, as a remedy for prostitution, is therefore unreasonable, because impracticable.

If the superstitious terror of the power of the priesthood —the dread of their supernatural *discernment*, and the fear of death were removed from the minds of the Mormon women, hundreds would obey the instincts of their natures, and Utah would become a pandemonium of licentiousness. Prostitution has its victims, and they are thousands; were polygamy as universal as monogamy, then polygamy would count its victims by millions.

The practice of polygamy among the Jews did not prevent prostitution. Judah went in unto Tamar; and Solomon needed to give the injunction, "Go not after strange women." Viewing Mormonism as a religion, it is still worse. None but *bad* men in the world encourage prostitutes; the Mormon *best* men practice polygamy; grant then for a moment that polygamy is a *less evil* than prostitution, it only proves that the Mormon *best men* are only one remove above the *world's worst!*

Even the Mormon women admit that it would be far better for the world were *monogamy* instead of *polygamy* the institution of God. A Mrs. Nixon, at Salt Lake City, told me, "I believe polygamy is an institution of God, Mr. Hyde, and I therefore submit to it; but *I have very often wished it were otherwise.*" This was wrung from the heart of a pure but infatuated woman; and must be echoed by all women's hearts. Let us compare, for a moment, Christianity with Mormonism, in this particular. *Christians* do not practice prostitution, but *monogamy. Mormons* do not practice prostitution but *polygamy.* In the non-practice of prostitution, they are therefore *equal;* but in as far as monogamy is superior to polygamy, and the Mormon women admit that it is, just so far is Christianity certainly superior to Mormonism. To blame Christianity because bad men encourage prostitutes, is ridiculous; and yet the Mormon Elders are constantly doing this. It is just as unfair as it would be to say Mormonism countenanced indiscriminate thieving, because William Nobody stole a horse. The general practice of the leaders is the exponent of the general principles of the body.

Whether viewed, therefore, in the light of the Scriptures, of nature, or of reason, polygamy is untenable and false.

IV. Polygamy is anti-Mormon.

1. There can be but one system called by one name. If one scheme be Mormonism, certainly the contradiction of that scheme can not be Mormonism too. The system first established by J. Smith was Mormonism. Polygamy entirely contradicts and opposes that system, and is, therefore, anti-Mormon. Those who received that system ought to reject polygamy. Smith, on p. 118, Book of Mormon, states:

"For behold, thus saith the Lord, this people begin to wax

in iniquity; they understand not the Scriptures; for they seek to excuse themselves in committing whoredoms, because of the things which were written concerning David, and Solomon his son. Behold, David and Solomon *truly had many wives and concubines, which thing was abominable* before me, saith the Lord; wherefore, thus saith the Lord, I have led this people forth out of the land of Jerusalem, by the power of mine arm, that I might raise up unto me a righteous branch from the fruit of the loins of Joseph. Wherefore, I the Lord God, will not suffer that this people shall do like unto them of old. Wherefore, my brethren, hear me, and hearken to the word of the Lord; *for there shall not any man among you have save it be one wife; and concubines he shall have none;* for I, the Lord God, delighteth in the chastity of women. And whoredoms are an abomination before me; thus saith the Lord of Hosts. Wherefore, this people shall keep my commandments, saith the Lord of Hosts, or cursed be the land for their sakes. For if I will, saith the Lord of Hosts, raise up seed unto me, I will command my people; otherwise they shall hearken unto these things. For, behold, I the Lord, have seen the sorrow, and heard the mourning of the daughters of my people in the land of Jerusalem; yea, and in all the lands of my people, because of the wickedness and abominations of their husbands. And I will not suffer, saith the Lord of Hosts, that the cries of the fair daughters of this people, which I have led out of the land of Jerusalem, shall come up unto me, against the men of my people, saith the Lord of Hosts; for they shall not lead away captive the daughters of my people, because of their tenderness, save I shall visit them with a sore curse, even unto destruction: for they shall not commit whoredoms, like unto them of old, saith the Lord of Hosts."

God threatens, according to Smith, "to smite them

with a sore curse, even to destruction," if they do thus take other wives. They have taken them: they will be cursed.

2. The Mormons try to elude all this by the words, "For if I will raise up seed, I will command you." A. B. does an abominable thing. For C. D. to do the same, it would be abominable too. If God were to command C. D. to do it, he would command an abomination. When God desires to raise up a godly seed, it will be as Malachi has said, "He made one!" If he were to institute any other method, he would contradict himself. There can be no evasion; the Book of Mormon curses them if they do it. Either they must cleave to their book, in spite of polygamy; or to polygamy in spite of their book. If polygamy be right, then the book is wrong, and Mormonism falls in its origin. If the book be right, then polygamy is wrong, and Mormonism falls in its present position. But whether it fell in the beginning, or since, it is equally fallen; and men are mad to adhere to a fallen system.

3. More entirely to enmesh himself, Smith pretended to get a revelation, February, 1831, in which he says that God commanded him, "Thou shalt love thy wife with all thy heart, and shalt cleave unto her, *and none else;* and he that looketh on a woman to lust after her, shall deny the faith, and shall not have the Spirit; and if he repents not shall be cast out." (Doc. and Cov., p. 124.) This was the pretended word of the Mormon unchangeable Lord in 1831; yet in 1838 Smith was cohabiting with several women!

4. In 1842, it began to be whispered at Nauvoo, that polygamy was a part of the Mormon faith. The Elders

strenuously denied it; and, in 1845, an appendix was added to the Revelations of Smith, in which the Mormon authorities state, although *most of them were polygamists at the time*, and they all knew they were lying! "Inasmuch as this Church of Christ has been reproached with the *crimes* of fornication and *polygamy*, we declare that we believe that one man should have one wife; and one woman but one husband; except in case of death, when either is at liberty to marry again." The writers of this infamous affair knew that Smith had children living, the offspring of polygamy, at the very day that they wrote it.

5. At length, in 1852, Brigham publishes to the world a pretended revelation, bearing date July, 1843, commanding polygamy, and asserts that *this* is the origin of their practice. This is another falsehood, as the pretended revelation itself proves. Par. 20 says: "And let mine handmaid Emma Smith receive all those who *have been given* unto my servant Joseph, and who are virtuous and pure before me." It is not said, receive all those who *may be;* or, *shall hereafter be;* but who "*have been given;*" not they they *shall be pure;* but "who *are* pure and virtuous before me." The tense is the past and not the future; and proves, therefore, that Joseph had taken *them previously;* that, previous to this date, their virtue and purity was questionable; that this pretended revelation was got up in fact only as a *mollifying plaster for Emma Smith!* If this revelation be the origin of modern polygamy, Smith practiced it before commanded, and was therefore an adulterer, according to his own showing. If he was commanded by a previous revelation, to pub-

JOSEPH SMITH

lish this revelation as the origin and defense of polygamy is deceiving the people; and this makes Smith an impostor. Either then he was an impostor, or an adulterer; and impostor he was in either case.

There existed another and still more forcible reason why the Mormons in Utah should not practice polygamy. By the census returns of 1851, made by the Mormons themselves, it was shown that there were in Utah 6,020 *males* to only 5,310 *females*, an excess of males over females of 710 persons. Now, when it is considered that some of those men had over twenty wives, and many from two to six wives each, it was defrauding so many more young men of wives; and, therefore, homes; and, therefore, happiness; and as the Mormon doctrine is "No wife, no glory; no glory, no salvation," it was, according to their own faith, building up their own kingdoms at the expense of the salvation of their own brethren. Damning hundreds to get glory!

Every physical and moral crime carries within it the elements of its own punishment. Polygamy is theoretically incorrect, and should, therefore, exhibit its fallacy when practically adopted. The worst argument against the Mormon polygamy is its practical results, as proven in chap. iii. Polygamy being theoretically erroneous, reasoning men and women should discard it as a principle; being actually debasing, they should reject it as a practice.

The charge of polygamy was invariably denied by the Mormons for fourteen years, *although it was true;* and it behooves every man to demand, "Are not the other charges made against them *equally true*, although they may have been *equally denied?*"

CHAPTER XIII.

FINAL SUPPRESSION OF MORMONISM.

Mormonism as a religion and as a civil polity—Cause of Mormon persecution at Missouri—At Nauvoo—J. Smith, a candidate for presidency of the United States—Smith a Mohammed—Brigham successor to his designs as well as office—His mismanagement — Famine *v.* ambition—His cause of fall—Mormon politics—The objects to be accomplished with regard to Mormonism—The Mormon polygamy—Ethical and legal crimes—Two methods of suppressing polygamy—Legislation and annexatian—Duty of Congress, in the matter—The advantages of annexation—On the women—On the men—Majority of Mormons foreigners—Poverty and discontent—Women would leave Utah—Many would apostatize—Effects of merely appointing a governor and sending troops—Mormonism as a religious evil—Means to uproot it—Duty of seceders—Of Christians—Its fundamental errors and weakest points.

WHAT shall be done with this strangely-infatuated people? This has become an important inquiry, as their position and developments will soon demand action.

There is a difficulty on both sides of the subject. The Mormons contend that the Constitution guaranties the fullest and freest enjoyment of religious opinion. Mormonism, say they, is our religion; to oppose our doings is an infringement of our religious rights, and that is violating the Constitution.

Others insist on viewing Mormonism as a civil polity

alone; and as such demand the interference of the federal power.

It is ridiculous to think that the government can have a desire to oppress any portion of its citizens, or that it has the slightest motive to limit human freedom in its broadest constitutional sense. If the doings in Utah compel the Congress to regard and act toward it merely as a civil polity, irrespective of its religion, the Mormons must remember that it is themselves who have united their ecclesiastical with their civil organization. As a church, they have the extremest right to worship whom and what they please. Rites the most ridiculous and fantastic; deities the most monstrous and fiendish; altars the most costly and magnificent; dogmas the most atrocious and profane; leaders the most bigoted or corrupt; people the most fanatic and suicidal may be tolerated as to religion. But when that religion nerves the arm and grasps the sword of secular power, it comes in contact with secular authority. Its claims of toleration then merge into assumptions of sovereignty, and wise men need to hesitate before acceding to its demands.

As a religion, Mormonism can not be meddled with; as a civil polity it may. The arm of government should never be stretched to crush *fanatics*, but the sword of justice must attack *conspirators*. Men have every right in the world to be the devotees of error; but no right at all to be the devotees of crime.

It has been their constant anxiety and incessant truckling for political ascendancy that has induced much of their sufferings already. The Mormons grasped at and obtained power in Missouri, and by force of numbers, knowing no motive other than self-aggrandisement, outvoted, and rose at the expense of all the other inhabitants. The same policy of political wire-working first incensed the mass of the Illinoians. It is folly to suppose that in the then new country, where every emigrant added to the value of property, and every new town enhanced every other town, that the whole mass of the people, comprising men of every sect and many of no sect at all, should persecute an industrious people merely on religious grounds. It is unnatural; it is absurd. The real secret was, the efforts of the Mormons to get the county-seat removed to Nauvoo, and thus to control the county. Those living in the immediate vicinity of Nauvoo, were enraged by the thefts committed on their property; but it was the Mormon political chicanery that induced their expulsion. Smith juggled so extensively and became so inflated by his success, that he presumed to offer himself as candidate for the presidency of the United States, in 1843, '44, and cursed the country for not promising him their support. He strutted from off the stilts of a religious impostor, to the balancing-pole of a political empiric, and fell. It was not for his religion or because of his prophetic pretensions, but for his political designs and his *modus operandi* in endeavoring to secure them. Having imitated Mohammed in his pretended mission and revelations, like him, having become the chief of a second Medina, he wished to extend the resemblance still further, and aspired to rule the continent. Brigham Young sympathises in his views and is sanguine enough to think that he can accomplish them. With more tact and greater pertinacity, he more carefully approaches the desired goal. His little world in

Utah grew too narrow for him, and he spread out his boundaries. San Bernardino on the south, Carson Valley on the west, and Salmon river on the north, were taken possession of. A settlement was sent into Nebraska to make a fort and permanent location, if possible. St. Louis and Cincinnati were created "Stakes of Zion, abiding-places for the Saints," in 1854. Missionaries were sent to the Indian tribes, to obtain their friendship and secure their support. Brigham said, "I will drive the wedge in with little taps; but will never draw back till the tree is split."

Hope beat high in Mormon hearts, that the Church would make a great move to retake Independence, Jackson county, Mo., which they believe they yet have to do, preparatory to conquering the world. War with England, the rising of the slaves, the triumph of the Saints, and the coming of the Messiah were prognosticated freely. The famine cooled down this boisterous effervesence. The pressure from outside began to bear heavily, and now the Carson Valley settlement is abandoned, San Bernardino is evacuated, the Saints at Cincinnati are recalled, and the St. Louis Stake is commanded to "come home." Brigham has withdrawn the foot he had planted so pompously, and, fearing difficulties at home, he is drawing his men around him. Still his ambition and belief remain unchanged. He is tired of the platform of his Tabernacle, or the paraphernalia of his endowment room; he covets the ermine and scepter of an emperor; and when he falls, it will not be because of his pretensions as a prophet, nor an infringement of his religious rights as a man; but for his criminal efforts to gratify his ridiculous ambition.

Having invested their religion with the Nessus shirt of political jugglery; having made their ecclesiastical influence the stepping-stone to civil power; not being content with supporting the laws, but covering, under a Jesuitically-assumed veneration for the *Constitution*, the most treasonable designs and oaths of conspirators; determining the overthrow of their country as the rubbsh on which to build their throne, and the center from which to sway their empire; inducing thousands of poor deluded men and women to sacrifice their all in order to embrace such objects; boldly defying the power of the government, and expelling its authorized agents; educating their children, as Brigham has said, "to be able and ready to carry fire and sword, if needs be, to the very gates of the capitol;" it is themselves who have divested their system of its religious character, and, therefore, subjected themselves to political interference. It is *themselves* who are guilty of placing their adherents in their dangerous position; and it will be themselves who must be responsible for the consequences. Their political ambition has ever been the curse of their system, and it will prove its downfall.

What shall be done? To answer this, it is necessary, first, to see clearly what are the objects to be accomplished. Mormonism is a moral, religious, and political evil. As a moral evil, it degrades women and curses the rising generation. As a religious evil, it dooms thousands of old and young to perdition, for its ablest polemic, O. Pratt, says, "The message in the Book of Mormon, if false, is such that none who persist in believing it can be saved."* As a political evil, it is a system

* Tract, "Divine Authenticity of Book of Mormon," p. 1.

of treason, sworn to subject the government, and hoping to usurp its place; an autocracy in the center of a republic.

The glaring moral evil of their system is polygamy. This is an anti-natural and a degrading practice; but still it is not a *crime* for the *Mormons* to be polygamists. There is no law against polygamy in Utah. There is a law against it in every other State and Territory, and, therefore, in every other State and Territory it is a crime. For it to become a crime, either Congress must enact a law against it extending over all the Territories, or Utah must enact such a law for herself. Until such a law be enacted it is no crime. Until it be made a legal crime, it can not be legally punished. Before the executive can inflict a penalty, the deliberative must prescribe one. Such a penalty has never been prescribed. So far, therefore, as polygamy is concerned, the people are *legally* innocent. The legislators of Utah are almost all polygamists; Brigham is too astute a tactician to repose much confidence, or elevate to much honor, any but those whose interests are inextricably enmeshed with that of Mormonism. They will never make polygamy a crime. If it be made criminal, Congress must do it. Till it becomes a legal wrong, it is only an ethical wrong; and for ethical wrongs there can only be ethical remedies. To attempt to adopt these in Utah would be folly. No man however informed or however eloquent would be heard. To call in question its propriety in Utah, would be as senseless as disparaging Washington in a fourth of July oration. They urge it as the perfection of purity. Outside Utah moral means may be effectual; but it has attained too strong a hold, entangled too many persons, and combined too many interests in Utah ever to be thus uprooted. Were it not for the fact of its being under the restraint of fanaticism, and all the Mormons being equally infatuated, it would fall to pieces of its own weight. It has become a cankering sore, but it is rigidly restrained to one spot; and excision is its only remedy. If, therefore, it is ever abolished, it must be by law. It must be made a legal wrong, or it better be let alone. Complete inaction as to Utah, or else thorough and vigorous action. It is mere child's play to blate at what can not be meddled with or improved. Polygamy must be either sanctioned or opposed; if it be sanctioned, and to ignore it is a tacit sanction, all is said; if it be opposed, it is a sign of imbecility if that opposition be not successful. For such opposition to be successful, it must be made a legal crime, and its penalty must be legally enforced.

It is a very important question, however, Is it the duty of Congress to suppress polygamy? Arbitrary exercise of power is a dangerous experiment, and would form a very dangerous precedent. Interference in domestic matters is contrary to the true policy of all governments; but do the affairs of Utah warrant this interference? Were a colony of Hindoos to emigrate to Nebraska in sufficient numbers to control the State Legislature, and to practice the burning of widows on the funeral pyres of their husbands, ought they to be interfered with? The society of "free love" was resolutely suppressed by law in New York; yet they manifestly had as much right to the enjoyment of their religious conception of marriage as any. To say that their numbers were insignificant and their organization feeble compared with that of Mormonism, only makes Mormonism the greater evil, and, therefore, more urgently demanding an effectual remedy. For government to attempt to punish without Congress previously legislating on it, would be an infinitely more arbitrary exercise of power than to confront the question and legislate at once. To send soldiers to endeavor to seduce Mormon girls, as some suggest, and by thus enraging the Mormons provoke murderous hostilities, is fiendish. In the name of humanity, if it be suppressed, let it be done legally, and not with the passions and injustice of mob violence. The great difficulty is polygamy, it can not be evaded; if its suppression be the object desired, it must be the object attacked. If it be not done with the temperate firmness of law, any other course will only aggravate the evil.

There are two methods of making Mormon polygamy criminal. The first is by enacting a law directly against it by Congress. This is the simplest method, but open to much dispute on the score of "legislating for the Territories." The second plan is to repeal the act organizing the Territory of Utah, and to place the Mormon settlements under the jurisdiction of the adjoining States, whose laws punish polygamy; or by Congress legislating for squatters on public grounds. This method would be as directly effectual, and not open to the same objections as the others. Annex the northern portion of Utah to Oregon, and the southern and western to California. Let these States call on the Federal Government for assistance to execute their law against polygamy. If the Mormons forcibly resist the execution of law, they become traitors *de facto* as well as *de volontas;* and the duty of the government will be evident, while the responsibility will be on their own heads. These policies will be effectual, and one of these will be the only *effectual* policy to adopt.

Not only on the sole ground of polygamy is such a course justifiable. The Mormons are conspirators; the real object of Mormonism is treason. The power they have so much misused may be legitimately wrested from them. They have used their freedom as a means of founding a political as well as an ecclesiastical autocracy. It may be urged as a dangerous precedent, but should a similar case occur again, it would be a precedent that would demand to be renewed. If Congress do not make such a law, or so repeal the organization, all other efforts at abolishing polygamy will be ineffectual. Out of Utah the Mormons do not practice it; in Utah they can neither be frustrated or punished. Not only would such a course accomplish this particular object, but it would also tend materially to the breaking up of the whole system. The Mormons owe their power to their isolation; destroy their isolation and you subvert this influence. Any thing that tends to bring Utah nearer to the rest of the world tends to complete the destruction of this system of folly and fraud. The Mormons fled from the world because their principles could not prevail where monogamy obtained. Their present seclusion disables any from inspecting their domestic arrangements; it prevents right minded women from using their influence, lending their assistance, offering their advice, or urging their arguments on the poor deluded wives. It prevents these wives themselves from seeing other and happier homes, mingling with other and happier hearts, being saddened by other and happier faces. It makes them grow accustomed to their lots, and habit speedily engenders a species of contentment. Break this seclusion and you break the chain of their thralldom. We can not bring the Mormons to the world, but it is easy to take the world to Utah by uniting Utah to others of the States. Any thing done to encourage emigration through Utah, or to facilitate communication and intercourse, will be the most effectual means of subverting this imposture. A wagon-road and weekly mails will be much; the late official appointments, if wisely sustained, will do much; a Pacific railroad would be more; annexation to Oregon and California would do more than them all.

It must be remembered that the vast majority of the Mormons are foreigners; that they have been in this country only for several years; that the majority of them have not made the first step toward naturalization; that they did not come here in the love of republicanism; that it is not this love that retains them here; that they are by predilection, by instinct, and by preference monarchical in their feelings; that they still cling fondly to their fatherlands; that they came "not to America but to Zion;" not in the admiration of American institutions, but in the confident expectation of assisting to subvert them; that were that system proven false, many of them would return again to old homes and old friends; that while here they are the dupes and victims of designing fanatics; and that these fanatics will force them into crime and danger if not prevented. These things must be remembered.

There are large numbers of persons very desirous but quite

unable to leave Utah, for lack of the necessary means. They, deceived by false representations, and cajoled by false promises, have spent their little all in toiling there; many of them going into debt in order to get there at all. With large families dependent on them, they have to labor wearily, to provide the barest subsistence for them; some of them just dragging out a wretched existence, and groaning in poverty and misery. Were Utah annexed to California and Oregon, the citizens of those States could not only offer inducements by land and otherwise for people to come to the western portions of their States, but also advance means to assist them. It might be done as a loan, it might be done as an act of charity, it might be paid by improvements. A dozen plans of "Emigrant Aid Societies" can suggest themselves to every one's mind. They are now a thousand miles from civilization. They need two months' food in advance, when it is more than they can do to provide a week beforehand. They need a wagon to carry that food, when many of them are sleeping in mud-hovels on stick bedsteads. They need a team to haul it, when they have now to go to the mountains and pick sage-brush and dried sunflowers for the scanty fuel to cook their shadow of a meal. They are poor and helpless, and helpless because they are poor. Could outfits be provided, and a brighter and better future shown to those poor unfortunates, hundreds of them would gladly leave. It is not *protection*, but *assistance*, that they require. The Mormons do not use any other physical restraint than by making and keeping them poor. Their chains are mental and moral duress, folly, and fanaticism. Not only are there men, but many women who are now suffering and sorrowing. When Colonel Steptoe's command passed through Salt Lake, dozens of women implored him to allow them to travel through to California under his protection. Six ladies were accommodated, who notwithstanding the ferocious denunciations, the malignant slanders and the soul-searing anathemas of Brigham Young and his compeers, left Salt Lake. Could fifty more have been taken, fifty more would have gone. If a means could be adopted whereby they might be assisted in leaving and protected from danger on the road, their reputations preserved from the attack of calumny or the taint of suspicion, and a hope of something brighter presented, hundreds would leave; joyfully leave. There are hundreds of as pure and virtuous women at Utah as ever lived, who would be a blessing and a comfort to as many single young men in the western States, and who only ask assistance to enable them to remove. Such a vigorous course of procedure would alarm many who are mere "summer Saints," who, while Mormonism pampers their pride, supports their idleness, or licenses their passions, will uphold it. These will willingly secede, and though their secession be no accession to the ranks of purity and truth, will still decrease the number and dispirit the remnant. The only argument that has persuaded the belief of others is the astonishing success of Mormonism. Their faith is dependent on this success. To arrest this progress would be to overturn their confidence. To prove by a firm, decided action that the authority of Congress is not to be defied with impunity, nor its institutions successfully outraged, will denude Mormonism of many of its votaries, not yet fatally entangled. This will render success easy, opposition ridiculous. These *desiderata* depend, however, on the boldness of the design, and the vigor of its execution. Vigorous and radical measures will have to be adopted; the sooner they are adopted the better will it be for the country and for the Mormons themselves. Thousands are swelling their numbers every year from Europe and the States. Hundreds are being born every year at Utah. Every year, while augmenting their force, consolidating their position, strengthening their influence, and increasing the number of polygamists, also confirms their audacity. The longer action is delayed, the worse matters become; the more expensive will be their subversion, and the more disastrous the finale. Whether Congress determines to act in the premises, or sanction, by their silence, all Mormon doings, remains to be seen. In great emergencies, tardiness is imbecility: energy is success. It is not to shed blood, but to spare it: not to sacrifice citizens, but preserve them. Let Brigham alone, and he will cause bloodshed in abundance by-and-by. To act vigorously now, is to prevent the fearful consummation of his intentions.

Notwithstanding all the bombastic menaces of Brigham, I do not think that they will resist *now*. They are not yet prepared to resist, but are steadily preparing. For this purpose are they calling in all their outer settlements, as San Bernardino and Carson Valley. It is but few men, however, who can not play at soldiers at parades and target excursions; it is but few men who will act as soldiers when soldierly daring is demanded. It is, therefore, not *force* that is demanded, but *firmness*. Every one must deplore the absurd and brutal violence suffered by the Mormons in Missouri and Illinois.

They have had already too many martyrs to their creed. Hundreds of women and children, whose only sin was their credulity, have already suffered fiendish inflictions of barbarities. It is not to re-enact such ruthless scenes of mob violence and madness; but with the gentle but unyielding arm of the country to maintain the dignity of the law. The rock breaks not the sea that dashes against it, *but it is the sea that breaks itself upon the rock.*

It is for the government to affix their boundary with reference to these people; to let it be distinctly defined, well-chosen, and resistless. So well-defined as to be unmistakable; so well-chosen as to be universally approved, and so resistless as to intimidate opposition. When the Mormons are made to feel that resistance is madness, Brigham is too *practical* a genius to command rebellion, or

"To let loose the dogs of war."

The mere appointment of a governor or the bare sending of troops to Utah can accomplish but little. Something *more thorough* is demanded. While the Legislature is Mormon; with the Mormon people to vote for and support them; with Mormon officers to baffle a United States appointed judiciary; with Mormon juries to perjure themselves, by disregarding evidence; and acquitting their friends and convicting their enemies; with the whole Mormon population to sanction and sustain them, very little can be done. Before requiring troops to do any thing it is necessary to state distinctly what they are to do. They can only enforce the law. The laws of Utah protect polygamy, and punish adultery with death:

they must enforce the law. The troops already sent will be quartered at Rush Valley, thirty-five miles west of Salt Lake City, and will only eat, sleep, parade, or punish refractory Indians. It is said they can protect judges from personal violence, but personal violence has never been employed. If they do any thing something must be prescribed, and until such a remedial law be enacted, they had better stay at home.

The new governor, all Brigham's vaporing to the contrary notwithstanding, will be courteously received at Salt Lake, but what can he do? The people are the Church; Brigham is the head of the Church and, consequently, of the people. They elect, under their Territorial constitution, their own Legislature; they are all Mormons, and are Brigham's most obedient votaries. In ecclesiastical councils all measures are discussed and decided, and are then only *enacted* at the Legislative sessions. On these measures they all vote in unison. The veto of the governor can be overruled by two thirds of the two Houses, but there every thing is done by the majority of the *whole.* Hence his veto power would be useless. *Their laws he must execute,* or else arbitrarily refuse. To subject the people to the arbitrary will of any individual is certainly improper, and the people would be justified in rebellion. Give him some well-defined law to execute; make polygamy a crime; be it his to preside over the enforcement of the penalty; give him something to do, and then there is some utility in his appointment. Else, very much perplexed and aggrieved, feeling himself unable to do, any thing when so much is expected from him, he will want to return before he is there one year, or else, like Colonel Steptoe, resign his appointment and advise that of Brigham Young. All the good a governor can accomplish, will be to intimidate immediate and active hostilities, while their preparations are maturing under his eyes, and their endowments being a portion of their *religion*, he will be unable to arrest their progress.

The slightest consideration must convince all that less than such measures can only result in failure, so far as the suppression of polygamy is concerned. Many women will, doubtless, without such a law being enacted, leave, but they will be a small minority. Many more will come in to supply their places. Many men may quit, but those who are fatally entangled must remain; and hundreds of enthusiasts are flocking from Europe to strengthen their confidence by augmenting their numbers. I am very much mistaken, if after completely investigating the affairs of Utah the new governor does not advise such a course of procedure as above suggested.

Mormonism is also a religious, as well as a political evil. Philanthropy and Christianity should feel that they have some duty toward the Mormons abroad. This strange delusion is not retrograding either in boldness of assertion or in zeal of proselytism, or in the enthusiasm of its neophytes, or in its disastrous tendency. The love for Smith is toning down into a deep reverence. As time passes he will become more and more venerated. The force of prejudice often dies with the person; the force of affection clings to the memory. It is more natural for men to love than it is for men to hate; and while others forget or despise Smith and his system, the

Mormons make *it* the one great object of their lives, and regard *him* as the regenerator of the world. They think that God has conferred upon *him* no ordinary authority, and sealed *it* with no ordinary success. They are willing to suffer any thing for this creed they neither understand nor fully obey; and are aching to retaliate the sufferings they have endured.

Bigoted in their faith, many have got beyond the pale of reason altogether. Like the Seekers of 1645, the Camisards of 1688, the Leeites of 1776, and the Wilkinsonians of the same year, the Mormons think they have received a supernatural testimony of the Spirit. This nothing can shake; being superior to all reason, it is unassailable by reason. Some have gone so far as to declare, "Even though Smith were proven a liar and were to acknowledge it, I would still believe him a prophet." (Sidney Rigdon, 1833.) "I would rather go to hell with the Mormons, than to heaven with the Christians." (Lyman Wight, 1842.) Men so completely sunk are completely hopeless. Such may see and suffer, while what they see and suffer only makes prejudice obstinacy. It is not toward these that useful efforts can be directed. There are thousands, however, who are not yet, but who are yearly becoming Mormons. Men of superior intelligence, of approved conscientiousness, and of deep sincerity, who are earnestly desiring to find truth, and restlessly roaming from party to party. These lend the prestige of respectability, the power of superior talent, the influence of position, and the assistance of wealth to the systems they adopt. Such hear Mormonism, are fascinated with its novelty, attracted by its pretensions, confounded by its sophistries, and seized hold on by its enthusiasm. They believe, obey, and are immediately set to preaching. Men in real earnest always arouse the sympathies of earnest men. Religious enthusiasm is a part of our nature; however dormant, it may be excited to fanaticism by a more active enthusiasm than our own. This is the case with these men, and it is the secret of Mormon success. There are more weak than wicked minds in the world; more fanatics than impostors.

These men demand our attention. They have not embraced Salt Lake Mormonism, but that taught outside Utah. This has combined Campbell's baptism by immersion for remission of sins with other dogmas, and many on hearing the Elders preach are struck with the apparent difference between the accusations and their style of address. Many admirable and scriptural objects have they incorporated in their system, *Bible bait* to catch the public ear, accompanied by piteous narrations of their persecutions, etc. They withhold the theories which constitute *Mormonism as it is:* the dogmas and doings denounced by all right-minded men. Many who embrace their ideal of Mormonism would not receive the reality. Their minds have to be Mormon-toned and Mormon-trained before they can be safely instructed in the real principles, sympathize in the positive hopes, or be initiated into the actual secrets of this system. Let the facts be circulated among such men; facts neither blackened by prejudice nor extenuated by partiality. Let them be circulated not with the narrow influence of individual exertion, but by the broad hands of general effort. Before they embrace the system, let them know what the system is, and not be entrapped by plausible falsehoods, and then lured to destruction by stra-tagetic man-management. There are hundreds who receive their doctrines in Europe who would be disgusted were they first to hear them in the filthy obscenities of Kimball, or in the menaces of Grant, or in the blasphemy of Young.

There are a great many persons who have been to and left Utah. It is a duty that they owe to God and humanity to let their testimony be known. They ought, every one of them, to write their reasons for leaving, the facts they have witnessed, the dogmas they have heard. Speak them, spread them, print them. Let them be so confirmed as to compel universal conviction as to their personal veracity, as well as the accuracy of their statements. While individual testimony is often suspected and discarded, every wise man can not but respect a "great cloud of witnesses." On as many of such as see this chapter, I would urge the importance of acting on this suggestion.

All fanaticisms feed on excitement; they must increase or they die out. Like a tumor, corruption must be in constant action or nature will heal it up. It is thus with Mormonism. There is no other system that has had so many apostates in the same length of time. Trying to maintain a constant extra-natural illumination and spiritual testimony, requires too unnatural a strain of the mental energies. It needs a con-stant and a constantly increasing stimulus, or it fades out. The accession of new members, boiling over with enthusiasm, and full of "testimony;" the enunciation of new dogmas, for the origin of which the Elders claim revelation to Smith;

the excitement of continual emigration to Salt Lake, and the stirring news from their Zion; the heavy tax on their purses to "support the cause;" the fresh arrivals of new Elders from Utah; the active exertions at opening meeting-houses, and their incessant controversy, all these things rekindle their zeal already in its decadence. To arrest this progress and calm down this excitement is to destroy the system. As fever will often delay death, so to check this fever is to accelerate dissolution. Stop the accession to Mormon numbers, and the "Churches" will soon die out of themselves. Mormon proselytism is not in a steady continuous stream, but in "fits and starts," just as their enthusiasm rises to the requisite temperature.

Any thing that will tend to cool the ardor or damp the energies of this system must tend to destroy it. All their Elders feel this. When Mormonism begins to stagnate, it perishes. Hence all their efforts are directed to *excite the people;* hence, too, the yearly appointment of scores of new missionaries, who replace those who may have lost their first warmth of zeal. Hence, also, all their preaching is doctrinal; moral teaching they despise. To make men *believe* their *theories* is their only object. Whether their theories make men and women holier and purer is a matter of indifference to them. It is not with them to convert souls, but merely to convince minds. This accounts for the startling numbers who enlist in all species of imposture, while despising religion. Men give up their *minds* to the molding hands of other men very willingly, when they will not give up their *hearts.* A philosophical hypothesis, a religious dogma, a scientific theory, or any mere object of belief, however ridiculous, will gather around it scores of devoted advocates, when very often the most correct principles of moral action will be neglected and despised. Thousands, too, will admit the force, admire the beauty, and even defend the claims of such well-springs of purity and happiness; but would never dream of making them their rules of action. Any system that promises a more lax regime of morality, that allows the gratification of more sensuous if not sensual appetites, that encourages levity, self-confidence, and vain glory, that bases its dependence on the observance of mere outward forms; neither reaching our deeper instincts of mentality, nor supplying the higher necessities of our souls, will always attract most disciples, and be most enthusiastically preached.

It is thus with Mormonism. It pretends to decry all regenerating change of the heart; makes conversion merely contrition for past sins, and a resolution of amendment in future. Salvation is then the simple obedience to certain ordinances. Remission of sins *is obtained by baptism;* the gift of the Holy Ghost is *conferred* by the laying on of hands of an Elder, quite irrespective of whether that Elder have any of the Spirit himself. To go to Utah is the next law of obedience, then the payment of tithing, then their secret endowments, and baptisms for the dead, then the practice of polygamy, and all the rest of their carnal observances. It is nothing but a long string of ceremonies and especial obediences. From the liberty and light of the Gospel, back into the vague symbolism and forms of Judaism, with its robes and allegories; sacrifices and costly Temple; glittering ornaments and golden vessels; regal priesthood and absolute authority have the Mormons stepped. It is a return to a lower law; and their members are accordingly all of the lower order of minds. They ought to have lived in David's day. They would have made excellent Jews. Jesus has come in vain for them, for they return to the "yoke too grievous to be borne." Unable to grasp or comprehend the higher or *spiritual* religion, they have gravitated to their own level, and reinstated the lower or *ceremonial* religion.

This necessitates, and seems to justify their polygamy to them; and it is why many good men practice it with, I am satisfied, the purest of motives. Purity of motive, however, in short-sighted mortality, does not always constitute purity of action. Re-adopting the formalism of Judaism, it is natural they should re-adopt the polygamy of Judaism; and wish women to become second Ruths, as they are willing to become a Boaz. Here is the great religious error of Mormonism. It is gradual training in these material views, a great deal more attention being paid to the Old Testament than the New, that has induced Mormon men and women to *sincerely* believe and obey the "authorities." As a natural consequence of their stand-point, they have adopted the *Aaronic* and *Melchisedec* priesthoods as those authorities; they have literalized all the Old Testament passages about the person of the deity, till Professor Pratt has got God into "the shape, appearance, and size of a man," Smith has given him many wives, and made him physically *beget* Jesus Christ; and Brigham has made him into being Adam himself. It is the re-adoption of this old ceremonial law, even to a belief in sacrifices of sheep and doves, that gives their system its partial consistency, and secures attention in the world, because affording many Scripture proofs and much specious controversial argument. The building a physical Zion, a literal gathering of the Jews to Jerusalem, a literal *separate hiding away*, and not *dispersion*, of the ten tribes, and their return to Palestine, etc., etc., are Mormon dogmas, and they inevitably follow the assumption of the old law, which was instituted as a course of tuition, and intended *only* as a "school-master to bring men to Christ." His is the higher law of perfect liberty; the practice of right more than the observance of forms, pure morals rather than mere dogmas, holy love of truth, and not implicit obedience to priesthoods.

These forms and ceremonies, priesthoods and dogmas, were but the abacus with which God has instructed his children in their arithmetic of religion. The love of the abstract principle has been diverted to attachment for the material object; and in the worship of the truth, they have ignorantly adored the symbol. As the perception of the concrete must precede the conception of the abstract, so must the material and symbolic precede the refined and spiritual. As children can not separate the idea of "one and one make two" from the marbles or sticks with which it was illustrated and by which it was taught; so children in religion had to be taught by means of forms and ceremonies, and now many are still unable to separate the two. When the child can perceive the abstract truth *as exhibited in*, but not *belonging to*, the material illustrations, then the material illustrations are discarded. So when men can appreciate the abstract truths of religion as *exhibited in*, but not *belonging to*, certain ceremonies, then the mere ceremonies are discarded. They cease to be more than the *representations*, and are no longer the *embodiments* of truth's. So purity was loved instead of the spotless lamb; the power of God, and not the power of priesthoods; universal worship, and not the Temple; the adoration of the Spirit, and no longer obedience to forms. Without these sticks and stones, God in the New Testament has come nearer to man, because, by his previous education, man has risen up nearer to God. To sink back into the mysticism and symbolism of the past, is a relapse into barbarism and ignorance. It is the return of the mathematician to the marbles and sticks with which he learned addition; and such a doctrine is therefore only as the drivelings of senility when sinking into second childhood.

It is on this radical and fundamental error that the whole of Mormonism is founded. Instead of ascending from the concrete and material to the abstract and spiritual, they have fallen from the abstract to the concrete. Like the children returning to the abacus of their infantile arithmetic, they have gone back to the symbols and forms of Mosaic religion. Many able and estimable ministers have completely failed in their opposition to this system, because they have not descended to Mormon ground. Fighting from different elevations, they only beat the air. It is not Mormon piety, but their contempt for it; not their moral theses, but their enunciation of *law* that arrests the attention of honest unthinking men and women. It is natural to prefer forms, because it is easier to *obey* than it is to *feel*; baptism of the body is easier performed than regeneration is obtained. A. Monod, the great French evangelical orator, uttered a wise remark when he said, "Les hommes aiment plus les sacrifices que la religion, parce que c'est plus facile de trouver *des victimes que des vertus.*"

To successfully controvert Mormonism, it must be met on its own basis. The key to the whole system is this re-adoption of the ceremonial law. Its whole authority depends on the pretensions of Smith. These are their fundamentals; and not only, therefore, the proper places to attack, but they are also, necessarily, their weakest points to defend.

LETTER TO BRIGHAM YOUNG.

Sir:—To perform an action without being prepared to assign the reasons inducing that action, is the conduct of a fool. I have renounced your system, and denounced your designs. My reason for doing the first is my conviction of your error; my reason for the last, is my desire to avert the sacrifice of your deceived followers.

I have not resolved on this important and final step without much deliberation; and I am entirely persuaded of doing my duty to God and man in taking it. To the full extent of my limited opportunities and abilities I have investigated your faith. Increasing insight into your dogmas produced an increasing conviction of your error. I carefully weighed my responsibility and decided on my course.

I have revealed the mysteries of your secret order with its treasonable oaths. I did it, sir, not to gratify a merely morbid curiosity of the public; but to show your adherents abroad, what are the schemes to which they are required to lend themselves; and what are the blessings that you assert God has in reserve for them. I have done so, also, to direct the attention of the government of the United States to the real character and object of your system. Not only that they should be beforehand prepared, but also that they might be induced to adopt vigorous measures, as to delay action is only to afford you opportunity to increase your numbers, and if you will not forego your treasonable intentions, to increase also the number of the sufferers. I feel perfectly sanctioned by God and reason in violating the oaths of secrecy; equally as much as I feel justified in disregarding my covenant of obedience.

That by this violation, I render myself liable to the penalty you have affixed to your obligations, I am aware; but I believe my duty surpasses my risk. If your system be true, it ought not to shrink from the broad glare of universal sunshine. If it be false, the more thoroughly it is known, the better will it be for yourselves and for mankind at large.

I have endeavored in the chapters on yourself, to render you as you are; neither distorted by prejudice, nor favored by partiality. I do not wish to unduly inflame men's anger, nor excite men's approbation toward yourself. You have made yourself notorious; and have, therefore, given yourself to the public. I do not cherish any feeling of enmity to yourself, or your adherents. I only wish that your really great abilities had been devoted to a worthier cause, and for the promotion of a nobler object; and only regret that you have so fatally involved your believers in your policy, who are so blindly infatuated in your interests.

That you are sincere in your confidence in Joseph Smith, and in your own pretensions, I believe and acknowledge; but, at the same time, that you are leading confiding thousands to misery and ruin, is evident. Charity for them would induce the frustration of your designs.

I admire the industry of your people, their notable labors and their general sincerity, but I deplore their delusion, and I denounce their deceivers. I have carefully chosen my course, and shall, with the help of God, pursue it.

That you will ever be made, in this life, to see your madness and its inevitable consequences, I can not believe. That you would forsake it if you did see it, I can not hope. One thing is certain, you have forged your own chains, as well as the fetters that you have fastened on your deluded people. You are as hopelessly your own slave as ever you wished to make others.

But while you can not retract the past, you are still able to prevent much sorrow and difficulties in the future. The political ambition of Joseph Smith entailed suffering, exodus, and death upon his blindly devoted and fanatically infatuated followers. Your political ambition will involve in the same disastrous consequences your still more numerous adherents. Your own wisdom must teach that your object of founding an independent kingdom is hopeless; and that to attempt it is to insure your own destruction. You must be aware, too, that while religious martyrs are pitied, political adventurers are despised; and that such a course will divest you of all sympathy, and hand you and your ambition down to universal execration and contempt. If you do push matters to so lamentable an extremity as to come into collision with the federal authorities, remember that it is YOU and not THEY *who will then be the real cause of the suffering and bloodshed that will ensue!* Were you the President of the United States to-morrow, and were such another system as Mormonism, with such another leader as yourself, to attempt to defy or outrage your country and its institutions, remember that you would be the first man to crush them, as you crushed Sidney Rigdon at Nauvoo! What you would yourself do as President, will be done by the President, should occasion require such energy and action. To oppose the government is to expose yourself; to oppose it so far as to shed blood, is to bring the blood that may be shed on your own hands and head. Wisdom should dictate caution, and caution would advise the renunciation of wild and impracticable schemes, which can only end in confusion, and involve the ruin of simple and devoted thousands.

Not alone could you prevent such ruin, but you could accomplish much good; and, instead of being remembered as only a curse to your race, leave some gleam of a better heart and a sounder mind. Your position would enable you to accomplish much toward the advancement of the interests of your country and the consummation of human progress. That you have energy sufficient to arrest and break up the whole system of Mormon *politics*, that you could quell the disturbance and control the shock which would ensue from such an attempt, that you could divert the attention and direct the power of your followers into a far higher and more rational pursuits, I do not for a moment doubt. That you have not sufficient moral strength to attempt it, I know. The most the world can hope and ask from you is to save yourself, and spare your believers from the suffering and destruction consequent on the struggle to which you are endeavoring to incite them. I will say nothing to you of the wickedness or of the treason of your effort to establish such a kingdom in the center of your country. All I urge on you is its folly and its impossibility. This, in your serious moments, you must feel. Those sanguine aspirants of your advisers, who really entertain the hope of ultimate success, confide too much on the neglect or the imbecility of their country's government. Such a confidence is ridiculous. Perhaps you may rely on supernatural assistance: if so, *where were your gods at Missouri, at Carthage, at Nauvoo?* Your Adam-deity, like the Baal of Elijah's day, was "sleeping or taking a journey."

It is not presumption in me thus to direct your attention to this subject. Having made yourself so conspicuous, you have given any one the right to address you. I have spoken to you as a prophet; as a man to a man I now write to you. I admire your genius, but I deplore its exercise. I no more dread your enmity than I fear your priestly anathemas. The slanders your coadjutors may attempt to circulate, I despise. You told the people once, that your "words were but wind;" as wind they may be safely encountered.

I confidently believe the time will come when honest men will be undeceived, desert your standard, and leave you forsaken and sorrow-stricken to remorse for the past and terror for the future. To this end I shall labor, and constantly and fervently pray that your power and your system may find a speedy and an eternal grave; that it may be sunk in the oblivion of its own mysteries, and be buried under the mountain of its own ignominy.

JOHN HYDE, Jun.

New York, *July*, 1857.

DICK'S WORKS.

THE

COMPLETE WORKS

OF

THOMAS DICK, LL.D.

CONTAINING

ESSAY ON THE SIN AND EVILS OF COVETOUSNESS; CELESTIAL SCENERY; SIDEREAL HEAVENS; PRACTICAL ASTRONOMER· THE SOLAR SYSTEM, WITH MORAL AND RELIGIOUS REFLECTIONS; THE ATMOSPHERE AND ATMOSPHERICAL PHENOMENA.

ELEVEN VOLUMES IN TWO· LARGE OCTAVO.

Full Sheep, $6. Half-Calf, $8.

Half-Morocco, $8.

NEW YORK:
W. P. FETRIDGE & COMPANY,
No. 281 BROADWAY,
OPPOSITE STEWARTS.

SARTAROE:

A ROMANCE OF NORWAY.

BY JAMES A. MAITLAND.

AUTHOR OF

"THE WATCHMAN."

"THE WANDERER."

"THE OLD DOCTOR."

"THE LAWYER'S STORY."

ETC., ETC.

NEW YORK:
W. P. FETRIDGE & COMPANY,
No. 281 BROADWAY,
OPPOSITE STEWARTS.

THE

WIFE'S TRIALS.

BY MISS PARDOE.

1 Vol., 8vo. Price 50 cents.

"Nor custom, nor example, nor vast numbers
Of such as do offend, make less the sin.
For each particular crime a strict account
Will be exacted." MASSINGER.

NEW YORK:
W. P. FETRIDGE & COMPANY,
No. 281 BROADWAY,
OPPOSITE STEWARTS.

WOODLAND CREAM.

A POMADE

FOR BEAUTIFYING THE HAIR,

HIGHLY PERFUMED,

AND GREATLY SUPERIOR TO ANY FRENCH ARTICLE EVER IMPORTED, AND FOR **HALF THE PRICE.**

For dressing Ladies' Hair it has no equal, giving it a bright glossy appearance. It causes Gentlemen's Hair to curl in the most natural manner. It removes Dandruff, always giving the Hair the appearance of being freshly shampooed. Price only 50 Cents. None Genuine unless Signed

FETRIDGE & CO., PROPRIETORS OF THE

BALM OF A THOUSAND FLOWERS.

FOR SALE BY ALL DRUGGISTS.

BEWARE OF COUNTERFEITS.

UNIVERSAL HISTORY,

FROM

THE CREATION OF THE WORLD

TO THE

BEGINNING OF THE 18TH CENTURY.

BY THE LATE

HON. ALEXANDER FRAZER TYTLER,

Lord Woodhouselee, Senator of the College of Justice, and Lord Commissioner of Judiciary in Scotland, former Professor of Civil History and Greek and Roman Antiquities in the University of Edinburg.

IN TWO VOLUMES, LARGE OCTAVO,

OF MORE THAN A THOUSAND PAGES, WITH COMPLETE INDEX.

PRICE, Cloth, $3 25. Sheep, $4. Half-Calf, $6. Half-Morocco, $6.

NEW YORK:
W. P. FETRIDGE & COMPANY,
No. 281 BROADWAY,
OPPOSITE STEWARTS.

"MOREDUN:"

A

TALE OF THE TWELVE HUNDRED AND TEN.

BY

SIR WALTER SCOTT, BART.

"We have received from FETRIDGE & Co., the enterprising publishers, a copy of the new *old* novel attributed to Walter Scott. The title of the work is 'Moredun,' and it is a tale of Scotland, the favorite field of Scott's prolific fame. Whether written by him or not, it is the *best novel which has appeared for many a month*, and must command a heavy sale."—*Woodstock Paper.*

"This work is selling very rapidly, and the first edition of 25,000 copies is nearly exhausted. The newspapers are discussing the merits of this work, and particular attention is paid to the following question, 'Who is the author?' The London *Literary Gazette* says, 'It is probable that this work was written before the "Waverly," which at once rendered Scott famous, and that he hesitated to publish it. Indeed, it is well known that the "Great Unknown" wrote several works, which, doubtful of his dawning genius for novel writing, he committed to the flames. It is more than probable, under the circumstances fully explained by M. Cabany—but which we have not space to enter into—that "Moredun" was spared.' At all events, the book is published by FETRIDGE; the curiosity of the public has been sufficiently excited to induce them to read it, and it will have a large sale; and we believe that most Scott connoisseurs will find in the plot and plan and style of the story enough of 'Scotiana' to impress upon their minds the fact that 'Moredun' is a genuine 'Waverly.' At all events, the book has merit enough of its own to render it generally attractive."—*Boston Sunday Dispatch.*

NEW YORK:
W. P. FETRIDGE & COMPANY,
No. 281 BROADWAY
OPPOSITE STEWARTS.

VALUABLE WORK,

PUBLISHED BY

W. P. FETRIDGE & CO., NEW YORK.

UNIVERSAL HISTORY,

FROM THE

CREATION OF THE WORLD

TO THE

BEGINNING OF THE EIGHTEENTH CENTURY.

BY THE LATE

HON. ALEXANDER FRASER TYTLER,

Lord Woodhouselee, Senator of the College of Justice, and Lord Commissioner of Justiciary in Scotland, and former Professor of Civil History and Greek and Roman Antiquities in the University of Edinburgh.

In *two volumes*, large octavo, of more than a *thousand pages*, with a complete *index*.

This important work has been stereotyped at considerable expense and is now published in the most substantial and attractive form, it

THE

PLANTER'S DAUGHTER:

A Tale of Louisiana.

BY

MISS A. E. DUPUY,

AUTHOR OF "OTELIA CLAYTON," "HUGUENOT EXILES," "COUNTRY NEIGHBORHOOD," ETC.

NEW YORK:
W. P. FETRIDGE & COMPANY
No. 281 BROADWAY,
OPPOSITE STEWARTS.
1857.

HAGAR THE MARTYR;

OR,

PASSION AND REALITY.

A TALE OF THE NORTH AND SOUTH.

BY

MRS. H. MARION STEPHENS.

WILL IS DESTINY.

Alas! O, alas! for the trusting heart,
When its fairy dream is o'er;
When it learns that to trust is to be deceived—
Finds the things most false which it most believed!
Alas! for it dreams no more!

NEW YORK:
W. P. FETRIDGE & COMPANY,
No. 281 BROADWAY
OPPOSITE STEWARTS.
1857.

SARATOGA.

A Story of 1787.

NEW YORK:
W. P. FETRIDGE & COMPANY,
No. 281 BROADWAY
OPPOSITE STEWARTS.
1857.

EVENTIDE

A SERIES OF

TALES AND POEMS.

BY

EFFIE AFTON.

"I never gaze
Upon the evening, but a tide of awe,
And love, and wonder, from the Infinite,
Swells up within me, as the running brine
From the smooth-glistening, wide-heaving sea,
Grows in the creeks and channels of a stream
Until it threats its banks. It is not joy,
'T is sadness more divine."

ALEXANDER SMITH.

NEW YORK:
W. P. FETRIDGE & COMPANY
No. 281 BROADWAY,
OPPOSITE STEWARTS.
1857.

THE ADVENTURES

OF A

ROVING DIPLOMATIST

BY

HENRY WIKOFF,

AUTHOR OF "MY COURTSHIP AND ITS CONSEQUENCES."

King.—What do you call the play?
Hamlet.—The mousetrap.
HAMLET, *Act* III. *Scene* 2.

NEW YORK:
W. P. FETRIDGE & COMPANY
No. 281 BROADWAY
OPPOSITE STEWARTS.
1857.

HOME SCENES AND HOME SOUNDS;

OR,

THE WORLD FROM MY WINDOW.

BY

H. MARION STEPHENS.

NEW YORK:
W. P FETRIDGE & COMPANY,
No. 281 BROADWAY,
OPPOSITE STEWARTS.
1857.

THE

OLD VICARAGE.

A NOVEL.

BY MRS. HUBBACK,

AUTHORESS OF

"THE WIFE'S SISTER," "MAY AND DECEMBER,"

ETC. ETC.

NEW YORK:

W. P. FETRIDGE & COMPANY

No. 281 BROADWAY

OPPOSITE STEWARTS.

1857.

Little Folks' Own:

STORIES, SKETCHES, POEMS, AND PARAGRAPHS,

DESIGNED TO

AMUSE AND BENEFIT THE YOUNG

BY

MRS. L. S. GOODWIN

NEW YORK:
W. P. FETRIDGE & COMPANY
No. 281 BROADWAY
OPPOSITE STEWARTS.
1857.

www.ingramcontent.com/pod-product-compliance
Lightning Source LLC
LaVergne TN
LVHW010131110826
845151LV00002B/328

* 9 7 8 1 4 2 5 5 3 9 4 9 8 *